I dedicate this book, in loving memory, to Marcus McCoy, and to the millions of unnamed children who have been discouraged, shamed, isolated, abused by, or because of, Religion.

Table of Contents

Trigger Warning

The Preface and Section I contain stories of emotional and sexual abuse, and violent crimes. They provide insight into my life and explain why I felt the need to write this book.. But they are not entirely pertinent to the rest of the book.

Should you feel, or fear being triggered, you can move on to Section II.

The point is to heal.

Preface

I did not realize I was emotionally, physically, and sexually abused; I just thought that was life. I did not understand that I was controlled, manipulated, and raped by my husband because we believed the Bible gave him power, and I must submit to him. I had no idea my Christianity was influenced, distorted, and politicized to condone such actions.

I never intended to lose my religion. It was an integral part of my identity. I had complete faith in the doctrine and believed it was God's flawless, divine word. Questions and doubts were eased by Bible verses and apologetics or dismissed as a lack of faith.

The dismantling of my faith began when I was confronted with the reality that much of what the Church and my Christian schools taught me was not holy or even accurate.

The revelations were sudden, but the acceptance was slow. I never consciously thought, "I will no longer be a Christian." In fact, after 25 years of deconstructing my faith, I still struggle with dropping that moniker. I am still a huge fan of Jesus. My problems with Christianity were never about him. They are about the hateful, judgmental, and sometimes murderous things done in his name.

My issues are not with Jesus' teachings. They are with the patriarchal, victimizing, abusive, hypocritical, bigoted dogma that is central to too much of Christianity. Jesus was the antithesis of all those things.

Realizing I could no longer believe in the god of religion was a process of examination, discovery, grief, and acceptance. There were many grueling years of embarrassment, cognitive dissonance, and disorientation. But they were interwoven with education, discernment, and grace.

Indoctrination is like an onion—it permeates all aspects of life, and its depths are only uncovered by peeling away another layer. My childhood centered on learning, accepting, and embodying Christian doctrine. A doctrine that said I was a second-class citizen, wholly inadequate, and not worthy of "God's love." They assured me my insatiable shame was normal.

They taught me that a righteous life was one of constant repentance for sins that I may have committed. I must accept my fate and punishment for every thought and action. Fear of upsetting this "God" consumed my life. A "God" who supposedly loved me so much that he regularly hurt me and called it "tough love." I was born a sinner. I deserved it all. It was such a heavy burden for a child to carry.

The god of my religion was the greatest abuser of all time and resembled my earthly attackers. Someone who claimed to love me unconditionally but was constantly destroying my life for every mistake, real or imagined.

My religion taught me that God justifies or ignores the actions of an abuser but punishes the abused for their reactions. Even the errors of an ignorant child were worthy of eternal punishment. All justified with, "We don't understand the ways of God."

I never decided to walk away from the Church. It was a slow realization that it was full of ego-driven tribalism and inconsistencies, and it justified ignorance, abandonment, and cruelty.

I did not even consciously embark on a journey to unravel my beliefs and study religions that span human history. But once the dome of indoctrination cracked, the glimmers of knowledge began peering through. And it became clear that most of what I knew was based on fairy tales, not facts.

I needed to know if there was any reality to my belief system. I had to find the truth about God, the Bible, and Jesus, if there was any—the truth about other religions, Heaven, and Hell. I did not realize this quest for information would become my passion: a passion for knowledge and to set the record straight. I wanted to bring awareness to the misinformed damnation and exclusion and the misogynistic manipulations and patriarchal domination that is the foundation of so much religious dogma. If the knowledge freed me of my shame, pain, and indoctrination, maybe it could do the same for others.

More than a quarter-century later, I earned my Ph.D. in Comparative Religion and wrote this guide for those questioning the dogma that shapes so many lives. This book is the examination of the theology that dominated my life, shamed me, and justified my neglect, abandonment, and abuse.

While I still believe in "God," my definitions have radically changed. My life evolved from a hellish existence of fear and indignity to one of faith, beauty, grace, gratitude, and love.

May your journey do the same for you.

Section I: How I Got Here

"I know God will not give me anything I can't handle. I just wish that he didn't trust me so much."
~ *Mother Teresa*

Chapter 1: Honor Thy Father?

My mom once confessed that getting married was the only way out of her family's home. My dad just wanted a naive, loyal woman. When they married, he was 24, and she was 21. She was already his second wife.

My mom was excited when she became pregnant, but that changed when he insisted on naming me after his first childhood crush. He stopped coming home at night once her baby bump grew.

They were only together for two years. After they divorced, their lives went in opposite directions. He became a thief, an influential drug dealer, and was nominated to be the Grand Dragon of the local KKK chapter. She became a fanatical, speaking-in-tongues, book-burning, Evangelical Bible college graduate.

Based on these descriptions, one could assume that one of them was terrible and one better. But they raised me between equal extremes of judgment and hate. Both stood in judgment of everyone they met. Both chose vengeance over forgiveness and justified it with their own god complex.

They were also similar in their relationships. After my mom, my dad had four more wives, totaling six marriages. My mom only remarried once but was engaged as often as my father married. She was the original runaway bride. Her closet was full of wedding dresses that were bought but never worn.

I was not taught forgiveness or how to get through times together. They only taught me how to run away. My dad always said, "When the going gets tough, the tough get going!" I only learned during the editing process of this book that others understood the phrase differently than me.

I was almost two when he took off, and he did not come back until I was seven. When he left us, he moved in with his soon-to-be third wife, and I became a thing of the past. I am fairly certain he only contacted me because he needed an alibi. Each time he picked me up for a visit, we stopped by his mistress' house on the way home to his wife. I sat on her couch watching TV while they retreated to her bedroom. After a while, he would appear, zipping his pants, buckling his belt, and informing me it was time to leave. I could never talk about these "rest stops." Until one day, he used me to get rid of his fourth wife.

Previously, she was the "rest stop," and it was time for that cycle to continue. He told me to tell her there was a new woman like I was divulging his secret. He knew the revelation would be incredibly hurtful coming from me, his 13-year-old daughter. He was such a coward.

A year earlier, I called him. I needed him to keep a secret and help me. Things had deteriorated between my mom and me, and I was running away. I needed a place to stay and for him not to tell her where I was. He agreed and came to get me.

While I was loading my stuff into his car, he called my mom and told her everything. They decided I would stay with him for two weeks as a cooling-off period, and I could bring my dog. I was furious with him for betraying me, but I had no choice but to remain silent. Staying with her was worse.

Two days before I was to return home, my dad came into my room. He sheepishly asked if we could talk. He sat on the edge of my bed, compassionately putting his hand on my leg. He explained he had just gotten off the phone with my mom, and she did not want me back. I could not live with her. I could not go home. He sat there tenderly, comforting me. He assured me that if she did not love me, he did, and he would be there for me.

The rejection sliced through my already damaged self-esteem. My mother did not want or love me. It confirmed my worst fear: I was unlovable. The revelation broke me, sinking me into a deep depression and crying for days.

How could my mother do that?

I later discovered she had never made that call. My dad called her, telling her I hated her and wanted to stay with him. She probably went through the same rejection and anguish as me, wondering how her daughter could ever say that.

With a broken heart and crushed ego, she agreed to let me stay. She hoped he could break my strong will and get me under control.

"Winning" me elated my dad. I would not be the same because he lied, but that never mattered to him.

This forever altered my relationship with my mom because there was always a part of me that wondered what really happened. Did he lie, or did she? I will never know, but I imagine the truth is somewhere in the middle. My dad wanted to win, and my mom was done losing every battle with me. Somewhere along my path, I gave up trying to understand and just tried to forgive them and heal.

Living with my dad went smoothly until I upset him. A few months later, in the middle of the seventh grade, we were moving to a neighboring city. So, I was changing schools. On my last day before the move, I stole a bottle of booze from my dad and stashed it in my locker. I thought I would be "cool" doing farewell shots in the bathroom with my girlfriends. I was busted when the teachers found out.

My dad did not care that I planned to drink or brought the bottle to school. What sent him over the edge was that I took his bottle. I stole from him.

I adamantly denied it until he told me the state recorded all alcohol sales, with the transaction dates and the store that sold it. He said he would return the bottle to the store and prove it was his. I did not know any better, so I believed him. He confidently announced that once his suspicions were confirmed—after all my lies—he would literally kill me.

My father did not use those words lightly. I knew he would kill me the moment he confirmed my lies. Fearing for my life, I started sobbing, begging for his forgiveness, and crumbling to the floor. I was terrified of his next move. He said nothing. He simply left the room.

We did not speak for three months. He funneled all communication through stepmother #3. During dinner, if he had something to say to me, he would leave the table, go into the kitchen, and summon her. She would return with his message. I would answer, and she would relay the information. His behavior was childish, but terrifying. My dad was a cold, frightening man. No longer speaking in my presence led me to believe he was calculating his revenge and my demise.

Then, my stepmother lost a hundred-dollar bill. He was sure I took it, which was his final straw. Full of rage, he spoke through his teeth, inches from my face. He said he was done, and I would die if I did not give it back.

This time, I did not do it. I pleaded with him to believe me, but after the bottle of alcohol, he would not. He said as soon as he had proof that I stole the money, he would beat me so badly that my body would be unrecognizable to the authorities.

He stood there, steely-eyed, fists clenched, hissing things like, "I will leave your bloodied corpse on the side of the road for the vultures to feed on. I will make sure it's dumped where your classmates will see your mutilated body on their way to school."

Then he would sit back and say, "But not today. Soon. As soon as I have proof…"

For the next three weeks, he randomly burst into my room in the middle of the night. Lit only by the streetlights coming through my window, he jolted me awake by mercilessly and diabolically shouting,

"Tonight is the night you're going to die!"

I hysterically begged and pleaded for my life. After I was sufficiently terrified, he would back out of the room, not uttering another word but never taking his eyes off me. I hid under my covers, using them to soothe and protect me. I lay there shaking and crying.

Then, one day, I arrived home from school, and my stepmother told me they had found the $100. Evidently, she put it in her jeans, not her purse. The night the money went missing, she took off her pants and threw them over the back of the couch. That caused the bill to slip out and drop behind the sofa.

There were no apologies, but the terrifying threats of a madman no longer awakened me. I survived but knew I had to return to my mom's ASAP.

He never laid a hand on me, but the scars left by his verbal abuse and terrorist-style parenting were permanent. After exactly a year, I went back to Mom's.

A little over a year later, I was feeling especially antagonistic and called him. I asked him if he wanted any copies of my prom pictures. He said, "Whoa, that's my girl! You landed a senior at only fifteen! Way to go, honey! Yeah, I'd love to see the pictures!"

I paused, then said, "Dad, I should warn you. The photos are black and white."

Confused, he said, "That's weird. You'd think nowadays, pictures would all be in color?"

I snickered—my heart racing—I delivered my punchline: "No, Dad, he's Black, and I'm White!"

I erupted in haughty, antagonistic laughter. He hung up, completely aghast.

Years later, I found out that when he hung up, he grabbed his rifles and handguns and was coming after me. He was irate, shouting he would kill my boyfriend and me. My stepmother only stopped him by threatening to call the police. Evidently, it was quite the scene.

My teens were rough. I was full of rage and resistance. And since I was upsetting my parents, they wanted nothing to do with me.

Throughout my rebellion, my mother kept her faith in God, believing everything would work out because of her faith.

Evidently, while I was living with my dad, "God told her," I would marry the Church's pianist. This "message" gave her hope and comforted her while I was subconsciously paying them back for my childhood.

Fast forward five years from her vision. I was an 18-year-old pregnant bride 40 miles south of that Church, marrying the pianist's music partner and best friend. It was not the Church's pianist I would marry, but the drummer.

I imagine a Monty Python-type scene with "God" telling my mom my future husband was on the church stage. She looked and smiled, seeing a prim and proper White boy playing beautiful music on the grand piano. "Oh, Thank God!" God smiled and responded, "No, Tanya, not him. Him...." Directing her to the jolly, round, Black boy, pounding away on a 9-piece Pearl drum set. I imagine her horror and her dismissing any such misinterpretation of her vision. She was not necessarily a racist, but she had her ideals, and Vince was not part of them.

Vince and I had discussed marriage. We even set a date. But when I discovered I was pregnant, I called it off. I did not want to be a pregnant bride.

In early August, I was five months pregnant and at work when I received a call from my mom. She had just seen Vince, and they discussed us "living in sin." She said, "I asked him how it felt to betray God, and he said with such conviction, 'I hate it!'"

Her voice pepped up. She joyfully said, "So, we got to talking, and we think you guys should get married on the original date you set, September 3rd. I will plan the entire thing! All you need to do is buy your shoes and show up! I love you, honey! You're getting married! Yay!"

I do not remember saying anything. I hung up, looked at my boss, and said with a fake, forced smile, "I guess I'm getting married."

She said, "Oh, that's fantastic!"

I looked away, pausing, "I guess?"

I loved Vince, but we always fought. I was not sure that I was ready to get married because they thought we were "living in sin."

The night before the wedding, I placated her and stayed at my mom's, appearing chaste and honoring tradition. My belly was protruding, but the illusion gave her peace. Before bed, I called Vince to say goodnight; he was drunk. Frustrated, I asked if he handled the wedding music. He was too drunk to understand my question, so he laughed and said, "What wedding? Who's getting married?"

Feeling completely insignificant, I burst into tears, told him to go to Hell, and that our wedding was off! I ran into my mom's room, looking for comfort and validation. She calmed me down, but instead of supporting my decision to call it off, she talked me into going through with it. I kept asking, "Are you sure? I don't think I can do this!"

She repeated, "Yes, everything will be fine in the morning. God's intention is marriage."

It could have been cold feet. It could have been a sixth sense. Whatever it was, I was scared.

I shook and cried as I took my first step down the aisle. I steadied myself and prayed. Trying to catch my breath, I whispered, "Oh, please, Jesus. Please come back soon. I cannot stay married to him for the rest of my life. If you are forcing me into this marriage, please don't make me endure it for too long. Please. Come back soon and spare me from this sentence."

Every Sunday, the pastor said, "Today could be the day! Jesus could return on this very morn!" And everyone would cheer. Jesus had to be returning soon! So, I had nothing to worry about.

My dad did not walk me down the aisle because I was unaware someone was supposed to "give me away." He did not offer; I didn't know to ask. I was just glad he was there without guns.

In hindsight, Vince checked all the boxes for my rebellion. He was everything that would infuriate both of my parents.

He was Black: Dad ✓

He was a drummer: Mom ✓

I was pregnant out of wedlock: Mom✓✓✓

With a Black guy's baby: Dad ✓✓✓

Forcing them to be together while enduring their hopes and dreams for my life being crushed: ✓✓✓✓

My dad only accepted Vince because I lied about his ethnicity for years, and they got to know each other over the phone. After the fiasco with the last Black boyfriend, I could not tell him about Vince.

When we got engaged, I had to tell the truth. I cushioned it by saying that Vince was biracial. My father chuckled and asked, "Is he French-Canadian?" I said no, but he continued like it was a fact. I do not know why he asked that, but it made everything OK in his mind, so I went with it.

Soon after that call, my dad invited us for a visit so they could formally meet. Right before we left, my mom called me. She was in full panic. She spoke to my aunt (my father's estranged sister), and they were convinced this "visit" was a trap. My dad would kill at least one of us, probably both.

I alerted Vince, but he brushed it off as nonsense. Before me, Vince lived a sheltered life, and his naivety was no match for my father's cruelty. Vince said the weekend would be a blast, and I wanted to believe him.

On our way, I remembered the warnings and everything I knew about my dad. As we neared his house, my palms became clammy, and my heart raced. Were my aunt and mom right? I brushed away the panic and focused on the monumental event about to happen. My father was meeting my fiancé.

When we arrived, my dad whisked Vince away to see his prized Corvette. Before I knew it, they were gone. My stepmom and I went inside to get something to drink and put away the bags. I sat at the kitchen table, sipping my drink, and it hit me.

Where were they? Oh, my God! It was a setup!

I started to shake; my stepmom was oblivious to my panic.
They were gone for what seemed like forever.
More time passed. I went to my old bedroom and crumbled.

This was it! My dad did it!

Was I next?

My stepmom was mysteriously absent, which only fueled my paranoia. I sat there sobbing in the same room my dad terrorized me years before. I knew better than to trust him!

Fear overcame me. My chest caved in. I heaved from the tears, shaking like a leaf. Suddenly, Vince burst through the door with a massive smile, looking like a kid on Christmas. Before realizing I was in complete meltdown, he shouted, "Oh my God! That was the coolest thing ever!"

Then, he saw me and dropped to his knees to comfort me. "Oh, my God! What's wrong, babe?" He had no idea why I was distraught. I collapsed in tears, hugging his head. I told him of my horror and how I thought we were both goners. He smiled and said it was one of the best times of his life. The exhilaration of going 140 mph in my dad's' custom '76 Corvette.

Our marriage only lasted 14 months. Once I was his wife, I became his property. My body was no longer mine but his to use as he wanted. If I objected, he used guilt and force or waited until I was asleep to have his way with me.

A year after the wedding, he got hooked on methamphetamine, which was my final straw. The Church said that I must submit to my husband, but I refused to deal with a meth addict with a toddler running around.

In the early days of our separation, he showed up unannounced. He kicked open the door, threw a Bible on the coffee table, and shouted, "In the name of Jesus, I command you to take me back!" I looked at him in complete dismay. He had lost his mind.

Years later, he called and said, "God told me we are to be reunited!" I laughed and said, "It would definitely take divine intervention for us to get back together!"

Because of our marriage, I learned not to allow someone else's version of God to decide my life.

Vince died of cancer just days before his 49th birthday. We stayed friends till the end.

My father was remarkably disappointed when I informed him

that the marriage was over. I was shocked but reassured him everything would be OK. With agitation in his voice, he told me that having a child complicated my life; I should have had an abortion.

I was speechless. I thought my divorce disappointed him. But he freaked out that I would be "strapped with a kid." Not just any kid. Joey was lifelong evidence of my most significant transgression: I was with a Black man.

My father had held my son. He bought Joey's baby monitor and stroller. Joey bounced on his knee. And now he was saying I should have had an abortion?

Just when I thought his words could not be any more hurtful, he said, "I know times are tough, but it's not too late to take care of things. I can help. The kid is under a year old, and you have the rest of your life ahead of you."

Then my father asked if I was interested in him "taking care of it."

I felt like an elephant jumped on my chest. I was horrified. Did I hear him right? The telephone line was quiet.

"Well?" He shouted.

I mumbled, "No, Dad, I'm good."

Aggravated that I did not accept his offer, he said, "Okay, well, let me know if you change your mind. I can make it quick and easy. You don't need this baggage."

We hung up, and that was the last time we spoke.

I had no idea at the time that he was a prominent meth dealer. When I was a kid, marijuana was his thing. He grew bored with that and saw potential in the emerging meth market. He collaborated with his youngest sister and her husband, and their business boomed for years. They dominated the Northern California meth industry. The stuff Vince got hooked on probably originated with my father.

Eventually, the DEA took him down after installing one of their undercover agents as my youngest brother's babysitter. My brother said when the DEA raided the house, they savagely beat our dad. They humiliated him, leaving him bruised and bloodied—all while my seven-year-old brother watched. My brother said he tried not to laugh at the spectacle. My dad was incredibly unforgiving and cruel to him, too. He thought Dad deserved every punch and Billy club hit he endured. That was the last time he saw our father. What an indelible image that must have been.

Our dad only spent a few years in prison. In 2003, after being estranged for more than ten years, he and his youngest sister spoke. He had lung cancer but was doing well. He told her that he knew where I was but said we no longer spoke because "I told her the truth about her mother, and she couldn't deal with it."

No, Dad, that's not why.

I had not spoken to my dad in sixteen years when he died. From cleaning out his house, I learned the cancer had returned. Based on how I found things and knowing him, he killed himself instead of enduring more chemotherapy.

In his last five years of life, he created a whole new life. He told people he was raised in Maui, not San Francisco. He claimed he had no biological children and was looking for "a loyal, honest lady."

Growing up, I heard stories, but it was not until a few years after his death that I grasped the magnitude of his immorality. I confirmed he killed two people and gang-raped (at least) one woman. He ended up declining the KKK nomination because he did not believe in "organized bullshit." Not because it was a racist and violent organization but because it was an organization.

My father hated religion. He claimed it was "a crutch for people who needed that sort of thing." Ironically, a drug dealer shunned people for needing a crutch.

Five years after his death, I tried to come up with something positive he did in his life—other than "his children." The question stumped me for months. He was rarely present and taught me so little, so producing anything positive was a genuine struggle. However, after months of contemplation, I finally had a few things.

My father taught me to ethically weigh marijuana, hunt, never say "hate" or "kill" because they are powerful words that lead to actions, and never pull a gun unless you plan to use it. In summation, he taught me to be true to my word by never issuing empty threats. Ironically, such an evil man gave me this moral and valuable lesson.

He also gave me the saying: "Justification is just like masturbation. You are only fucking yourself!" Another nugget of priceless wisdom.

Chapter 2: Honor Thy Mother?

My grandmother was 41 when she had my mom. When my mom was born, my grandmother had a 21-year-old daughter, 17-year-old and 11-year-old sons, and two other children who died as infants. It was the 1940s, and my grandmother assumed she was on her way to menopause, not another baby.

The house was full, so my mother's "bedroom" was a corner of the kitchen. As a child, she did not realize her predicament, but as a teenager, it humiliated her. She never talked about her childhood, except that her mother once threw a shoe at her head and that she hated her parents. There were many family photos until my mom was about six, and then they stopped entirely until her late teens. Pictures often show only the happier times of our lives.

Because of her childhood, she was woefully unequipped to raise a child, let alone one as strong as me. My mom had severe control issues, and if she could not control me, she had no use for me.

She used "God" to control me, praying that her will be done and for me to be "fixed." My mother thought God would heal me after she looked the other way when her married boyfriend molested me. I was three and four. We stopped going to every therapist who said my actions resulted from abuse.

She hoped God would save me, as she ignored all the signs of her husband raping me.

When she could no longer endure the results of her inaction, lack of protection, and denial, she prayed God would fill my voids. She jumped headfirst into her faith to live with her denial. She begged God to help while she abandoned me.

My mom thought "God" would fix everything.

What I needed was love. I needed compassion. I needed "God," but only because God is love.

I may have been restored if she had acted in love instead of relying on a Being.

It would have soothed my wounds if she loved me instead of turning her back on me. If she would have surrounded me in love, I may not have been abused.

She could have loved me if she loved herself.

If it were not for her religious indoctrination, she would have known it was up to her to love and protect me.

Instead, she hoped some guy in the sky would magically intervene.

God is a verb, not a noun. God is the action of love, not a Being you reach out to for your every whim and wish.

She left her daughter to the wolves, hoping the Angels would step in. She saw her only child deteriorate before her eyes and closed them. When the pain became too much, she dropped to her knees but focused only on her pain and ignored mine.

God is present in every act of love, yet she rejected love and chose isolation and judgment.

It is not possible to pray away the pain. We must do something. We cannot hope that everything will be okay. We must act so that it will be. We are here to help, not stand idly hoping someone else will.

I do not know where or who I would be if she did not just close her eyes and pray. I spent many years pondering the should've, would've, and could've and only found those thoughts to be a waste of time, energy, and tears—as useless as her thoughts and prayers.

What happened, happened, and no amount of prayer can ever change that. What I do with my experiences is what matters.

Chapter 3: Me, The Seeker

I was six when my mom remarried, and as a new family, we started attending Church. After a few months, I became curious as to why people walked to the front at the close of each service. My mom and stepdad said they were accepting Christ. They said if I was interested in accepting him, too, I should walk forward the following Sunday.

All week, I eagerly waited to find out what was going on with all of this "accepting Christ." I could not wait to go forward like everyone else!

When the call came the following Sunday, I pushed through the pew and dashed to the front. A sweet, elderly, stereotypical church lady greeted me and took me to a small side room. She spoke softly, showing me some Bible verses, and then took my hand to pray. I kept waiting for the big revelation, but nothing happened. After we prayed, she patted my hand, smiled, and sent me back to my seat.

I walked back with my head down. I felt like I missed something.

Wasn't I supposed to "accept" something? Shouldn't I walk away with something?

My mom was so excited and beamed with pride, making me feel worse. As I approached, she asked me how I felt. I looked up at her, perplexed, and felt like a failure. I said, "I don't know. What was supposed to happen?"

Seeing my confusion, she knelt, stroked my arm, and said, "You just accepted Jesus as your personal Lord and Savior!"

It suddenly made sense! I immediately perked up. "That's what this was about?"

With the warmest smile, my mom nodded and said, "Yes!"

I was overcome with relief but disappointment because I had expected to get something. Regaining my composure, I looked up at them and matter-of-factly said, "Oh. I did that weeks ago."

They stood there dumbfounded as I confidently walked out of the Church, looking for lunch.

Jesus was my (imaginary) best friend. I was an only child with two working parents. As a latch-key kid, I spent afternoons alone and terrified, locked in the house, waiting for one of them to get off work. However, even after they came home, I was still isolated. I despised my stepdad, and my mom was in her own world. So, Jesus was my father, friend, and confidant.

I stared out my bedroom window every night, looking at the moon and talking to Jesus. I was so enthusiastic that I carved "I ♥ Jesus" into my wooden windowsill. My mother later confessed she was furious but could not scold me for proclaiming my faith and love.

I was eight when I took my first communion, and at that age, it traumatized me. I sat there sobbing, with the juice cup in one hand and the wafer in the other, like an ugly face, uncontrollable drooling, kind of sobbing. My mom asked if I was okay, and with snot dripping from my nose, I mumbled, "I can't do this. I can't eat my Savior's bones and drink his blood!"

She dismissively laughed. "Those aren't really his bones and blood, honey."

I snapped back, "I know! They represent his bones and blood. I can't do it. Thinking about all the pain he went through makes me too sad. I can't do it, Mom."

She leaned over, whispering, "'Through his stripes, we are

healed.' 'Do this in remembrance of me.' It's a celebration, Sheri. It is also a commandment. It's okay. The Holy Spirit is moving in you, and it's beautiful. It's okay. Jesus did this for you. You can do this for him."

I begrudgingly put the wafer in my mouth but could not chew. The tears would not stop. In the middle of a sermon, I sat towards the front, crying my eyes out with a soggy wafer melting in my mouth. Only when I choked could I drink "the blood." It was always just grape juice, but the blood imagery seemed to overtake reality. It quenched my mouth enough to wash down the wafer so I did not cause a bigger scene by choking.

Drinking the juice was difficult, but I did so out of need, not desire. Thinking of it any other way caused too much pain.

And then, just like that, it was over. My mom beamed with pride. I felt like I crossed a significant milestone—one of the difficult hurdles one must do during their lifetime. I sat there wondering, why do they make us do such horrible things?

Enrolled in a Christian school in the second grade, my entire world was the Bible, Jesus, and the Church. We attended Church at least three times a week. Regularly, the pastor came over for dinner, prayer, and Bible study.

Being faithful congregants, we took part in all the church functions. I enthusiastically joined the Missionettes (the Church's version of Girl Scouts). I excelled in getting my badges, Honor Star pins, and sash. My mom sang in the choir and cooked for all the events.

I was in the holiday performances, singing and acting in lead roles. My family was active and comfortable. So much so that when I was baptized, the pastor started telling stories and forgot to lift me out of the water. My arms flailed. He looked down and said, "Oh ya!"

Laughing, he raised me as I gasped for air. The congregation reacted like a family laughing at inside jokes. My best friends, first "boyfriend," and most fun childhood memories were at that Church.

Then, when I was ten, we changed churches. We went from a 300-person Assemblies of God sanctuary to Bethel, a mega-church (in its time) with over 2500 members. I went from a youth group with a couple dozen kids to one with a couple hundred. These kids grew up together and made it clear there was not room for me. This was their church home, not mine. Around the same time, I switched schools and entered the same situation as a new student. I started there in the fifth grade, and most students had been together since kindergarten.

My stepdad and mom were always separating, but my mom spent every penny making sure I received an excellent education. They raised me in a barely-above-poverty, revolving door of a home. These facts only further isolated me at school because most of the kids were from healthy, wealthy, stable families. For me, it was the trifecta of loneliness. My primary years were full of being bullied at school, snubbed at Church, and ignored at home.

While my education was above par in English, math, and biblical studies, it was thoroughly inadequate in history and science. The Bible was a textbook. Life-altering moments occurred when I realized I was well-educated and woefully ignorant.

I learned in my twenties that Adam and Eve were not Earth's first inhabitants. I believed childbirth was painful because of Eve's sins until I learned animals also feel pain. I believed we could not have evolved from apes because there were still apes. In my thirties, I learned men and women have the same number of ribs.

I spent my childhood being educated with bias, indoctrinated by half-truths, and having faith without logic. I was surrounded by hypocrisy and fake smiles insinuating perfection but only covering up lonely, tumultuous lives. The messages always lacked God's absolute love for everyone and everything. All I ever heard was: "God will love you if…"

It was easy for me to love God because I felt so much love during prayer. But rarely from people proclaiming themselves to be his followers. The Church mainly offered fear, judgment, and a mob mentality. The us-against-them mindset perpetuated cliques and isolated everyone else.

Deciding who gets into Heaven is the ultimate superiority complex, driving sanctimonious wedges between everyone. As a child, it only instilled sorrow and fear. The thought of my loved ones

burning in Hell engulfed me in sadness. My nightly prayers were full
of angst. Every night, I prayed for my father's salvation. The Church
assured me if my best friends did not accept Jesus as their Savior,
"God" doomed them to eternal damnation. I pleaded with God to
spare their souls.

While my father was a lost cause, I could not understand how
"God" could doom my friends. They were good people, kind, giving,
and supportive. But because they did not go to Church or say the
"sinner's prayer," God would cast them into the Lake of Fire?

At fourteen, while at Bethel's summer camp, I sat on the cathedral
floor with my head resting on the pew, weeping. My heart ached to
hear that everyone I loved faced eternal damnation. I collapsed in
sorrow. This verdict of doom caused overwhelming tears but, more
consequentially, questions.

Why do we worship something so cruel and absolute?

If I, as a mere mortal, have more compassion than "God," why
should I love him?

Even as a child, it made little sense to me. How could "God so
loved the world" be true if there were so many restrictions and the
path so narrow to whom was loved?

"God's love" was frightening, controlling, and abusive. I knew
this kind of "love," and it made me cower in fear. This "god" was an
asshole, and as I grew, I saw no validity in praising "him." Religion
tried to scare me with the apocalypse, burning in Hell, and even
losing my mother. But they could not get me to worship a Being that
was not worthy.

But…

I knew they were wrong. I knew there was some "thing" that was
superior to humans. Something more significant than those beliefs.
Something higher than bigotry and judgment. Something more than
Santa Claus or an unstable lawman in the sky.

Instead of striving to love more, we created a god that justifies
loving less. In humanizing God, we limited love to the realms
of human dysfunction. We created a possessive, jealous, abusive
relationship with love.

Religion claims "God" is our protector unless you anger him.

Then, he is our worst nightmare. That god resembles my father or the Mafia, not a Superior Being.

My mother would say, "Your father loves you as much as he's able." But that is true of everyone. One must learn to love in all situations, not just when convenient. Religion is supposed to teach these lessons because if they are not taught at home, fear and isolation take hold. Some will seek knowledge and grow; others succumb to ignorance as their fate.

I have so many regrets about who I was as a teenager, but I am thankful things did not worsen. I could have ended up as a heroin-addicted prostitute. They could have found my corpse in a gutter.

There were no cell phones or internet, so when my mom was done with me, I was of no concern. Months would go by without communication. During my son's teenage years, I concluded my mother could not have loved me.

When Joey was running the streets as a teenager, every time I heard an ambulance or police siren, my heart dropped. I did not sleep a whole night between the ages of fifteen until he entered the Navy. At least I had MySpace and cell phones to check on him.

During the most challenging times of Joey's teen years, I reached out to Vince. I asked him how my mom could have loved me and abandoned me. He told me her faith got her through the darkest times. He reassured me that her love and trust in God enabled her to release me to his control.

My mom had hoped that kicking me out at sixteen would break my will. She thought a few nights on the streets would force me to see things her way, and I would have to come home. She totally underestimated my resolve and rebellion.

Instead of crumbling and begging to return, I got a job and an apartment. Rather than succumbing to her demands and surrendering to her ideology, I started my life on my terms. Even though I lacked support, I stood firm.

The strings attached to her "love" were nothing more than shackles. I spent years fantasizing about the love parents were supposed to give their children. I got none from either parent, so I did what they taught me: walk away and not look back. My parents were incredibly determined, so I got a double dose in my DNA. However, throughout most of my life, I felt weak and unworthy.

Having Joey saved my life. Becoming pregnant and being his mom forced me to straighten up. I would protect and spare him from the pain I incurred. I would do everything to be a better parent than I had. Joey was my world, but I was alone and lost in every other aspect.

I spent most of my twenties as a young single mom. I worked and partied hard. I tried to fill the voids and loneliness with many friends and whatever boy toy I could find the time to play with. As I approached my thirties, I felt more alone than ever.

While I never lost my faith, I only attended Church a few times in over a dozen years, and my nightly prayers were merely habits. Seemingly, my prayers went unanswered, but I felt like they were a spiritual insurance policy. So, I never stopped praying.

My mom would pray for electronics, even citing the serial numbers for what she was asking. She prayed her friends would clean their houses and that she would lose thirty pounds. She asked "God" to save me from my heathen lifestyle and to protect Joey despite my sins. It always seemed like self-absorbed wants and desires, not communing with God.

Bored with it all, I prayed a new prayer. I asked what I should pray for.

Should I pray for my friends and loved ones? For the world? Should I ask forgiveness for always screwing up? Or is this just a wish list of the things I want? Tell me, God, please! What am I supposed to pray? *Can you please answer this one request?*

Frustrated, I rolled over and tried to sleep. Tossing and turning, Mathew 6:9 came to mind. I tried to sleep, but the verse kept echoing in my head. I know hundreds of scriptures but cannot tell you the source—which chapter and verse. I was curious but was too tired and frustrated to inquire further. I figured it was my dirty mind messing with me. I laughed it off and rolled over.

After over an hour of sleeplessness, I got out of bed and grabbed my Bible. Turning to Matthew 6:9 (KJV), I saw this:

> *"After this manner, therefore, pray ye: Our Father which art in*
> *Heaven, hallowed be thy name..."*

Chills flooded my body; every hair stood on end. I continued to read as my eyes welled up with tears. "Thy kingdom come, thy will be done on Earth, as in Heaven. Give us this day our daily bread. And forgive us our debts as we forgive our debtors. And lead us not into temptation but deliver us from evil: For thine is the kingdom, and the power, and the glory, forever. Amen."

I knew the verses well. I can recite them in English and French. But rereading them, after praying so desperately, gave each line a new meaning. And wow, my prayer was answered! I was literally given, "Pray like this..."

From that moment, "Thy will be done" became my mantra. My mom always said, "You've tried it your way and always failed. How about doing something new and trying God's way?" Which meant her way. But, seeing those verses with fresh eyes and a rebounding faith, I decided to try Jesus' way.

I would no longer fight my way through life. I would no longer struggle down paths that only caused me to fall face-first. I would no longer believe; I only knew what was right. Because my mom was right, my way only led to suffering.

It was not about closing my eyes and walking mindlessly. It was about finally opening them and seeing clues for direction. I would no longer demand my way and lack patience for anything else. From that point forward, I would try to live my life in wonder—in the flow. Instead of trying to swim upstream, I let it take me where I was supposed to go.

When I was 23, I saw a quote on the corner of page 12 in the San Francisco Chronicle. I tore it from the page and saved it as a reminder. It is now tattered and taped for protection. It was from a then-unknown spiritual teacher, Deepak Chopra. "Be mindful of meaningful coincidences. They are clues to fulfilling your deepest dreams and desires." It was a meaningful correlation after receiving the Lord's prayer that night.

Judaism, Christianity, Buddhism, Hinduism, and Islam all have philosophies of "surrender." Jesus' opinion on the matter is clear. He gave us a prayer of surrender. "Thy will be done" releases your control and aligns you with the universal flow.

It is not about "thoughts and prayers" because the only prayers that were ever answered—and even those rare—were questions of why? And how? No personal requests, wants, begging, or pleadings were ever answered. In hindsight, every "divine intervention" or "miracle" I received was related to actions I took, not from idly sitting by with "thoughts and prayers."

And it is not about predestination or some man in the sky pulling our strings like a puppeteer. It is about synchronicity. Like jumping into a river and seeing where it takes you. Not mindlessly floating feet-first, but swimming with the current, headfirst, present, and completely aware, enjoying the beauty and wonder of it all.

Sometimes, rough waters reveal an opportunity for growth; other times, an unexpected opening reveals a beautiful new journey. Although seeing an upcoming cliff can be terrifying, I have learned that somehow, someway, a lifeline always appears, and sometimes, a miracle.

As a control freak, this lesson is hard for me. But life has repeatedly shown me that by living in the flow, my needs are met, and it will be okay. It gave me purpose through the pain, healing in the discovery, and unexpected joys and growth. It has not been easy, but it was worth it.

Section II: Before We Go Any Further

"The truth will set you free, but first, it will piss you off."
~ Gloria Steinem

Chapter 4: What's The Problem?

The biggest lie ever told: God created humans in his image. That fabrication alone has caused more death and destruction than all the natural disasters combined. Creating a god in our image gave him all the flaws of humanity. We transformed a Light of Love into the darkness of rage, judgment, and hate. We created a god as small and petty as we are.

We fight and kill over religion, yet no one knows if there is a God—all concepts are just beliefs. However, I, like millions of others, have concluded that the god of religion is inconsistent and utterly flawed.

Religion was always the Public Relations Manager for God, and it has utterly failed. They constructed a man that resembles people I try to avoid. Abrahamic religions (Judaism, Christianity, and Islam) envisioned the universe's most powerful man as narrow-minded, jealous, volatile, unforgiving, racist, misogynistic, and, frankly, a murderer.

A god who is responsible for everything but accountable for nothing. A god that ignores dying children but opens parking spaces and wins football games. A god that hates everyone you hate and agrees with everything you believe. Religion created a god of cliques, "blessing" believers while damning everyone else to Hell.

Nothing worthwhile is ever easy, and that is especially true of integrity and righteousness. Much of religion has conveniently forgotten this and lazily stands in a place of judgment. If this "God" does not make us more accepting and loving people, why should we acknowledge it? How can it be superior if it does not cause us to grow beyond the security of our tribalism and fear?

These questions divide believers and non-believers. For some, faith conquers all issues. For others, there are too many unanswered questions to buy anything religion is selling. Expanded awareness coupled with repressive philosophies are creating a mass exodus from religion.

Doctrine is questioned and abandoned for more personal experiences. Spirituality supersedes dogma. More people now believe we should dismiss anything not scientifically verifiable. The religious climate is thawing, causing the Orthodox to dig in their heels and try to reclaim their supremacy and forcing many to navigate the uncertainty of their faith, alone or in hiding.

With so many religiously unaffiliated, should we assume we have evolved so significantly that "God" is no longer necessary? Or are people fleeing because religious leaders refuse to release their grasp of control, status, and superiority? The most consequential change is that we are finally seeing through religion's veil of symbolism, power, and hypocrisy, which they purposefully concealed.

Most people agree there is probably something out there. Something that is greater than us and our understanding. Since the dawn of man, we have tried to describe and label it. Since the first written text by the Sumerians, there were Beings labeled as gods. We have portrayed "God" as a man with a white beard, a woman with eight arms, a piercing light, an energy, the Sun, a warrior, an animal, or something resembling aliens.

Since the beginning of time, we have searched for something superior and beyond us; it is instinctual. This desire advanced humankind and enabled the technology that propels humanity. We know more about celestial bodies than our oceans because we historically looked to the sky for answers. For greater knowledge of life beyond us, we have walked on the moon, landed spacecraft on Mars, toured Neptune and Saturn, and are exploring the universe.

This instinct is natural and often beneficial. Studies show (Koenig) that people of faith heal faster and have an overall brighter outlook. Most people need to believe in something, if only for comfort and support.

It is not always a god. For some, it is faeries, nature, vampires, aliens, astrology, mysticism, energy, or science. Regardless of our beliefs, since we started walking this planet, we have intuitively searched for something extraordinary. Archeologists discovered ancient cave art depicting higher beings that were carbon-dated to over 300,000 years ago. It is deeply rooted in our nature.

There is something beyond our imagination. Some thing that drives our intention, creativity, and compassion. The same power that supports all living creatures' desire to live, thrive, and survive. A universal consciousness that comes from something greater than us. Something that enables all sentient beings to feel compassion, joy, and love.

Most reasonable people can agree on these basic premises. It is when laws, judgment, and tribal rage enter the god equation that people question and ultimately turn their backs and walk away. When religion is "crowd control," it has failed.

Organized religion has lost sight of its only proper purpose: to teach us how to love our neighbor.

The more significant problem is that religion's faults cause us to question "God" instead of our own perceptions. We fault "God", but we have failed. We argue and wage wars over beliefs instead of standing in amazement, pondering the wonder of our creation and the oneness of us all. Too many believe we are the guardians of righteousness; sadly, that belief is often used to demean others. We must remember that they are all just beliefs, and everyone has them.

When we try to define, comprehend, and justify "God," we fail. Our ancestors failed when they turned human history into an allegory for God's will. When we refuse to acknowledge the ancients' reasoning was based on ignorance, we further the demise. When we humanize something superior to humans, we diminish the Divine. We contain everything within our limited knowledge.

Beliefs are personal, and as a society, we fail when we try to take something personal and create a mass doctrine that fits everyone. This applies to every belief, but we rarely see such rage outside of religion (and politics). We never see wars, murders, suicides, and government involvement over what food, music, occupation, or even shampoo is the best. We have accepted our differences in those areas but refuse to accept any discrepancies with "God." Religious beliefs are just opinions fueled by faith.

However, when religion is your identity and it is questioned, it can (and often does) incite rage. This is called cognitive dissonance, and it is often so strong that when our beliefs are challenged, fights ensue, relationships end, and resentment is all that remains. Most religions demand blind faith, which causes people to believe they are sinning for even questioning. We forget that it is all being taught by humans with a human perspective.

Realizing my view of God was derived from thousands of years of men's perception, not an infallible doctrine or absolute truth, completely altered my life. I had to reexamine everything they taught me, but more importantly, I had to accept the findings. Each lesson came with waves of emotions, leaving me shocked, saddened, and angry but also hungry for more information.

I turned away from God because of the Church. "God" has been misrepresented because of the laws and politics of men, not because of a lack of miracles that reinforce the possibility of something extraordinary. The problem is the god portrayed in religion is not supreme at all.

I wanted more; more than someone's opinion, agenda, hallucination, or a revised history.

Was that even possible? How would I find truth in the unseen? Could opinion ever translate to fact, and if so, whose view is correct?

I had uncovered too much hypocrisy, inconsistencies, and myths labeled as historical facts. I could no longer remain mindlessly faithful.

Philosopher René Descartes said, "If you would be a real seeker after truth, it's necessary that at least once in your life you doubt, as far as possible, all things."

Embarking with some cynicism sharpened my focus and established my goal of knowledge. I had to overcome my frustration when reality did not align with my beliefs and not try to justify or maintain my beliefs because of my indoctrination.

I used the universal benchmark for Truth: it must be valid in all scenarios, to all people, in all eras, cultures, and geographies. What was true for a U.S. citizen must also be true for the tribes in the Amazon. What was true in 3000 B.C.E. must remain true today. Focusing on religion, I knew my task was monumental, but I had to try.

I wanted to quit hurting and heal. I wanted to stop blaming someone or something for all my problems. I wanted to feel whole, even though they had assured me I was inadequate, incomplete, and unworthy. I did not care where the journey took me. I had no preconceived notions about what I would find, and I held no prejudices about those findings—they just had to measure up to "truth."

Chapter 5: My Disclaimers

Generations before me would not discuss religion or politics. So, early on, I knew I was breaking ancestral rules. The guidelines were in place to avoid confrontations and ensure peace. However, that only proved to deepen the indoctrination and isolation. It prevented new information, collaboration, and opposing views. It enabled the mentality that only your beliefs were correct.

With that in mind, I knew I had to establish some guidelines and make some clarifications early in the book. We all have preconceptions of "God," which is why I have used quotation marks. To differentiate between the "God" taught and the God that is love.

So, before we go any further, let's ensure we are on the same page and start this exploration looking in the same direction. To understand my journey and references, you will need to understand my perspectives. "God" is such a volatile subject. I want to be clear where I stand to avoid any unnecessary offenses.

Starting with the reference to "Religion," I am talking about Judaism, Christianity (Catholicism and Protestantism), and Islam unless otherwise noted. All three faiths worship the God of Abraham and have the same roots. The differences are more significant between Eastern and Western Religions than between those three—regardless of what they and our media say.

Early in the writing process, I struggled with pronoun usage. I no longer believe that "God" is male or female or any human form. But for ease of writing and organization, I use masculine pronouns.

I understand the patriarchal and personification issues with doing so. Still, since they own most of the mess, they should be called out accordingly. I honor and appreciate the divine feminine but switching "God" to feminine pronouns would often implicate "her" and not "him." I did not want pronouns to distract the message (There's already enough information to digest!), and I hoped with this clarification, they will not.

No one truly knows what "God" is or if "it" even exists. The discovery of that knowledge is, at a minimum, our life's journey. I am not arguing if there is a divine Spirit; there is. Instead, I am documenting the colossal mess we made of "God." And despite the human errors in perception, there is still something phenomenal out there.

I expose the baseless arguments, distortion of scripture, and human influence that are prevalent in religion. When I use the word "God," it represents a higher power/energy: a benevolent source. God is not the entity that solely exists in the Torah, Bible, Qur'an, or Vedas.

"God" has been called El, YHWH, Jehovah, Krishna, Allah, and the Holy Trinity, to name a few. Regardless of the name, the core messages are the same: "Love one another" and "Let go."

If they all have the same tenets, why are we so divided?

Organized religions are all a little right and a lot wrong, and they are not fully revealing or encompassing "God." Religion elevated humanity's failures, closed-mindedness, and bigotry, and those are solely ours to own.

I was raised as an Evangelical Protestant. There is now a vast distance between me and that denomination, and I try hard not to allow it to influence me, but I still have that background. This journey enabled me to get a closer look at other world religions but through the eyes of a Protestant. My beliefs, criticisms, basis, arguments, and knowledge all have that foundation, so my opinions

Chapter 5: My Disclaimers

and analysis may be positively and negatively skewed.

I tried to approach everything with an open mind, but it was still a mind that had a lifetime of indoctrination. Deconstructing your religion is a lengthy process because it is often so deeply ingrained in our psyche that we are unaware of what they constructed and what is real. The realizations are part of the journey. I will no longer put God in the box humans built or have blind faith in our perspectives and interpretations. God receives credit or condemnation for everything— man's ultimate scapegoat.

We have ruined God, and I am placing the blame where it is due. Ironically, the perception of "God," perpetuated by religion, is precisely what most founders like Abraham, Moses, Jesus, and Muhammad warned against and, according to scripture, came to correct. The power, greed, and the philosophy of fear and shame are as present today as they were then. As believers, we forget the directives of compassion and love, only remembering what is convenient and what feeds our ego.

Our egos have been the source of our failures since Adam and Eve. Scripture claims if they did not yearn for equality with God, we would still be in the Garden. Throughout history and religious teachings, we elevated humans to divine positions. So, millions of people look to humans, instead of logic and love, for all the answers about "God."

The word "ego" also has different meanings. When I use the term, I am implying something that creates separation. I am not speaking clinically, but spiritually. Wayne Dyer said it is an acronym: "Edging God Out." But the ego edges everyone out. It claims you are the best, ahead of the rest. Or it says you are last and alone. It tells you whatever you will believe. The ego is within us, and its goal is separation.

Because of my life, I would not have believed I was better than everyone else—that contradicted everything I was told. The ego accomplished its separation by affirming that I was a total piece of shit, which I readily accepted.

Others might only believe their ego if it assures them they are the greatest, separating them from others deemed unworthy. We see it in the caste systems, class warfare, and cliques. Eckhart Tolle said, "All you need to know and observe in yourself is this: whenever you feel superior or inferior to anyone, that's the ego in you."

Lester Levenson said, "Every problem is an ego problem. In order to have a problem, there has to be an ego-frustration."

But it is not all bad. The goal is to ensure the ego remains in check, driving you to be the best you can be at love, charity, and compassion. When the ego is in control, winning is all that matters. When religion is founded on the ego, it requires someone to be right and others wrong, and when that happens, people die.

When we proclaim authority on righteousness, we fail to realize many profound and true-to-the-soul philosophies exist in each religion and science. If we opened ourselves beyond our belief system, we could only become more knowledgeable and loving.

If everyone embraced and learned from each other instead of insisting on a single belief as the only path to "God," we would become more compassionate humans and a better functioning society. Personal growth leads to interpersonal growth, resulting in a stronger and more loving family, culture, and planet. Isn't that what a God would want? For all his children to love each other?

But anytime anyone says they have the only answer to every question and excludes people who disagree, it is not of God; it is pure ego. When a religious leader says, "They're going to Hell because (fill in the blank)," it is the antithesis of love. The goal of all religions is devotees, but when tribalism, fear, and dominance are how you get them, it is a gang, not God.

Jesus was a man of inclusion, not exclusion, so using his name for separation is an oxymoron and blasphemous. Jesus' greatest commandment was to love each other. Therefore, any action or feeling of superiority directly contradicts the founder of Christianity.

With so many discrepancies, it is no wonder people are leaving religion. When anyone claims an all-knowing, infallible status, as most religions do, a single inconsistency calls everything into doubt. We must always remember that humans are always fallible.

When we forget our fallibility, we look to others for answers instead of focusing on what matters: being kind to one another. Instead of "WWJD = What Would Jesus Do?" It should be "WWLD = What Would Love Do?" We should always focus on love: How can I become more compassionate and helpful?

Long ago, the Church brushed away compassion, love, and generosity teachings. Their pious, controlling attitudes cause us to doubt God instead of humanity.

Historically, the Church alienated anyone who exposed their hypocrisy and closed-mindedness. Well, I see it, and so do millions of others.

This life affords us daily opportunities to heal and grow. While the journey was long and arduous, I am thankful for each step. As you go through this book, I encourage you to embark on your own exploration. Some information may shock you and seem unbelievable because it is not what they usually teach, but that is the point: going beyond the indoctrination and agenda-driven dogma.

Look deeper into the subjects and ask questions. It is how we all grow; in the worst-case scenario, it starts conversations. Even if you disagree with what I say, please read the entire book. I experienced the shock, dismay, anger, and denial you may feel. I took time to process, understand, and absorb the information. This was a journey, and how I came to my conclusions was a process. Where the book starts is not where it ends.

Open your mind, release any guilt or prejudice, consider logic and what feels right, and decide for yourself.

Section III: Sin

"So, the Pharisees and teachers of the law asked Jesus, 'Why don't your disciples live according to the tradition of the elders instead of eating their food with defiled hands?' He replied, 'Isaiah was right when he prophesied about you hypocrites; as it is written: 'These people honor me with their lips, but their hearts are far from me. They worship me in vain; their teachings are merely human rules. You have let go of the commands of God and are holding on to human traditions."
~ Mark 7:5-8

Chapter 6: Me, The Sinner

I was 21, madly in love, and moving with the man of my dreams from California to Florida. Glenn's family owned a business in Florida, and his grandmother was in her 80s, so it was time for him to take over. I welcomed the adventure. Everyone else thought I was nuts.

Glenn left his third wife for me, and I moved across the country for him. In hindsight, I totally understand their concern. But then, I was so in love, and no one could stop me. I was different!

I was an idiot.

My mom lost her mind. She feared God's judgment on my soul. So, I quelled her fears by lying. I assured her I was getting my own apartment until we were married. I figured she was across the country and would be none the wiser, until she decided to visit for Christmas.

Luckily, we were already planning to move, so I told her he and I would live together at that point. I hoped my three months in Florida were easing her into me "living in sin." Regardless, it was Christmas, and it would be a glorious time! She planned for a full two weeks. I was concerned but hoped we would make wonderful memories. I had so few from childhood.

I was in complete denial. The first night, Christmas Eve, she kept me up till 3 a.m. trying to convince me Glenn was not good enough.

She pleaded, "You should marry a doctor or a lawyer!" I was numb to her judgment. He loved me, and I was happy.

Glenn arranged for "Santa" to bring Joey his presents on Christmas morning. This Santa needed no costume. Both his hair and his long beard were silver. He had a big round belly, drove a red pickup truck, and delighted in his life's purpose: bringing joy to children on Christmas.

I was elated, and there was no way my mom would ruin this holiday. Glenn and I guaranteed that Joey would have an exceptional Christmas. It filled me with joy and happy tears, knowing my son would have so much more than I ever did.

Santa parked a few doors down, appeared from his fully decorated truck, and began walking down the sidewalk, ringing his Christmas bell. The moment was magical. Kids ran out of their homes, and he greeted each of them with a belly roar, "Ho! Ho! Ho! Merry Christmas!" When Joey saw him, he bolted out the front door, running as fast as his little four-year-old legs could carry him.

Joey tripped, fell face down, jumped up, and continued his Olympic-style sprint to Santa. He leaped into Santa's arms, and on perfect cue, Santa exploded in deep belly laughter, "Merry Christmas, Joey!"

I was in full glory! My son's smile was forever imprinted on my heart. It was going to be the best Christmas of my life and something Joey would surely remember for the rest of his. Hand-in-hand, Santa and Joey walked to the house as tears of joy fell down my cheeks. This is what Christmas was supposed to be about: joy, love, and the wonder of it all!

Behind me, however, was something completely different. My mom had stayed inside, sitting in the couch's corner, staring off into the distance. When Santa came inside, Joey sat on his lap to open presents. Joey excitedly squealed as Santa pulled each gift out of his big red bag. He cackled joyfully, clapping his little hands, bouncing on Santa's knee. The joy was palpable. My mother donned her fake smile.

After Santa left, we opened the presents from each other, and

Joey received two Christian fairytale books from my mom. They were the Christian versions of "Goldilocks and the Three Bears" and "Little Red Riding Hood." I glanced through the books and showed Joey the pictures. I noticed stuff like, "If Goldilocks had prayed, God would have told her which bed to sleep in." Or "If Little Red Riding Hood wasn't a sinner and had God's protection, the wolf couldn't get to her!" I glanced at Glenn, and we exchanged looks of Wow!

The shock on my face was apparent, making my mom seethe. I feared these books could cause damage. They were twisting classics, albeit already twisted stories, to teach children to fear this all-powerful and mean "God." Joey just turned four, and she wanted me to read these to him.

The room became full of tension. My joyous Christmas was over. My mom leaped from the couch, shouted, "If you teach him about Santa, he will never believe in God!" and stormed into her bedroom. Glenn and I sat there, stunned and silent.

After her outburst, I did not see or speak to her for two days. The day after Christmas, Joey went into her room for a few minutes and told me she was reading the Bible.

I was folding laundry when she appeared on the third day. She approached the doorway of my bedroom, Bible in hand. She maniacally screamed, "You're going to hell, and you're taking my grandson with you!" I stood there, in the middle of folding a towel, with my jaw dropped. I had no words. My shock and silence further enraged her. She began pacing up and down the hall, flailing her arms and shouting, "Get me out of this den of sin!"

Within the hour, I was driving her across town to a hotel for the remaining ten days of her trip. It was a 45-minute drive, and not a word was spoken. She picked a dated, two-star airport hotel in the middle of nowhere. As we pulled in, I asked, "Are you sure you want to stay here, Mom?" She shouted, "Yes!" and opened the door with the car still in motion. I slammed on my brakes. She bounced off the door as she leaped from the car. She silently regained her composure, grabbed her bag, and slammed the door. It would be over three years before we spoke again.

Exactly three years later, I broke my foot in half, trying to escape a wasp. As I said, holidays have always been challenging. The doctors claimed I would never walk "normal again." The best-case scenario was a bad limp. They said to throw away all my high heels, confident the damage was permanent.

Glenn reached out to my mom to let her know I was in surgery and the implications of the accident. When she heard it was "just" my foot, she interrupted, said it was not that serious, and hung up on him.

A few months later, she finally called. After some small talk, I confessed my relationship was in trouble. She gasped with delight and sighed, "Oh, praise God!" She boasted about enlisting her entire prayer group to help end my sinful relationship. She sighed as if she had just gone from poverty to wealth. "Oh, thank you, Jesus!" She said with a song-like quality in her voice.

I was utterly dismayed. I had not spoken to this woman in over three years. And all she could do was tell me how happy she was that my relationship was in jeopardy. She bragged about praying for my broken heart. My mother and her friends were hoping for the destruction of my family.

My son loved this man! I loved this man! How could she do this to her daughter?

As she outlined her efforts and was giddy over her "success," I tried to process the conversation.

According to my mom, I cannot be in love without the Church's ordination.

She disagreed with my relationship.

Did that justify praying for its demise?

How could this be godly?

Jesus never wished for anyone's pain. He said to love unconditionally. But with her and her faith, there were no concerns about my feelings. Just the rigidity of her dogma. Her daughter's heart was broken, and dreams crushed, and all she could do was thank "God."

Regardless of my horror at her joy, I needed her. I had nowhere else to run. Glenn was cheating on me (shocker!), and I could still barely walk, a fact he used to justify his affair. I was leaving him as quickly as possible. I had to run home to mommy, even if it meant running into the arms of someone who prayed for all my pain.

In trying to understand this and her, I researched what exactly was sinful and what it all really meant. Understanding this was an essential step. Her beliefs about sin adversely affected our relationship because it justified her abandoning me.

Religion uses sin to separate us all, forcing us to fit into two categories: right or wrong, holy or unholy. However, while we are here, it is only human judgment, and humans only have the power we give them. The problem with human judgment is that it always leads to (some degree of) persecution, separation, and hypocrisy.

The Gospels state there is no room for human judgment, but we constantly measure who is "worthy" and who is not in our society. In 1 John 1:8-10 we are told:

> If we claim to be without sin, we deceive ourselves and the truth is not in us. If we confess our sins, he is faithful and just and will forgive us our sins and purify us from all unrighteousness. If we claim we have not sinned, we make him out to be a liar and his word is not in us.

Focusing on the sins of others is the driving force behind most religions.

When an angry mob brought an adulterous woman to Jesus, he condemned the crowd. *"He that is without sin among you, let him first cast a stone at her"* (John 8:7).

Even though the mob demanded him to, Jesus did not judge, scold her, or agree with them. He looked at her and told her to leave and sin no more.

There was no flogging or lingering penance. Simply, try not to do it again. Jesus did not turn her away, lecture, repudiate her, or perpetuate the crowd's agenda. Instead, he addressed the crowd's hypocrisy and focused the judgment on them.

"Do not judge, or you too will be judged. For in the same way you judge others, you will be judged, and with the measure you use, it will be measured to you. Why do you look at the speck of sawdust in your brother's eye and pay no attention to the plank in your own eye?" (Matthew 7:1-3)

Focusing on the sins of others places you on a direct path to hypocrisy, invalidation, and shame.

My mom was an example of this. Ten years after her death, I learned my mom was a liar and hypocrite. When I was a teenager, she constantly left me home alone for the weekend or sometimes a week; she was getting drunk and sleeping with most of the men in my aunt's small town. She was doing the same things she disowned me for. She kicked me out of the house for eating a pot-laced cookie and having sex with my boyfriend. Throughout my twenties, she disowned me every time I dated. Her prayer journals detailed her obsession with my sex life while enjoying her own. The hypocrisy would be comical if it were not so traumatizing.

In her twisted views, she loved me enough to save my soul, even if she was so careless with hers. My mom tried judgment, fear, and isolation to control me, driving me further away from her and her God. If her actions represented "God," I wanted nothing to do with him. Any god that told a mother to abandon their child, to be discarded like trash, is not worthy of praise.

Through this journey, I saw her humanity and could separate her from her distorted beliefs. People she trusted led her astray. Because to be genuinely God-like, one must address everyone, in every situation, with love. Love does not control or judge. Love accepts and affirms.

Chapter 7: What Exactly is a Sin?

Let's begin with the basics…

Per Merriam-Webster's Dictionary (2023), a sin is:

- An offense against religious or moral law
- An action that is or is felt to be highly reprehensible <it is a sin to waste food>
- An often-serious shortcoming: fault
- Transgression of the law of God
- A vitiated state of human nature in which the self is estranged from God

You might think (at least I did) that if they labeled something a sin, it was always a sin, but that is incorrect. Throughout the ages, the "sins" humans imposed on society run the gamut. Most would view these "sins" as ridiculous.

Cutting one's hair or shaving, wearing clothes of mixed fabrics like polyester, and having a child born with any abnormalities were sinful and carried significant penalties. Also sinful was touching a menstruating woman, tattoos, and seeing a family member nude. Religion created these laws to ensure that certain tribes were separate and superior to others, and these laws are obviously not divine directives that prove one as righteous.

Religion admonishes all theories of evolution yet has undergone its own, proven by the ever-changing "sins" they taught us to avoid. These transformations would be comical if the laws did not perpetuate superiority, judgment, and hate and cost lives.

Historically, religious leaders used the culture and ideologies of the era to dictate what was sinful. This perspective leads many to believe that labeling something a "sin" was used to control the masses. When personal hygiene and (ignorance of) women's health are conditions for eternal salvation or damnation, there is a problem.

Most people would say, "Well, that was then, and we have grown and learned." However, our position of judgment and often hateful ways toward anyone outside our belief system are evidence of the contrary. This behavior proves we are still people of ancient minds, with tribal motives, and using "God" to justify our actions.

Chapter 8: Sinful Foods

Genesis said we have dominion over everything on Earth and can eat anything *"except the fruit that grows on the Tree of Knowledge."* (Gen. 2) Leviticus and Deuteronomy get more specific. Forbidden animals included those that "chew the cud" (the ruminants: regurgitate and swallow again—cows, goats, sheep, etc.), split-hoofed animals (the ruminants, pigs, buffalo, llamas, deer, etc.), and scavengers (shrimp, lobster, crab, etc.). They were all considered dirty.

Christians believe Jesus lifted the prohibition, and Jewish dietary restrictions no longer apply. Jews and Muslims do not acknowledge this. However, the Church continued to label foods as sinful, but for entirely different reasons.

When potatoes arrived in Spain mid-sixteenth century, the Church classified them as unhealthy and sinful. They labeled the potato the "Devil's Root" or "Devil's Apples." This belief caused approximately 150,000 people to die of starvation during a crop famine across Europe and Russia. The Church blamed and charged more than 50,000 people with witchcraft and burned them at the stake. Eventually, the Church changed its position and lifted the restriction, giving it its blessings.

Then Ireland's potato crop failed. The Catholics claimed it was divine punishment for eating it, and many accepted their fate and died. The Protestants blamed the famine on the Catholics, claiming it was because of their flawed religion. Some Protestants demanded conversion to Protestantism before giving starving children life-sustaining food.

Consider the absurdity of this "sin" while eating your next order of French fries, potato salad, or baked potato. More than 200,000 people died because the Church claimed eating a potato caused eternal damnation.

They believed the tomato was sinful from the late 1700s through the early 1800s. After discovering the fruit, the New American Christians saw it as beautiful and tempting, so they considered it immoral. They categorized it alongside dancing, drinking, and playing cards. In 1834, they learned it had medicinal benefits, so the fruit was no longer sinful.

The Church considered chocolate a sin for longer than marijuana has been. For over 5000 years, shrimp, lobster, bacon, and ham were an abomination and remain so in most religions. The Bible declares them an abomination four times more than same-sex activity. However, Christianity overlooks these laws so they can focus on other "abominations" while eating their bacon-wrapped shrimp.

A common perception of religion is that anything that gives us pleasure is considered sinful. In most cases, this observation aligns with history. Ironically, sugar was never a sin, yet it was a primary reason for the mass kidnappings of Africans and their subsequent slavery.

Evidently, the cold-hearted cruelty of human ownership lacked the same eternal implications as eating chocolate or a tomato. The destruction of families and the deaths of millions of people through torture and mutilation was godlier than eating a potato.

Sadly, even now, people use the Bible as their defense and justification for elitism and discrimination. Historically, it is only a sin if it does not suit your agenda.

I wonder which "sins" of today will be viewed with equal absurdity by future generations.

Chapter 9: In the Beginning, There was Racism and Sexism

The first sin is "The Original Sin," as detailed in Genesis 3. In this story, Eve disobeyed God by eating from the "Tree of Knowledge." The serpent tempted Eve with ultimate equality with God — knowledge, power, and superiority. This story originates in Judaism, but only Christianity believes the serpent was Satan.

We are supposed to believe there was a talking snake and questioning that is a lack of faith. However, since talking snakes only occur in imagination and animation, we can surmise the talking serpent is metaphorical.

In this first story of sin, the snake symbolizes our ego — our thoughts tempting us with pride, power, and knowledge. It is a cautionary tale of what happens when these things control our lives. Ironically, those qualities are the goal within religious leadership, but outside of their governance, it is a sin.

The penalty for Adam and Eve's disobedience was separation from constant communication with God, painful childbirth for Eve, and banishment from the Garden of Eden. When God confronts them, Adam blames Eve, and Eve blames the serpent. Biblically, this is the first "warning from God" about the "power of women." It is also the first: "It wasn't me!" We will never know if Eve ate the fruit first and then coaxed Adam. Or, if this was the baseline, establishing the derogatory tone towards women and diminishing their role in society—most modern scholars believe the latter.

Adam and Eve's story begins with her considered "lesser." Eve was a "gift" from God, not an equal partner, but a gift. This doctrine established an ownership mentality so profoundly rooted in our psyche that only in the last 50 years have women finally gotten their voice and freedoms and seen their worth. Men assumed the power of "God" to fulfill their ego and diminished the God-ordained giver of life. Then, they completely disregarded her, claiming all life came from Adam—though his rib—not Eve.

Ancient Jewish folklore tells of a woman before Eve named Lilith. She and Adam were made from the earth simultaneously (Rosh Hashanah). Lilith demanded equality, refusing to lie underneath Adam during sex and insisting on being "on top." When Adam protested, Lilith left him. Adam pleaded with God to make her return, so God sent three angels to coax her. When she refused, she was cursed.

The biblical foundation for this story is the different creation accounts in Genesis: *"So God created mankind in his own image, in the image of God he created them; male and female, he created them."* (Genesis 1:27)

Then, in Genesis chapter two, Adam is alone. Verse 18 says, *"The Lord God said, 'It is not good for the man to be alone. I will make a helper suitable for him.'"*

In 4000 B.C.E., the Sumerians claimed Lilith was a night demon. She was the source of sudden infant death syndrome (SIDS) and men's nocturnal emissions—they blamed her for him spilling his seed. She was the scapegoat for all of men's sexual weaknesses. Labeled a succubus and baby killer, she was the villain and victim of the patriarchy. Independent women who did not want to be servants to men must be demonic.

A text published in the Middle Ages, "The Alphabet of Ben Sira," told of Adam being sexually inadequate. The Jewish leadership considered it satire since men were surely not weak and sexually incompetent. Lilith made a pact with God: "… it created me only to cause sickness to infants. If the infant is male, I have dominion over him for eight days after his birth, and if female, for twenty days."

Once the boy is circumcised, Lilith loses control.

In the Jewish Kabbalah, she is a serpent that tempted and mounted Eve. Menstruation is supposedly Lilith's evil seed. In some texts, she is Cain's mother.

For thousands of years, religion demonized strong, independent, non-subservient women. In Lilith's case, literally. Whether fact or fiction, it is the perfect allegory used by the patriarchy, both as a warning for feminists and as a justification for men's lack of control.

One Sunday, the pastor said, "Oh, men! Where would we be without our wives?" Someone from the congregation shouted, "Still in the Garden of Eden!" Everyone roared with laughter. Sadly, religion's depiction of women adversely affected our societal standings, and the Bible justified our degradation.

Coupled with manufactured "sins," religion furthered a doctrine that kept women submissive, just as the patriarchy intended.

The second sin was Adam and Eve's first-born son, Cain, killing their second son, Abel. Cain was a farmer and Abel a herder—their offerings to God were according to the fruits of their labor. Abel offered an animal sacrifice, and Cain offered fruits and grains. The legend is that Abel gave wholeheartedly, while Cain gave out of obligation. When God realized this, he scolded Cain and applauded Abel. Cain was overwhelmed with jealous rage and killed his brother.

Per the texts, God marked Cain and sent him away. Genesis 4: 9–16 details the story.

They did not understand skin color, so they assumed it originated with sin and canonized the ignorant belief that people of color were cursed by "God." This is, by far, the most detrimental, cruel, and ego-driven misconception religion has ever perpetuated, costing millions of lives. Sadly, it continues today.

The implications of this ignorance are vast, affecting billions of people throughout history. This belief is so ingrained in us we forget where it originated: a lack of understanding and placing our ignorance in a box labeled "God."

The Bible reinforced Black skin as a mark, or a curse from "God," in the story of Noah and his son Ham: "The Curse of Ham." Noah had three sons: Shem, Japheth, and Ham. The Bible asserts we are all their descendants because everyone else perished in the flood.

The Bible documents the first caste system, supposedly dictated by "God" via Noah. Shem's sons were to be free men. Japheth's sons were the nobles, and Ham's sons were to be enslaved. Because of Noah's flaws, millions of people have suffered. The event is detailed in Genesis 9:20–27:

> Noah, a man of the soil, proceeded to plant a vineyard. When he drank some of its wine, he became drunk and lay uncovered inside his tent. Ham, the father of Canaan, saw his father naked and told his two brothers outside. But Shem and Japheth took a garment and laid it across their shoulders; then they walked in backward and covered their father's naked body. Their faces were turned the other way so they would not see their father naked.

> When Noah awoke from his wine and found out what his youngest son had done to him, he said, "Cursed be Canaan! The lowest of slaves will he be to his brothers." He also said, "Praise be to the Lord, the God of Shem! May Canaan be the slave of Shem. May God extend Japheth's territory; may Japheth live in the tents of Shem, and may Canaan be the slave of Japheth."

What we know from this scripture is that Noah got drunk and passed out. What happened next has many interpretations. Some scholars say the text is exact, and Noah was naked and exposed, and Ham publicly ridiculed him. Other theories claim Ham sodomized or castrated his father. There are even some theologians who believe, according to Leviticus, to "uncover the nakedness" of a man meant to have sex with his wife, meaning Ham had sex with his mother. Others speculate Ham practiced black magic and cursed Noah with temporary sterility.

Ultimately, most scholars believe we should take the scriptures literally because seeing someone naked was considered a major sin. Some Muslims still believe this sin is punishable by death, as dictated in the Bible.

Regardless of the assumptions, Noah cursed Ham's first-born child, Canaan, when he awoke and realized what had happened. There is much debate about why he cursed Canaan instead of Ham, but most surmise it was because Ham received God's protection during the flood.

In an apparent preservation of Noah's religious image, drinking was ritualized, negating his sin of drunkenness, and adding to Ham's crime. With this revision, Ham disrespected his father and a sacred ritual. In the end, Canaan and all his descendants, identifiable by their Black skin, were cursed, slaughtered, or enslaved. These descendants became known as the Canaanites and were the focus of many war stories in the Old Testament (O.T.).

Jewish folklore alleges Ham had sex on the ark (which was prohibited), so "God" turned him Black, or children conceived on the ark were born Black. These ancient stories fuel man's desire for superiority and racial discrimination. For over 4000 years, Jews, Christians, and Muslims have cited "The Curse of Ham" as a justification for the caste system and the enslavement of people of color.

The Canaanites are infamous in the O.T. as the tribes' "God" sent the Israelites to slaughter. Racism is never overtly taught, just its undertones which justify annihilation. The first seven books of the Bible detail God's alleged rage against them—the Israelites were "ordered" to slaughter them all. "Canaanite" was a generic designation for any non-Israelite. Ham's descendants were also linked to the Tower of Babel, and Sodom and Gomorrah. They labeled an entire race as evil and justified their mistreatment because of Noah's drunkenness and not understanding skin pigmentation and genetics.

After "God's" attempt at ethnic cleansing, five of the six Canaanite tribes survived. Seemingly, "God" is highly inept. God receives credit or blame for all the world's events, but "he" totally failed at this. We failed. We failed at the atrocity of ethnic cleansing. And no one could prove themselves as "God's" favorite children, or there would be only one surviving race.

But since ancient times, we have succeeded in ignorant rhetoric and justifying ego-driven supremacy and hate—all in the name of "God." Proof of its success is that so many generations accept it. Even today, when the facts prove otherwise, we see endemic racism and declarations of supremacy, claiming appointment by "God."

Worldwide, Protestantism is the exclusive religion for White supremacy groups. As late as the 20th century, the Southern Baptist Convention believed "Blacks" had their own Heaven. The SBC only relinquished its racist ideology in 1995. Before the 1960s, most Protestant churches banned Black people from serving as clergy, and some churches practiced racial segregation until the late 1990s.

In 1978, the Latter-day Saints (Mormons) repealed their ban on Black people in the priesthood. The president of the Mormon Church claimed "God" commanded him to extend the ministry to all honorable men.

What a fickle "God" we conceive.

The Canaanites were Semitic and created symbols that later became the alphabet. Adapted by the Greeks and Romans, it influenced many cultures, including Western civilization. The Canaanites were politically active, including membership within the Pharisees (the religious authority enforcing Jewish law).

In approximately 1200 B.C.E., during and after the attempted genocide, the Canaanites vanished and reemerged as the Phoenicians. The Phoenicians were superior traders, sailing ships from Asia to Britain and as far as 2500 miles along the African coast. The Phoenician's stellar business acumen provided them with a large military. It transformed the capital of Carthage into a vast empire.

"Phoenicians" comes from the Greek word "phoínios," which means purple. Phoenicians discovered purple dye. The Canaanites/ Phoenicians worshiped the god Baal, which fueled the Israelite's justification for eradication. When the Israelites left Egypt and set their sights on conquering Canaan, it was an established culture for over 400 years; they had their own religion. When the Canaanites refused to convert, the Israelites vowed their eradication. The Bible details an extraordinarily volatile and insecure "God" who's Hell-bent on mass destruction.

Can you imagine a religion conquering and slaughtering nearly everyone in the U.S. and claiming "God" ordered it? The United States is less than 250 years old. We look at other religions and their supposed "calls from God" and claim our God would never act like that. However, the Bible starts with a god whose primary goal was to conquer and destroy vast portions of his creation. It is as if God said, "Oops! I did not mean to create those people! Can you kill all of them for me? Thanks!"

Man is fickle. Hate is fickle. God is love.

The proof that this is a manufactured ideology and not a directive from God is in archeological evidence, DNA, and logic.

In Africa, they found remains of humanity's oldest ancestor (commonly referred to as "Eve," ironically enough). Carbon dating showed that she lived between 100,000 and 200,000 years ago.

- Our DNA reveals we all originated from dark-skinned Africans.
- No mentally stable (human) parent could ever imagine condoning the slaughter of their children.

But a greater force full of love, a perfect Being, is diminished to uncontrollable acts of anger and rage? This Being allegedly orders the annihilation of not just one of his children but all their children. And then he supposedly tells us he marked these people for easy targeting? That is evil and illogical, and man's attempt to justify their ignorant, deplorable actions.

We have ruined God.

Chapter 10: The Top Ten

The scholars, theologians, archeologists, and religious leaders who studied the history of the Ten Commandments had difficulty putting all the pieces together. They struggled to fit them nicely into one story and align with religious text. This section took me down rabbit holes of confusion and once again forced me to set aside everything they taught me for the facts.

Then, I had to understand the disjointed, distorted, and agenda-driven alterations occurring throughout history, which many tried to hide. For the first time in history (in most cases), information is available to anyone seeking it. Uncovering the parts of history they concealed for centuries despite their availability was challenging.

The Ten Commandments are not the Bible's first nor the only laws. The first was the Seven Laws of Noah. They were given to the "Children of Noah," or everyone, because of the flood. God supposedly gave the first six to Adam and Eve. After the flood, Noah added the seventh, claimed them as his own, and made them official.

These laws were the foundation for all biblical commandments. In Judaism, if any non-Jew adheres to these mandates, they too will reach righteousness.

Prohibition of:

1. Idolatry

2. Murder
3. Theft
4. Sexual Immorality
5. Blasphemy
6. Eating flesh taken from an animal while it is still alive
7. Establishment of courts of law

The Ten Commandments appear twice in the Bible: Exodus 20:1-17 and Deuteronomy 5:6-21. There are a total of 613 commandments. However, ten were far more manageable and easier to adhere to across the ages. Today, they are the foundation of Judaism, Christianity, and Islam. However, they did not gain prominence in Christian law until the fourth century C.E.. They were not official Christian doctrine until the Lateran Council in 1215.

The Council of Trent in 1545 and the Second Vatican Council in 1962 reconfirmed them. The Vatican periodically confirms there's agreement on the commandments. Really?

The story of the Ten Commandments, perpetuated by Hollywood, leads us to believe these laws were prominent and integral in early Judaism. In reality, they are merely ten out of the 613. In the New Testament (N.T.), Jesus said no law held more importance than to love God and your neighbor. For Christianity, this proclamation meant the dismissal of the other 603 laws since the top ten covered it.

According to the O.T., Moses received the entire Torah, not just the Ten Commandments. Moses was on Mount Sinai for 40 days and nights, but modern Christianity only tells of receiving ten. Emphasis on these laws and only these laws became the official separation between Jews and Christians. They declared the 613 commandments in the Torah only applied to the twelve tribes of Israel and not followers of Christ.

In Judaism, three times a year during high holidays, they recite Exodus and Deuteronomy, which includes all the commandments. Jews believe the Ten Commandments are the foundation for all the others but are not the only laws given to Moses.

History shows that unless a commandment suits the Christian agenda, usually with feelings of superiority, they do not abide by or recognize any of the other 603 laws. We use a commandment like "men are not to lie with another man" as judgment and discrimination against gay people but conveniently forget they considered a menstruating woman in public a more grievous sin.

The abominations included masturbation, porn, cheating on taxes, tattoos, and playing or watching football on Sundays. For thousands of years, adultery was punishable by death. We conveniently stand in judgment of others while flirting online with a stranger as our significant other sits alone in another room.

Religious law promotes hypocrisy because we select which rules to obey and ignore. This hypocrisy is why Jesus said love is the only thing that matters. Because if love is all you do, everything else falls into place.

This story of the Ten Commandments asserts the finger of God wrote them. A common fallacy perpetuated by Hollywood and art is there were five commandments on each tablet. However, scholars state each tablet included all ten. There were two tablets because the culture and era dictated that important text be written in duplication.

Allegedly, the text penetrated each side of the tablet but was legible from both sides. The tablets were a miracle in every sense—stone tablets illustrating the physical proof of God. So, of course, they disappeared.

The Ten Commandments are broken down into two sets of five laws. The first set deals with religious laws, and the second is moral laws. The religious laws dictate how to respect and worship God. The moral codes ensured social harmony. Do not lie, cheat, or steal because it could disrupt tribal peace.

The Ten Commandments vary over time and are the product of hundreds of years of debate. Martin Luther scolded the Catholics for not really following the commandments, which started his separation and reformation. But even with just ten, they differ according to denominations. Each set of commandments addresses the needs of the author's beliefs, culture, and agendas.

There are three versions of the Ten Commandments based on Exodus 20:2-17: Philonic, Talmudic, and Augustinian:

- Philonic (Phi) from first-century writers Philo and Josephus is the oldest division. It adjusts the third verse to be the first, verses 4–6 become the second verse, and so on. Protestants (except Lutherans), Greek Orthodox, and Hellenistic Jews generally follow this breakdown. Most include the prologue in verse two as part of the first commandment or as a preface.

- Talmudic (Tal): The third-century Jewish Talmud has verses 1 and 2 as a declaration, not a commandment, and combines verses 3–6 as the second commandment.

- Augustinian (Aug): This fifth-century breakdown starts with the Talmud's second commandment and adds an extra commandment by dividing the covenant of envy into two parts. Roman Catholics and Martin Luther used this division. However, Roman Catholics used Deuteronomy for the Ten Commandments, and Luther used Exodus.

Confusing, right? I did not know the Top Ten were changed to fit their desires.

Here are their breakdowns.

First Commandment:

Hebrew: *I am the Lord thy God, who brought thee out of the land of Egypt, out of the house of slavery.*

Catholic: *I am the Lord thy God. Thou shalt not have strange gods before me.*

Protestant: *Thou shalt have no other gods before me.*

This revision shows the evolution of the faiths. Since Christians were not the Israelites, the verse was unrelatable, so they changed it. They renumbered the commandments and used them to bolster the Christian message. Eras dictate interpretations and laws, and doctrine is altered accordingly.

While it does not appear in the Hebrew version (it is their second), the key words are "before me." Back then, there were many gods. The

O.T. lists many of them. The lesser gods helped with harvests, rain, and daily survival needs. Those gods just could not precede the God of Israel. If "God" were first, other gods could maintain their purpose and value.

Allowing other gods was about compromise and mass appeal. We see this tactic throughout history when conquerors try to recruit and merge ideologies—what can be adjusted to minimize the impact on daily public life?

This commandment is, "My God is better than your god," and if that were understood, there would be no problems. However, history proves this mentality can be deadly.

An example of how complicated this commandment can get is how it reconciles Jesus, Mary, and the Saints. They became intercessors, literally coming before him, resulting in thousands of years of hatred, cultural separation, and religious wars.

Second Commandment:

Hebrew/Protestant: [1] *Thou shalt have no other gods before Me. **Thou shalt not make unto thee a graven image, nor any manner of likeness, of any thing that is in Heaven above, or that is in the Earth beneath, or that is in the water under the Earth; Thou shalt not bow down unto them, nor serve them; for I the Lord thy God am a jealous God, visiting the iniquity of the fathers upon the children unto the third and fourth generation of them that hate Me; and showing mercy unto the thousandth generation of them that love Me and keep My commandments.***

Catholic: *Thou shalt not take the name of the Lord thy God in vain.*

Judaism and Islam consider the veneration of any object a violation of this law. The Amish and some sects of Islam also include photographs. The worship of images is still a large part of the schism between Catholics and Protestants. Early Protestants burned images, artifacts, and sculptures—anything breaking this law. As a kid, most churches we attended looked more like corporate offices, not

1**Bold** indicates the Hebrew version, and plain text indicates the Protestant version. Both as bold text means alignment.

cathedrals.

Augustine of Hippo (Saint Augustine) said, "He who worships an image turns the truth of God into a lie."

While the wars over this have (relatively) subsided between Catholics and Protestants, this commandment remains significant and divisive between Islam's Sunni and Shiites and prompted some terrorist attacks.

The Catholic version changed the second commandment from graven images to taking the Lord's name in vain, the Hebrew and Protestant's third commandment. To compensate for this omission, they moved up the rest—changing the fourth commandment to the third, the fifth to the fourth, and so on.

For almost a thousand years, the Catholic Church successfully concealed its elimination of the second commandment. The Seventh General Council in 787 virtually omitted or falsely explained it away. Their concealment was so thorough that it was not uncovered until 1563. Martin Luther found it several decades after his initial protest.

If the Catholic Church were able to continue prohibiting the public from reading the Bible, they could have forever concealed their omission. The Protestant Reformation started a literal "opening of the books" and, in doing so, opened a massive can of worms. The Catholic's defense was, "The honor paid to sacred images is a 'respectful veneration,' not the adoration due to God alone." And "whoever venerates an image venerates the person portrayed in it."

The flexibility of "God's Law" amazes me.

Third Commandment:
Hebrew/Protestant: *Thou shalt not take the name of the Lord thy God in vain; **for the Lord will not hold him guiltless that taketh His name in vain.***

Catholic: *Remember the sabbath day, to keep it holy.*

Besides disregarding the second commandment, the Catholics condensed their third commandment. The Catholics called this edit meaningless because the numbers associated with the commandments were only for reference and study purposes. Here, the Church admits to altering biblical text and dismisses it as insignificant yet denies it anywhere else.

This law initially meant taking an oath in God's name, "I swear to God"—not profanity, as we are told today. The intent was to prohibit using God as your credibility.

Taking an oath with your hand on a Bible breaks this law. Ironically, government facilities usually display the Ten Commandments and then ask you to break one to validate yourself.

In 1500 C.E., the Puritans and Henry VIII changed this commandment's meaning to using God's name outside the Church. In Latin, "profane" means "outside of the temple," and before this revision, just saying "God" was not necessarily a bad thing. Over the last 500 years, the commandment's meaning evolved to curse words involving God's name(s).

Fourth Commandment:
Hebrew/Protestant: *Remember the Sabbath day to keep it holy. Six days shalt thou labor and do all thy work. But the seventh day is the Sabbath in honor of the Lord thy God; on it thou shalt not do any work, neither thou, nor thy son, nor thy daughter, thy manservant nor thy maidservant, nor thy cattle, nor thy stranger that is within thy gates; For in six days the Lord made the heavens and the Earth, the sea, and all that is in them, and rested on the seventh day; therefore the Lord blessed the Sabbath day and hallowed it.*
Catholic: *Honor thy father and thy mother.*

In 324 C.E., Emperor Constantine moved the Sabbath from Saturday to Sunday. He reasoned that Jesus' resurrection happened on a Sunday. So, he altered a 2000-year-old law and changed the Sabbath from the last day to the first day of the week. Even if religious leaders objected, it would have been in vain. Roman law always eclipsed religious doctrine.

This commandment's importance is to remind us that no one enslaves us; God freed us. It urges us to remember and honor that.

In early colonial America, the Puritans made adherence to the

Sabbath paramount. On the Sabbath, one could not work, travel, cook, clean, laugh, play, walk, or swim; doing so was a crime. The punishment varied according to the severity of the offense but could involve fines, imprisonment, beatings, and death.

Church attendance was also mandatory, and violations could result in death. They heavily enforced these laws on Native Americans, and this was part of their forced conversion.

Sex was also prohibited, and the Puritans believed a child was born on the same day it was conceived. So, a child born on Sunday was proof of a crime.

Returning on a Sunday from a long deployment at sea, a Naval Officer kissed his wife. They charged him with "unseemly behavior."

The Colombian Centennial's December 1789 issue stated George Washington was accused of traveling on a Sunday.

A "Sunday Exception" is in the American Constitution: Article I, Section 7. They removed the word "Sabbath," but many of its laws remain. Nineteen states still prohibit alcohol sales on Sundays. As late as 1985, Texas banned the purchase of pots, pans, and washing machines. Car dealerships in Texas, Illinois, Indiana, Maine, and Utah still observe Sabbath law.

North Dakota retailers may open at noon on Sundays. Bergen County, New Jersey, only allows grocery stores, amusement and entertainment facilities, and restaurants to be open on Sundays. Because, regardless of the Sabbath, servants must still serve.

The Puritan enforcement of these laws enabled the wealthy and powerful to observe the Sabbath while forcing the marginalized to work and cater to them. Eventually, these laws helped construct the first set of labor laws, allowing everyone a day off. In the 19th century, they overturned mandatory church attendance since it violated religious freedoms.

Biblical law continues to structure and form U.S. law, even though our founding fathers intended to prohibit it. Americans (hypocritically) look at other countries where Religion influences their governments and condemn it with superiority and disdain. They claim we would never allow such a thing.

Fifth Commandment:

Hebrew/Protestant: *Honor thy father and thy mother; in order that thy days may be prolonged upon the land which the Lord thy God giveth thee.*

Catholic: *Thou shalt not kill.*

Honoring family elders was critical to keeping tribal order. Its placement as the first of the moral commandments confirms its prominence. Chaos would ensue if children were left to their own accord or did not learn from their elders. This commandment is essential to any society, crossing all religions and cultures throughout history. We see the results of a lack of parental influence in films like *Lord of the Flies.*

Even young male elephants who have lost their parental figures run amok, out for destruction, filled with anger and rage. Orphaned males lack the compassion developed in family units. Similarly, humans lacking parental involvement also exhibit elevated levels of rage.

This commandment assumes the parents act in love, not teaching judgment and hate. However, parents frequently pass on their ignorance and fears to their children, and it often starts with Religion.

Knowledge and critical thinking have always threatened the orthodoxy. Critical thinking and faith rarely mix. Religious scripture was intended for peace and goodwill but was distorted by the powerful and used as crowd control.

Based on English laws, the early American Puritans set up state-run education facilities to support their values and indoctrinate children, ensuring generations were taught their Christian philosophy.

In 1636, the Puritans in Massachusetts voted to establish "The School of Prophets," a divinity school that grew into Harvard College and Harvard University. The early Fundamentalists founded Harvard, Yale, and other Ivy League schools as programs for "unruly" children. They believed the commandments justified detaining children. They listed the scriptures in the state law.

These institutions established a doctrine to prevent deviations from the Puritan value system. They were founded on the most extreme interpretations of the Bible. In 1646, the Massachusetts colonies implemented the "Instruction for the Punishment of Incorrigible Children" law. This legislation required parents to teach their children to accept the Puritan value system. Failure to comply was punishable by death.

The Massachusetts Capital Laws:

13. If any child, or children, above sixteen years old, and of sufficient understanding, shall CURSE, or SMITE their natural FATHER, or MOTHER; he or they shall be put to death: unless it can be sufficiently testified that the Parents have been very unchristianly negligent in the education of such children; or so provoked them by extreme, and cruel correction; that they have been forced thereunto to preserve themselves from death or maiming. Exod. 21. 17. Lev. 20. 9. Exod. 21. 15.

14. If a man have a stubborn or REBELLIOUS SON, of sufficient years & understanding (viz) sixteen years of age, which will not obey the voice of his father, or the voice of his mother, and that when they have chastened him will not harken unto them: then shal his Father & Mother being his natural parents, lay hold on him, & bring him to the Magistrates assembled in Court & testifie unto them, that their son is stubborn & rebellious & will not obey their voice and chastisement, but lives in sundry notorious crimes, such a son shal be put to death. Deut. 21. 20. 21. (1929)

Most of the United States' Founding Fathers were against the Puritan societal concepts and were home-schooled. Ben Franklin fled from Boston to Philadelphia to avoid the Massachusetts school system. He spent the rest of his life criticizing Harvard and the Boston clergy. The Northwest Ordinance and the Reconstruction Amendments prevented extreme ideologies from spreading and controlling the land.

Ironically, conservatives now fear these institutions because they believe it leads to liberalism and the abandonment of faith. Centuries later, religious influence still tries to mold society into more Heliocentric, despite our Founding Father's attempts to prevent it.

Sixth Commandment:
Hebrew/Protestant: *Thou shalt not kill.*
Catholic: *Thou shalt not commit adultery.*

The Bible states unlawful killings are grievous moral sins. The intention of this verse is often debated. Most agree the term "to kill" means murder. Lawful or justified killings are considered necessary and often "ordained by God," like war, the death penalty, or self-defense.

A significant biblical contradiction is Moses. After receiving the commandments, with "Thou shalt not kill" being a major one, "God" supposedly ordered him to slaughter thousands of people. A human parent would never ask such a thing. Yet we conceive a god so small that murdering his "children" was common in biblical days.

In 1947, Louis Fisher said, in his book about Gandhi, "The shreds of individuality cannot be sewed together with a bayonet; nor can democracy be restored according to the biblical injunction of an 'eye for an eye' which, in the end, would make everybody blind."

Early humanity conceived a god equally primitive, full of rage and jealousy — a "Supreme Being" who constantly fears isolation and becoming inconsequential.

Really? God?

They also include suicide, assisted or otherwise, in this commandment. It demands that life-supporting measures be given regardless of the patient's condition. This philosophy was tested in the 1998-2005 Terri Schiavo case in Florida, which drew national attention. The Church claimed it was "God's will" for Terri to remain alive, regardless of her ten years in a vegetative condition.

Why is this life so important if Heaven is glorious and God so loving? Even when the merciful thing to do is to let them go. The Church prefers a dying person to suffer rather than letting them die peacefully.

Although, I would fear meeting their god, too.

It does not take a religious person to know that taking another life is wrong. It does not take Religion to value life. Ironically, Religion has caused most of the killing.

Instead of love, we hate. Instead of acceptance, we separate. We do this. Not God.

Seventh Commandment:
Hebrew/Protestant: *Thou shalt not commit adultery.*
Catholic: *Thou shalt not steal.*

The "Nash Manuscript," from second century BCE, shows they viewed adultery as worse than murder. For over a thousand years, adultery (the 7th) preceded murder (the 6th) on the list.

Adultery was a sin throughout the ages, not because of a breach of loyalty and trust but because it violated another man's property. In the Bible, adultery was a sin only for women. A man could not commit adultery since he was the property owner. Men had many wives, but they forbid women to stray.

This law was essential to keep tribal unity. It could be catastrophic for a woman to bear another man's child—the implications of family inheritance would cause chaos within the tribe. In the fifth century, when inheritance was not an issue, adultery lost its importance. The Puritans reinstated it in the 1500s and considered it a grievous sin, punishable by death.

During the Victorian Compromise, adultery remained a crime, but they only prosecuted it in "open and notorious" circumstances. One could be acquitted of murder if their spouse's affair caused public shame or notoriety.

The Bible commands men to love their wives. Still, given the era and culture, it was obviously about the treatment of women, not fidelity. A man could have up to eighteen wives. Scripture includes the wife on the list of property in the tenth commandment.

Today, in most countries, a wife labeled and treated as property would be offensive and illegal. Religious lawmakers and leaders distort the biblical definition and try to mold it into their agendas. I chuckle every time I hear a politician claim they are doing God's will by outlawing same-sex marriage. "Marriage is between one man and one woman!" Most of the Bible is the antithesis of that.

Luke 16:18 states,

> *"Anyone who divorces his wife and marries another woman commits adultery, and the man who marries a divorced woman commits adultery."*

Catholics still admonish it, but most Protestants disregard it and have no qualms about multiple marriages while judging someone else's definition of it.

Christianity, Orthodox Jews, and Muslims consider all sexual acts outside of marriage a grievous sin—often prohibiting holy communion until they repent and are forgiven by the Church. Adultery is breaking a vow to God, so it should be a greater sin than fornication.

This law covers thoughts and actions, so masturbation, pornography, and lust, as well as prostitution, rape, and incest, are adulterous.

But biblically, this law did not apply to men.

Eighth Commandment:
Hebrew/Protestant: *Thou shalt not steal.*
Catholic: *Thou shalt not bear false witness against thy neighbor.*

This commandment's intention was malice. Many theologians surmise its purpose was to prohibit the stealing of people—abductions into slavery. In biblical times, no one would go hungry. They fed people experiencing poverty. They condoned taking sustenance as a means of survival. Taking property in "obvious and urgent necessity…to provide for immediate, essential needs (food, shelter, and clothing)" was not considered stealing. (Archdiocese)

People experiencing poverty had the right to eat from the fields until they were full. They just could not take anything with them.

This ensured everyone was fed, the poor were not forgotten, and it safeguarded landowners against greed. Studies prove poverty breeds theft—most people steal to survive or feed their families. Ensuring everyone was safe and fed left only malice to be addressed. Like the other moral laws, compliance was essential to tribal unity and peace.

The poverty laws are now ignored, but it was a mandate for everyone, especially the Church. Everyone was to give to the poor, to set aside crops for them, and failure to do so was sinful. Tithing resulted from this commandment, but they were supposed to give it to people in need, not build mansions or buy private jets.

Its importance was diminished because it is the antithesis of capitalism and the "fend for yourself" mentality. Neglecting people experiencing poverty contradicts the basic tenets of all formalized religions. We have failed to care for our brothers and sisters, our greatest sin. No honorable leader, Christian or righteous man, should ever allow an empty stomach or a cold ground to sleep. Ironically, Conservatives proclaim faithfulness as they shun and slander the starving and homeless.

Churches have used water hoses on the sleeping homeless to remove them from their sidewalks. Mega churches remained empty while flood waters rose, and people drowned. The purveyors of God's message treat God's least fortunate with disdain, disregard, and complete disrespect. It is thoroughly anti-Christ, anti-Bible, and anti-God. It is shameful.

"A society will be judged on the basis of how it treats its weakest members." ~ Pope John Paul II

This commandment also directs business owners to balance their profits with the good of their employees. They should honor contracts, pay their employees a reasonable wage, and be honest. Employees are responsible for a full day's work and honesty.

It also commands wealthier nations and individuals to help developing countries in economic recovery and stabilization because it benefits all of God's children. Too many supposedly faithful leaders rarely adhere to this moral obligation; unless it involves colonization, then they have no problem heeding "God's call."

Ninth Commandment:

Hebrew/Protestant: *Thou shalt not bear false witness against thy neighbor.*

Catholic: *Thou shalt not covet thy neighbor's wife.*

There were no Sherlock Holmes, lie detectors, camera phones, or video recorders in ancient times, so a person must be impeccable with their word. Bearing false witness or spreading lies could be catastrophic.

This law includes all untrue or hateful speech: slander, bragging, boasting, mockery, flattery, exposing secrets, and believing and/or disseminating information without valid or sufficient evidence. Internet bullying is an example. We also see this in our politics and news media.

This commandment is the basis for perjury laws worldwide.

The Catholic version took a part of the tenth commandment and made it the ninth. There is no separation of sentences in the other breakdowns. Other than to compensate for their alterations, there is no apparent reason for doing this. History proves it would not be for women's protection or to hold them in high regard.

Tenth Commandment:

Hebrew/Protestant: *Thou shalt not covet thy neighbor's house, thou shalt not covet thy neighbor's wife, nor his manservant, nor his maidservant, nor his ox, nor his ass, nor anything that is thy neighbor's.*

Catholic: *Thou shalt not covet thy neighbor's goods.*

To covet is to envy or lust after something or someone; it is not an action but intent. To envy another's life or possessions often leads to adultery, theft, and social breakdown. Envy's power is that it rarely remains just thoughts but leads to actions. This law is why Muslims wear the Hijab—to cover their beauty and not induce envy or lust. Bans on dancing are because of modesty laws.

The Catholic version leaves out critical information needed to understand this commandment. Consumerism and capitalism are founded on envy. The U.S. Bishops define envy "as an attitude that fills us with sadness at the sight of another's prosperity."

"Keeping Up with the Jones," or now the Kardashians, is based on wanting to have more than the next guy. People will sleep on the streets for Black Friday or the latest technology release. The consumer holidays celebrate the need to be the envy of everyone else—the first one with the newest toy.

The foundation of the "Prosperity Churches" is envy. They claim that if you "live right," God financially blesses you, and you will have everything you dream of. Their teachings directly contradict this commandment and most of Jesus' teachings.

"Again, I tell you, it's easier for a camel to go through the eye of a needle than for someone who is rich to enter the kingdom of God." (Matthew 19:24)

Sadly, this sin's biggest perpetrators scream at someone else for "sinning." Shouting condemnation for everyone else's actions while standing in their Louis Vuitton's, shaking their Rolex-gilded wrist in disgust from their diamond-crested pulpit of hypocrisy.

Chapter 11: Does Religion Define Morality?

Short answer: No. The ethical guidelines of the Ten Commandments also align with other beliefs, varying only slightly per region and culture, and maintain the same theme: Love each other.

Religions try to stand in moral superiority, claiming they are essential for spiritual health and growth and establishing the foundation of social justice. However, most would agree hurting others is wrong. It does not take Religion for people to have empathy.

To prove this, atheist organizations compiled their own "Ten Commandments."

The God Delusion, **by Richard Dawkins**

1. Do not do to others what you would not want them to do to you.
2. In all things, strive to cause no harm.
3. Treat your fellow human beings, your fellow living things, and the world in general with love, honesty, faithfulness, and respect.
4. Do not overlook evil or shrink from administering justice, but always be ready to forgive wrongdoing freely admitted and honestly regretted.
5. Live life with a sense of joy and wonder.

6. Always seek to be learning something new.

7. Test all things; always check your ideas against the facts and be ready to discard even a cherished belief if it does not conform to them.

8. Never seek to censor or cut yourself off from dissent; always respect the right of others to disagree with you.

9. Form independent opinions on the basis of your own reason and experience; do not allow yourself to be led blindly by others.

10. Question everything.

The Good Book: *A Humanist Bible*, **By A. C. Grayling; The Good 8:11:**

1. Love well
2. Seek the good in all things
3. Harm no others
4. Think for yourself
5. Take responsibility
6. Respect nature
7. Do your utmost
8. Be informed
9. Be kind
10. Be courageous

These come with a postscript that everyone should "at least sincerely try." And a final thought: "Add to these ten injunctions this: O friends, let us always be true to ourselves and to the best in things so that we can always be true to one another."

Christopher Hitchens's "Ten Commandments"

1. Do not condemn people on the basis of their ethnicity or their color.

2. Do not ever even think of using people as private property, or as owned, or as slaves.

3. Despise those who use violence or the threat of it in sexual

relations.

4. Hide your face and weep if you dare to harm a child.
5. Do not condemn people for their inborn nature-why would God create so many homosexuals only in order to torture and destroy them?
6. Be aware that you, too, are an animal and dependent on the web of nature. Try to think and act accordingly.
7. Do not imagine that you can escape judgment if you rob people with a false prospectus rather than with a knife.
8. Turn off that fucking cell phone-you can have no idea how unimportant your call is to us.
9. Denounce all jihadists and crusaders for what they are: psychopathic criminals with ugly delusions. And terrible sexual repressions.
10. Be willing to renounce any god or any faith if any holy commandments should contradict any of the above.
11. In short: Do not swallow your moral code in tablet form.

The Satanic Temple's Seven Fundamental Tenets:

1. One should strive to act with compassion and empathy towards all creatures in accordance with reason.
2. The struggle for justice is an ongoing and necessary pursuit that should prevail over laws and institutions.
3. One's body is inviolable, subject to one's own will alone.
4. The freedoms of others should be respected, including the freedom to offend. To willfully and unjustly encroach upon the freedoms of another is to forgo your own.
5. Beliefs should conform to our best scientific understanding of the world. We should take care never to distort scientific facts to fit our beliefs.
6. People are fallible. If we make a mistake, we should do our best to rectify it and resolve any harm that may have been caused.
7. Every tenet is a guiding principle designed to inspire nobility in action and thought. The spirit of compassion, wisdom, and justice should always prevail over the written or spoken

word.

It is not Religion that keeps us from hurting others; it is love.

Chapter 12: The Rest of the Commandments

Judaism believes there are three types of sin, or "avera," which means transgression. Intentional sin is "B'mezid," an accidental sin is "B'shogeg," and unknowingly sinning is "Tinok Shenishba," which applies to non-Jews who did not know any better. None of these sins resulted in eternal damnation.

Of the 613 commandments in the O.T., Moses received 611 on Mount Sinai. Two other laws were given directly from God: "Be fruitful and multiply" and the circumcision of male children, completing the 613 commandments.

Documenting these laws was a strenuous task. They struggled with what would count as commandments, and if every one was for every person.

Were they only for Israel or everyone?

If a commandment were from God, would it apply to everyone for all time?

How would they count each commandment, each verse, or each prohibition?

After World War 2, many tried to add one more, mandating the continuation of Jewish life, therefore never giving Hitler a posthumous victory. But 613 remains the complete list.

The rules address everything the ancient people questioned and every variation of the Ten Commandments. There are a lot of laws demanding sympathy, care, concern, and empathy. There are also commands to destroy, conquer, and have complete apathy towards enemy tribes. If you were a Canaanite who was captured and survived the genocide, they required you to work until death, unless injured.

Another arch nemesis was Amalek, and the laws included all his descendants, whom "God" commanded to be annihilated. The entire nation of Amalek was unforgivable, and they should be slaughtered. To add emphasis, they repeat "without mercy or forgiveness" when addressing rival tribes.

There are laws stating the rule of law surpasses everything, whether rich or poor. A Judge must be righteous and never accept testimony from a lone witness.

A lot of our modern judicial systems were built on these ancient laws. However, since most of the rules were based on religious dogma and tribal rivalry, death was the ultimate and (often) penalty.

Judaism, and therefore Christianity, have barbaric roots. Deuteronomy 13:6-9 states:

> *If your very own brother, or your son or daughter, or the wife you love, or your closest friend secretly entices you, saying, "Let us go and worship other gods" (gods that neither you nor your ancestors have known, gods of the peoples around you, whether near or far, from one end of the land to the other), do not yield to them or listen to them. Show them no pity. Do not spare them or shield them. You must certainly put them to death. Your hand must be the first in putting them to death, and then the hands of all the people.*

With pious attitudes, Christians condemn Muslims, asking, "How can you say Islam is the Religion of peace, but it says to kill people? Where did you get this crazy ideology?"

An honest response could only be: "The Bible. Mohammad commanded us to honor the Bible's commandments. The Bible states, multiple times, to kill anyone who doesn't believe in YHWH."

We disregard so much of the Bible, and inevitably, what we "obey" only serves to isolate ourselves and maintain our tribes. In any religion, when we use separation instead of love, it is not of God; it is our ego. We focus on the redeeming commandments, forgetting that atrocities are also commanded and disregarding the ones that no longer suit us. We make "God's word" a buffet. We proclaim divine purpose and intervention when we find something we particularly like (which often justifies discrimination).

The commandments continue...

We must lend to low-income people without interest and not demand repayment. Unless it is an "idolater," then we must do the exact opposite, with as much harshness as possible. The U.S. is driven by our capitalistic system, making us all idolaters of the All-Mighty Dollar.

The courts must impose the death penalty by burning, stoning, the sword, or strangulation, except for the blasphemers and idolaters who were to be hanged. Most Christians support the death penalty because of this commandment, even though it is what killed Jesus. The Bible also says no one should be executed based on circumstantial evidence, and we forget that commandment, too.

Honesty, integrity, and empathy in business are also addressed. We must keep our scales and weights accurate to ensure justice and avoid theft. Do not withhold wages or fail to pay debts. Do not overcharge or underpay. Release all loans after seven years—a law that remains in our credit system.

It estimates the value of each human and mandates purchasing slaves according to custom. Do not work them oppressively or allow others to do so. When the enslaved person is freed, give him gifts— do not send them away empty-handed unless they are Canaanites.

For over 50 years, the Church banned bankers from communion because of their "sinful" status. In contrast, Jesus broke bread with the bankers of his age.

The Church declared interest on any loan was sinful.

How does that work in today's economy? Matthew, the

inspiration for the first book in the N.T., was a tax collector, but 1800 years after Jesus, these people were no longer worthy. The pendulous nature of sin can last a lifetime or a millennium. It is the Church's agenda that decides.

They also established general laws of daily life: a.k.a. "Don't be a dick" rules. These include not standing by if someone is in danger. We must designate cities of refuge and allow access to those in need. Do not allow pitfalls and obstacles to remain on your property. Make a guard rail around a flat roof. Do not put a barrier before a blind man or give them harmful advice. Help others unload their goods. Do not destroy fruit trees, including during war. A King must not have too many wives, horses, silver, or gold. Do not break oaths or vows, and be a person of your word.

These commandments are usually ignored while focusing on the "sins" of others.

We are to love, and these laws reinforce that.

Chapter 13: The Patriarchy

Historically, cleanliness laws were essential to all tribes and religions because of germs, diseases, plagues, and misogyny.

Judaism once considered women "unclean" after giving birth and, depending on the child's gender, mandated isolation for 33-66 days. Once the isolation ended, women must present three offerings: one for forgiveness, sin, and a sacrifice to God. This commandment was enforced for over a thousand years. Mary, Jesus' mother, obeyed these laws and was isolated for 33 days after giving birth (Luke 2:22).

Armed with more knowledge, people asked religious philosophers to explain this law. They answered that since childbirth is so painful, women would surely swear an oath to God to make the pain stop. The leaders feared that the oath would include abstinence.

I swear to God, I will never have sex again if you make this pain stop!

The theologians surmised her promise to God, spoken out of duress, would inevitably lead to her sinning. Women were imprisoned, forced to beg forgiveness, and killed a bunch of birds to ensure their husbands would "get some" again.

The penalty's length was different because they were happier when a boy was born. *"Every first-born male that opens the womb shall be called holy to the Lord."* (Luke 2:23)

A more comfortable environment meant she was less likely to keep her oath and return to her husband, sanctioning a lesser penance. A girl's birth was considered a disappointment, which could cause a woman to remain chaste, requiring more time to recover from the "misfortune."

For over 5000 years (and still in many countries), they considered female births more of a curse than a blessing. A girl's life was one of servitude and degradation, all ordained by the Bible.

Biologically, females have a greater chance of surviving the birth process than males, so historically, women held a slight majority. This natural pattern ensured a greater chance of reproductive availability since women can only get pregnant once per year. However, for the first time in history, because of religious doctrine, males now out-populate females. (World Population Prospects, 2022, 2023)

For thousands of years, Religion commanded women to be secondary and the weaker sex, resulting in ordained subordination, mutilation, and often murder, and now we see the consequences worldwide. Religion (allegedly backed by "God") altered the perfect pattern of nature and, with their own hands, destroyed the giver of life: the daughters of God.

The sin of uncleanliness also pertained to menstruation, masturbation, sex, nocturnal emissions (wet dreams), skin ailments, bodily fluids, and exposure to sacrifices. They refer to penile and vaginal discharge as "leaking" and include semen and menstruation. Penance for any such occurrence was seven days of isolation, and on the eighth day,

> ...after that, they will be ceremonially clean. On the eighth day, they must take two doves or two young pigeons and bring them to the priest at the entrance to the tent of the meeting. The priest is to sacrifice one for a sin offering and the other for a burnt offering. In this way, he will make atonement for them before the Lord for the uncleanness of their discharge. (Synopsis, Leviticus 15)

That is a lot of dead birds because of a woman's monthly fertility cycle. The recurring nature of these laws kept women begging for forgiveness and ashamed of being a woman.

The beliefs of the powerful dictated what was sinful. A gift from God one day could become a deadly sin the next. What was once idol worship is now found in every aspect of Christianity. It is all evidence that our religious laws are fluid and fallible.

We often judge everything in terms of black and white: white being good and black being bad. We ignore or conflate the gray in the middle with either holy or unholy. Nothing in nature lives by such radical concepts. Our ego will not allow us to say, "I don't know." And what we do not understand must be evil. It is such a small way of thinking.

Chapter 14: The Unforgivable

The Bible states there is one "unforgivable" sin: blasphemy. We often declare something blasphemous, but it is usually just an ego-driven demonstration of our perceived status. One's beliefs about blasphemy vary as much as denominations and religions. The answer is somewhere in an extensive list of anything attributing evil to, dismissing, mocking, or ridiculing Jesus, the Holy Spirit, and/or God.

Some might call this book blasphemous. However, my irreverence is towards Religion, not God, so that is my loophole. Religion is littered with inconsistencies because it tries to address every question for every aspect of life. It gets messy, which is why only love matters.

Today's primary definition of blasphemy is "irreverence toward a deity or deities and, by extension, the use of profanity." Profanity is blasphemous?

How can the Church assign such a lethal law and make it meaningless by adding profanity? The only reason our curse words have meaning is because, at some point, someone added a negative connotation to those words. Religion would have to decide which words, for which era, are good and evil and then assign the law to those words. How can this be something that concerns God? The essence of the law should have been, "Calm down and don't say something you might regret." Instead, the Church uses it as another form of control.

Understandably, profanity is socially unacceptable, but that should not make it a sin. A worthy God would care how we treat each other, and that's how sins should be determined—not by the Church's whims and certainly not by social decorum. Eternal consequences for social etiquette make God a snob.

Blasphemy or other "unforgivable" sin directly contradicts "unconditional love." Nothing is unforgivable if there is no condition for God's love. The two are mutually exclusive. To love is to forgive. Mortals inflict pain and judgment, hold grudges, and abandon. Not the source of love. A God, as anything other than unconditional love, is unworthy of our consideration, praise, or Jesus' sacrifice. A god as flawed as us is inferior, not superior.

We ruined God because we made God in our image.

Chapter 15: Fornication Under Consent of the King

The Bible details forbidden sex in every combination and predominately addresses men. It prohibits sex with a man's mother, stepmother, stepsister, sister, daughter, granddaughter, with a woman and her daughter or granddaughter, aunt, uncle's wife, son's wife, wife's sister, another man, uncle (women), another's wife, menstruating women, or animals.

Augustine of Hippo is considered the Doctor of Christianity. St. Augustine's doctrine permeates all levels of evangelicalism, and his beliefs are seen throughout Christianity. However, Augustine's early years were as a pagan and a sexual hedonist. His mother eventually coerced him to regain his Christian upbringing. He spent fourteen years with the love of his life, with whom he had a child, but his mother disapproved of her.

Part of his reconversion included entering a loveless, arranged marriage. His mother selected a Christian woman she considered more suitable and socially acceptable. When she became betrothed to Augustine, this "woman" was ten years old, and many historians believe they started having sex upon engagement. Others claim he took another lover until his future bride "became of age," which was twelve. Eventually, he ended the engagement, choosing celibacy.

Augustine considered a significant religious founder of

Christianity and appointed a "Saint," was a pedophile and a massive hypocrite.

Augustine decided sex was the root of all evil and labeled it the Original Sin. He changed the original sin from disobedience to God to sex without intent to procreate. He condemned all forms of affection and called sex a failure of the mortal self.

He boasted of his sexual escapades, then asserted sex was among the worst sins. Before his conversion, his famous prayer was, "Grant me chastity and continence, but not yet." Much of Purity Culture is based on his teachings—the rantings of a man who spent most of his life as a hedonist.

Augustine's insatiable sexual appetite was dwarfed by the need to please his mother. His emotional baggage, guilt, and shame had implications that eventually reached the bedrooms of millions of Christians. He was the epitome of the recovering addict who doggedly judges everyone else who still does what he used to do, like the ex-smoker who hates anyone who smokes. But with Augustine, he became the leader of Christianity, affecting millions of people across dozens of generations. His doctrine made the gift of sex a dirty, shameful, conditional act.

Fornication is defined as "unlawful sexual intercourse" or the original Greek meaning, "to consort with prostitutes," which, in ancient Greece, meant sex with boys. The Grecian history of sexual escapades and our current definition of "fornication" or "prostitution" do not align.

The question posed by the Church was, "What is unlawful"? In biblical times, it meant adultery or pederasty, which is sex between an older man and a young boy. Today, it means "sex between unmarried people." Another demonstration of evolving laws.

The Bible is not as modest as Augustine's followers. *There she lusted after her lovers, whose genitals were like those of donkeys and whose emission was like that of horses."* (Ezekiel 23:20)

Lot's daughters had sex with him. The Song of Solomon is ancient erotica. Most of the O.T.'s leading men slept with queens, slaves, and prostitutes. After they conquered another tribe, they raped the women and girls.

If we view the central message of the moral commandments as "do not harm," sex can quickly become sinful. If your needs exceed others, it will cause pain, which is immoral. It goes against the beauty of the interaction if you lie to fulfill those needs. However, an honest, adult rendezvous, or expressing and sharing love with someone, should have no shame or condemnation. God made us sexual creatures.

Religion holds hostage our most intimate needs (connection, beauty, oneness, ecstasy, creation), demanding their sanction and control through their ordination of marriage. A healthy and honest (adult) sexual relationship can make you feel closer to "God" than an unhappy marriage.

The restrictions on our most intimate connections reinforce the conclusion that Religion labels anything that makes us happy a sin. Marriage became another way for the Church to discriminate and separate the "holy" from the "unholy." Religion manufactured laws to assume power and mandate our sex lives via a marriage license.

King Solomon had 700 wives and 300 mistresses.

They do not teach this history in Sunday schools, churches, or prayer circles. But if one of your founding fathers is famous for his sexual escapades with Queens and Pharaoh's daughters, it's incredibly hypocritical to make sex a sin.

Solomon is remembered for his wisdom and is revered as a godly man in Judaism, Christianity, and Islam. He is also the original author of the "Deadly Sins." When documenting these sins, he proclaimed there were *"six things the Lord hateth, and the seventh His soul detesteth."* (Proverbs 6:16-19)

They were:

1. A proud look.
2. A lying tongue.
3. Hands that shed innocent blood.
4. A heart that devises wicked plots.
5. Feet that are swift to run into mischief.
6. A deceitful witness that utters lies.

7.   He that sows discord among brethren.

Approximately 600 years after Solomon, they altered the list. They added adultery, fornication, uncleanness, lasciviousness, idolatry, sorcery, hatred, variance, emulations, wrath, strife, sedition, heresy, envy, murder, drunkenness, reveling, "and such like" as sins resulting in the banishment from Heaven.

Only about 800 years separated King Solomon and Saint Augustine. These men are stunning examples of the constant evolution of Religion's sexual sins.

Sex makes the religious so uncomfortable that even Jesus' humanity was stripped, and his sexuality was debated for millennia. The Church cringes at any thought of Jesus enjoying his human form and all the ecstasy our body gives us. They are OK with the pain, but Jesus feeling pleasure is unseemly.

Their message is that denying our nature makes us godlier. We hate ourselves, our bodies, and our natural desires because of this. It is destructive and causes internal shame and disgust. God does not shame his creation; we deny its divine greatness.

The primary scripture used to propagate this anti-sex ideology is,

> *Flee sexual immorality. Every sin that a man does is outside the body, but he who fornicates sins against his own body. Or do you not know that your body is the temple of the Holy Spirit who is in you, whom you have from God, and you are not your own? For you were bought at a price; therefore, glorify God in your body. (1 Corinthians 6:18-20.)*

Religion made God the ever-present parental figure. Making our bodies the Temple of God is like thinking of your parents during sex; it is the ultimate *eww* factor. Sex is a gift from God, enabling a beautiful connection between two people. But we turned it into: "Be careful! He is watching!"

Also used is:

> *"It's good for a man not to touch a woman. Nevertheless, because of sexual immorality, let each man have his own wife, and let each*

woman have her own husband." (1 Corinthians 7:1-2)

Paul was addressing the immorality within the Church. His message was: If you cannot abstain, please go to your wife, not little boys.

Evidence that it is us, not God, who has issues with sex is in our anatomy:

- The clitoris is the only thing on the body solely for pleasure.
- Men have a spot in their anus near the prostate, which brings more pleasure than any other erogenous zone.

These facts should force us to question the "sin" of fornication and homosexuality.

Would a supreme creator put something on our body that gives us immense pleasure and bans us from using it? Would the argument change if it were on our arm or leg? It makes no sense to have something put there by God, and its only purpose is pleasure, but we cannot use it because it is a sin.

What a sadistic god man conceives.

This belief completely disregards and denies the gifts God gave us. We are told to ignore, deny, and subjugate who we are. Our natural desires, given to us by God, are considered disgusting and sinful and should only be controlled, not enjoyed.

The American Evangelicals are especially devout followers of Augustine, so fornication was always an enormous deal in my childhood home. It was not just me that my mom tried to control. She regularly ended friendships and relationships because she viewed their lifestyles as sinful. Or because they just disagreed with her beliefs. But fornication was always the leading cause.

No one was immune from her judgment and ostracization. My mother missed my son's entire childhood because she disowned me so many times. She believed any affiliation with someone "living in sin" would affect her relationship with Christ.

For many years, I blamed "God" for causing this. The more my mom grew in her faith, the further she moved away from me. She regularly abandoned me in the name of God. She shouted scripture and lectured me, and I only thought she sounded insane. My logic and her fanaticism conflicted in every way. I will never understand how disowning your child could be God's will.

The biggest problem with these fabricated laws is that people believe them and genuinely fear for their loved ones. The believers will do and say anything to "save" people they love. They think if they cannot save their loved one, an incomprehensible, eternal pain is imminent. I experienced this fear, and it was terrifying. But it never felt legitimate, and I started questioning the entire belief system.

Religion uses our fear and uncertainty about death as crowd control. Believers worry about their fate but also can become consumed with fear over a loved one's soul. Religion wants us to believe our lives of (roughly) 80 years have eternal ramifications. The punishment is not for just a lifetime but for eternity. It does not get much scarier.

In the last months of my mom's life, she admitted that disowning me was her way of controlling me. She also conceded it never worked. She thought she could "make me see the light" and step in line with her beliefs if she took away the only thing she had—her.

The abandonment was traumatizing. There were so many things my mom never taught me or my son. All because she genuinely feared for my soul. There was so much unneeded pain because she trusted her pastor.

My grandson was born "out of wedlock." He was a gift who instantly stole my heart. He was born on Valentine's Day.

His mother wanted him christened before his first birthday. She called me to discuss the ceremony, explore options, and get input. As a Protestant, I explained we did a Dedication Ceremony rather than a Christening.

The Dedication is a prayer by the pastor, usually during or after a Sunday service. The congregation supports them by joining in the prayer. Its purpose is to pray for good health, success, and a faithful walk with God.

When we dedicated Joey, the pastor said, "This is an anointed man of God!" Those words comforted my mom, who held them tightly for the rest of her life. My willingness to raise him in Church, beginning with his Dedication, enabled her to forgive or overlook my indiscretion and "sinful" life.

After I explained the ceremony, my grandson's mother wanted the same thing for him. We chose Joey's childhood church. She was 800 miles away in Virginia, so I offered to arrange things. The new family was coming to visit the first week of January, so we set a tentative date.

I called the Church, and they eventually transferred me to the pastor's executive secretary. I explained the situation and asked when their next scheduled dedication ceremony was. The secretary was sanctimonious, asking questions about the parents' walk with God and their current religious standing.

I was not expecting an inquisition when I asked for a prayer over a child. I explained Joey's history with the Church and that they were in the Navy, so they did not have a home church. And, because of the Church's influence, at one time, Joey wanted to be a pastor. I knew she wanted their marital status, and I was dodging it with ducks and weaves.

She finally directly asked if they were married. They loved each other, but their relationship was toxic. They broke up every other week. They discussed marriage but knew they were not ready. When the secretary pressed me for an answer, I lied and said they were engaged. With an overt tone of disappointment and disgust, she said they were unwilling to hold a dedication ceremony for my grandson until his parents were married.

Her attitude stunned me, but I persisted. We agreed to talk in a few days after she consulted the pastor. She assured me things would not change, but I could call her in two days.

I was working, so I immediately refocused on my job. As time passed, my anger steeped. By the time I was driving home, I was livid.

I had never written a complaint letter, but as soon as I got home, I grabbed the laptop and composed an email to the Church. After some research, I found the secretary's and pastor's email addresses. The email below was in their inbox the following day.

Naomi,

> I spoke with you today regarding the Dedication of my grandson. Your Church was the preferred location because my son grew up attending CCC. They were going to drive from Norfolk, Virginia, to hold this special ceremony at CCC.

> I am writing to you today to let you know how terribly disappointed I am in your policies/beliefs. You informed me that my grandson could not be dedicated until my son was married. I feel those comments were completely judgmental and hypocritical. I do not want my son to marry this girl; it would be a disaster and end in divorce within months. I believe a vow to God is a far bigger issue than fornication. Through your judgment, you are depriving an innocent child of a special prayer. Did Christ ask his disciples only to bring him the "holy" children when he wanted to pray for all of them? Did Christ not welcome every sinner, whore, and thief?

> How dare you stand in judgment of my son and his family and not welcome them with open arms! Christ said, "Above ALL, love one another." I might understand the bigotry from a stranger on the street, but to come directly from the pastor's office is truly gut-wrenching. This is precisely the reason I left the Church. Because of people like you, God has morphed into what man deems godly, certainly not what Jesus said or did. Man has ruined God, and CCC is a direct representation of this.

> I have no doubt that when Christ returns on His Holy Day of Judgment, He will AGAIN destroy the temple and spit at the priests for their immorality.

I will say a prayer for you and your organization.
Sheri

She called the next day and said she spoke to the pastor, and they agreed to do the Dedication, but under the circumstances, they could not hold it during their Sunday service. They would do it after a Wednesday night's service. It was their attempt at compromise, but it was the continuation of judgment, offensive behavior, and a weak attempt at appeasement. I calmly but coldly told her I would consult the family but doubted they would be interested after her initial reaction.

Their pious attitude disgusted and offended me. What upset me most was it was contrary to Jesus' teachings. However, I now see without that incident, this book would not exist. I went from saying nothing (other than with friends) to standing up and holding the Church accountable for their bigotry, judgment, and segregated behavior.

To follow Jesus means to follow his order to love. Instead, religion molded Jesus into a judgmental bigot. When love is your focus, you rise above condemning others. The ego clouds your vision, giving you a sense of superiority and closing your eyes to your faults.

My journey will continue until I die, but my search for what a "sin" is complete. Like everything else, we make it far too complicated and continually look for loopholes.

There are not any.

You will be judged by how much you love. Did you serve the weakest among you? Were you selfish in your acts, love, and time? Did you try your best to love in all circumstances?

"Sins" that demean God's creation, intrude on healthy relationships, divide over beliefs, or condone someone's pain should be wholly ignored.

How you were born has no implication on your soul. What matters is what you have done with your life since birth.

Sin is inflicting pain. It is simple.
Just love.

Section IV: Animals

"We patronize the animals for their incompleteness, for their tragic
fate of having taken form so far below ourselves. And therein we
err, and greatly err. For the animal shall not be measured by man. In
a world older and more complete than ours, they are more finished
and complete, gifted with extensions of the senses we have lost or
never attained, living by voices we shall never hear. They are not
brethren, they are not underlings; they are other Nations, caught
with ourselves in the net of life and time, fellow prisoners of the
splendour and travail of the Earth."
~ Henry Beston

Chapter 16: My Best Friends

I am one of those who say "Hi!" to animals. That is sugar-coating it—I talk to them. I never expect a response (I am not crazy), but since animals sense tone and energy, sometimes a few kind words can turn a scared creature into a friend. Jewish philosopher Martin Buber said, "An animal's eyes have the power to speak a great language."

Animals try to communicate with us in many ways, but our egos often silence their voices.

Milne, creator of Winnie-the-Pooh, said, "Some people talk to animals. Not many listen, though. That's the problem."

As a child, I wanted to be a veterinarian. I abandoned the ambition once I learned I must euthanize animals. They explained it was often the best thing to do, but me killing an animal for any reason was a deal breaker.

We always had a pet. My dad went for the unusual side, owning an alligator, ocelot, cockatoo, piranha, and at least one dog. He built giant fish tanks, filling them with fish from around the world.

Some of my dad's favorite stories were about his animals. He often spoke of his alligator biting the dog's tail and the dog dragging the gator in circles around the yard. He claimed they did this all day, every day. It was their little game. They played until the alligator grew too big, and my dad had to remove it. But not before it bit off my dad's little toe.

On another occasion, one of his (drunk) friends almost lost a finger to the piranhas because he doubted their veracity and ability to break the skin. He received fourteen stitches and a gaping scar to remember his poor decisions.

Animals were always attracted to my father. He was a whisperer. He honored and respected animals for their strengths and weaknesses. He did not afford humans the same grace.

My dad's first cockatoo would spread his beautiful, broad, white wings across my father's chest and sleep for hours. Or give anyone (who would dare) a sweet kiss with his beak. The cockatoo's name was Fred, and he was with our family for over 25 years.

My mom was a "clean freak," so animals were contradictory to that lifestyle. However, she loved them and knew they brought me happiness. After a few incidents with stray cats, we stuck with dogs. My first dog, Mandy, was my best friend. She was a Lhasa Apso/ Poodle mix. She was a puppy from a close family friend, looked like a little gremlin, and we were inseparable. After school, she and I played until my mom returned from work. Every day during those lonely hours, Mandy kept me company. There were only three TV stations, no personal video games, and I could not leave the house. So, I occupied my time by playing hide-and-seek with Mandy.

It still amazes me that she grasped the concept. She would sit in a room, giving me enough time to hide, and then she would come looking for me. I was wise to her sense of smell, so instead of immediately finding a spot, I spent most of my time running in circles, trying to throw her off. She, of course, found me every time and would jump and bark at her accomplishments. After celebrating, she would run off and hide, and I would search for her.

"Animals are such agreeable friends—they ask no questions, they pass no criticisms." ~ George Eliot

During an awful fight with my mom, I decided to run away. I was twelve, but I was sure I could make it if Mandy were with me. My mom saw the absurdity of my logic and would not let me leave

Chapter 16: My Best Friends

with the dog. There was a slight tug-of-war between us, with Mandy caught in the middle. We quickly realized the insanity.

We both let go, and Mandy took off, terrified. I went running after her, and so did my mom. She and I chased Mandy around the front yard, running in circles, going nowhere. Both of us were trying to catch her and win this ridiculous power struggle. Now, it makes me laugh to think about what the neighbors and that poor dog must have felt. Mandy was running from us, looking back, confused and scared, seemingly thinking, *"What the hell is wrong with you guys?"*

My mom always disliked Mandy. She complained that Mandy was too independent and unloving. She never saw our friendship, so she did not understand. It frustrated her that Mandy was my dog and not hers.

Then, one day, I came home from school, my mom was unexpectedly home, and Mandy "had run off." My mom was unfazed, but I was shattered. I posted signs and, for weeks, looked for her. She was never seen again. My best friend was gone.

The days filled with Mandy's friendship were suddenly empty. After losing her, I started sneaking out of the house while my mom worked. I met new friends and started getting into trouble. It exemplified "Idleness is the root of mischief."

My mom once joyfully announced her new theory: since "dog" was "God" in reverse, dogs were God's unconditional love on earth. She was practical and conservative, so saying something so whimsical made me think she went mad.

However, Jean Houston, an American author involved in the "Human Potential Movement," agreed with my mom. "The illuminated ones can take any form—a man, a woman, a child, an elder, or even a dog. It's not inconsequential that the English language allows for the dyslexia of the spelling of the word dog: God spelled backward."

I see the correlation in hindsight and a lifetime of love from my dogs. A dog is our best friend and our protection. They are always happy when you come home, love you unconditionally, and offer unconditional forgiveness. A dog's love for their human is genuine, a godly love. There are no other animal relationships with humans like there are with dogs.

My dog Bailey made me smile and laugh daily. He was the sweetest soul I ever knew, a little Being full of love. I am so thankful for him because there were days I thought I could not smile, but he helped me to. He predicted my every move, and he mastered my routine since I am a creature of habit. He knew when I was sad, sick, or happy and looked at me like I was crazy when I danced. He looked just like Mandy and, like her, he was the best friend I could ask for.

Philosopher Alfred A. Montapert said, "Animals are reliable, many full of love, true in their affections, predictable in their actions, grateful and loyal. Difficult standards for people to live up to."

I struggle to use the proper term when speaking of our pets; typically, we are called their owners or masters. We are so conditioned to our superiority that we label them as property. The proper terminology should be more like companion, helper, loved one, four-legged family members, or, in my case, my little monsters.

Between animals and humans, I prefer animals. They are much better friends, and their feelings are real.

Chapter 17: Do Animals Have Souls?

Our pets were family. So, I was stunned to learn that a lot of Christians do not believe animals have souls.

"If there are no dogs in Heaven, then when I die, I want to go where they went." ~ *Will Rogers*

Anyone who thinks they are soulless has never really looked an animal in the eyes. Animals love, honor, and give life. They fear, defend, and experience sadness, jealousy, loneliness, anger, and joy. Many animals use tools and have planning and problem-solving abilities. They dream, snore, catch colds, and get the hiccups. They bring us companionship, lower our blood pressure and stress levels, work for us, and give of themselves all that is asked of them. Except for cats, they are only here to remind us that we are mere humans and not really needed on this planet.

Anyone who is not entirely self-absorbed and has spent time with an animal can conclude that they are not mindless, soulless creatures only looking for their next meal or mate. They are part of a community, working together to live, survive, and thrive—with lots of love and play deeply intertwined.

"If having a soul means being able to feel love and loyalty and gratitude, then animals are better off than a lot of humans."
~ *James Herriot*

We must understand what a soul is to decipher if animals have them. I define a soul as our essence. I believe our soul is not what we do but who we truly are. A soul is not dependent on religion but what makes us yearn for and seek something greater than ourselves. It is the infinite part of our being.

Webster's Dictionary defines a soul as:

- The principle of life, feeling, thought, and action in humans, regarded as a distinct entity separate from the body, and commonly held to be separable in existence from the body, the spiritual part of humans as distinct from the physical part.
- The spiritual part of humans regarded in its moral aspect, or as believed to survive death and be subject to happiness or misery in a life to come: arguing the immortality of the soul.
- The disembodied spirit of a deceased person: He feared the soul of the deceased would haunt him.
- The emotional part of human nature; the seat of the feelings or sentiments.
- A human being; person.

Clearly, the church influenced our dictionary. The explicitly human definition shows our attitudes of supremacy. Issuing such a definition justifies reckless behavior. Our narcissism is causing the destruction of our planet and everything that coexists with us.

"Because we have viewed other animals through the myopic lens of our self-importance, we have misperceived who and what they are. Because we have repeated our ignorance, one to the other, we have mistaken it for knowledge." ~ Tom Regan

Based on his religious beliefs, Dr. Duncan MacDougall of Haverhill, Massachusetts, tried to prove the existence of the soul and inadvertently added to the notion that animals lacked them. MacDougall documented the loss in body weight at the time of death to be three-fourths of an ounce or 21 grams. He conducted this experiment on fifteen dogs and noted, "The results were uniformly negative, no loss of weight at death."

These findings fueled the church's stance and MacDougall's beliefs that animals were soulless. As soon as they published his results, it was challenged because they euthanized the dogs. Since the dog's death was not natural, like the humans, they could not verify the results. MacDougall's theory has been debated ever since, but somehow, the church still uses it as proof that God only loves us.

They used to believe animals had souls.

> I also said to myself, 'As for humans, God tests them so that they may see that they are like the animals. Surely the fate of human beings is like that of the animals; the same fate awaits them both: As one dies, so dies the other. All have the same breath; humans have no advantage over animals…A good man takes care of his animals, but wicked men are cruel to theirs. (Ecclesiastes 3:18-20)

The Bible says our worth is measured by how we treat animals. "A good man takes care of his animals, but wicked men are cruel to theirs." (Proverbs 12:10)

And "Speak up for those who cannot speak for themselves. Protect the rights of all who are helpless." (Proverbs 31:8)

We are alerted to the potential of evil when someone is cruel to animals because it signifies emotional and psychological issues unless it is "approved by God."

Religion cannot even decide if animals predated man. Genesis 1:24-27 and Genesis 2:18-19 contradict each other. Genesis 1 claims man was created after animals, but Genesis 2 says it was before. Most scholars agree that chapter one is chronological, and chapter two is topical. Regardless, we know from science that humans were a late addition to this planet. Before us, billions of creatures, great and small, roamed this Earth for millions of years.

As with most things we encounter, we have little respect for the creatures that preceded us. They mastered their part of this planet long before we entered Earth's history. But we tightly hold that it must be divinely appointed because we can dominate these creatures.

Our (supposed) divine appointment is purely ego-driven. We've diminished their place in this world and their very Being. Far too many people believe animals are soulless, pain-free creatures, subjected to our every whim, want, or obsession, and do not deserve our respect.

Animals enabled us to farm and domesticate livestock, resulting in our evolution from hunters and gatherers to farmers and tradespeople and, ultimately, to modern civilization. The world's primary energy source fueling our lives is the remains of animals living millions of years ago: fossil fuel.

It is convenient to think animals are insignificant because envisioning a Being with a soul would be difficult as we dine on their flesh and wear the carcasses. It is much easier to declare dominion over an insensitive creature. People of color were also considered soulless, which justified and perpetuated the slave trade.

Grocery stores enable us to detach from what we are eating. We are not forced to consider that before it hit the supermarket shelves and our table, it was alive, with feelings, and a family. Using animals as a food source is one thing; using them as a trophy, property, or subjects for abuse is another.

"Let us remember that animals are not mere resources for human consumption. They're splendid beings in their own right, who have evolved alongside us as co-inheritors of all the beauty and abundance of life on this planet." ~ Marc Bekoff

The ancient part of humans, what drives us to religion and tribal mentalities, gives us solidarity and family bonds, are distinctly animal. Prides, packs, herds, pods, flocks, and swarms are all communities. Within these groups are levels of defense against intruders, familial structures, those that tend to food, and those that lead. Their communities can appear chaotic from a distance and within our limited understanding. But animals perform fantastic feats of organization, communication, and accomplishing unified goals, with less internal conflict than humans.

Tecumseh Fitch, a psychology lecturer at the University of St. Andrews in Scotland, stated, "The recognition by neuroscientists that the brain mechanisms underlying pain, pleasure, fear, and lust are the same in humans and other mammals underscores our similarity to other species and is extremely important." (Berridge, 2011)

Charles Darwin recorded grief, jealousy, and joy in various species. Still, he was silenced by societal fears of anthropomorphism. Because of the similarities he saw, he theorized that we must be related and eventually concluded that we evolved from apes. "Darwin wasn't just provocative in saying that we descend from the apes — he didn't go far enough," said Frans de Waal, a primate scientist at Georgia's Emory University. "We are apes in every way, from our long arms and tailless bodies to our habits and temperament." (Lovgren, 2005)

The physical differences between animals and humans cause us to think there are few similarities. But in fact, human and animal DNA are virtually identical. All the building blocks are the same; they are just organized differently. The arrangement of the DNA dictates the species. We are 98.8% like our closest relative, the chimp. The differences between rats and mice are ten times greater than between humans and chimps.

As our science and technology advances and animal studies increase, we will undoubtedly discover how alike we are rather than how different. We share a 75% identical DNA placement with mice and dogs, 90% with cats, 80% with cows, 70% with fish, and 60% with the fruit fly. Genetic research is being conducted on fruit flies aimed at helping children with Down syndrome and other congenital anomalies.

They are a part of us, and we are a part of them. Our failure to recognize this is ego-driven and will only result in more deaths — theirs and ours.

Chapter 18: But Can They Take a Joke?

Jonathan Balcombe, an ethologist, author, and Director of Animal Sentience at the Humane Society Institute for Science and Policy studied laughter in animals by conducting tickle tests on rats.

What a job.

Balcombe, in an interview with the Huffington Post, stated:

> ...There's some decent evidence for that also in great apes. A gorilla who loves to run along with the keeper on either side of the cage bars–kinda sad that the gorilla's the one in the cage– and then the gorilla will suddenly stop, and the human keeps running by and that makes the gorilla roar with laughter or show a mirthful response like our laughter. The challenge of any question about the inner experience, emotion, and feelings is they are private. You know we cannot just go up to the rat and say "how ya feelin?" "Oh, I'm laughing. I just love this being tickled." But what we can do is we can observe how they behave. The fact that they are drawn to it, they come back to the hand, it's magnetic for them, that certainly suggests strongly that it's a positive thing. They like it, so we can undoubtedly measure that. The fact that they make the same kinds of these chirps during this tickling that they make when they're rough-

and-tumble playing, it's something they also seem to gravitate towards. The same kind of chirps they'll make when they're enjoying perhaps food or a sexual encounter. So, you know there's a lot of ways of amassing evidence to support this.

Cara Santa Maria, the journalist conducting the interview, reminded us we are told not to anthropomorphize animals; Balcombe responded,

We can't help making the connection, and it's important to make the connection. I think the power of recognizing that another species has a mirthful response or is clearly enjoying something, we see ourselves in that. We realize even though we can't get in the rat's body, we can't get in the dog's or the chimpanzee's or the orangutan's body, we can see that that being (and I think that that's the right word, not that thing, that being), that individual with a biography, not just a biology, is experiencing something akin to what we have. What we consider such a human trait, laughter, has its origins in the evolutionary tree, as it's seen in orangutans, gorillas, chimpanzees, and bonobos. Findings show that what we have considered distinctively human laughter, such as regular, stable voicing and consistently regressive airflow, are indeed traceable to the ancestors of the great apes.

Jaak Panksepp, a professor at Washington State University in Pullman, also studied tickle-induced laughter in rats. He was asked how he knew the rats laughed and were not complaining. He noted that the chirps originated in the same part of the brain tied to "reward activity." His 1998 video documented the rats chasing his hand when he stopped tickling them; they could not get enough. Based on his studies, Dr. Panksepp developed antidepressants for humans, which are in the testing phase.

Animals also feel grief. NPR interviewed Barbara King, author of *How Animals Grieve*, to discuss her studies. King states:

My definition of grief requires that an animal's normal behavior routine is significantly altered, and that she shows visible emotional distress through body language, vocalizations, social withdrawal, and/or failure to eat or sleep. So, while I do need to follow consistent criteria in describing grief, I don't need to know what an animal is thinking, any more than I'd need to know what a person is thinking, if he shows marked emotional response to a death.

We humans grieve differently than other animals do: using language, enacting symbolic rituals like funerals, and with an acute awareness of our own and other's mortality. Other animals don't do those things. But many other animals do love. My book is as much about love as it's about grief, because it's from love that the grief emerges.

Scientists assert there are approximately 8.75 million species on this planet, most of which have not been discovered. (2011) If we have not even figured out what is on this planet, how can we assume we know everything's desires, motivations, and means of communication?

We cannot.

Chapter 19: But...Humans are Superior!

William Ralph Inge, a professor of divinity at Cambridge and the Dean of St. Paul's Cathedral, said, "We have enslaved the rest of the animal creation and have treated our distant cousins in fur and feathers so badly that beyond doubt if they were able to formulate a religion, they would depict the Devil in human form."

For over 2,000 years, Christianity used humanity's emancipation from nature as a stance of superiority. Other religions across the world revere animals and sometimes consider them gods. The Dalai Lama said, "Killing animals for sport, for pleasure, for adventure, and for hides and furs is a phenomenon which is at once disgusting and distressing. There is no justification for indulging in such acts of brutality."

An overwhelming majority of Christians rejected their oneness with nature and negated our history and correlation with it. Our feelings of supremacy and failure to realize animals' significance have led to mass extinctions and ecological disasters. I cannot understand how we can claim that God created everything and then dismiss and destroy these creations as soulless and dispensable.

What spoiled brats we are.

Church leaders use Genesis 1:26 as their pretext for our supremacy.

"Then God said, 'Let us make man in our image, in our likeness, and let them rule over the fish of the sea and the birds of the air, over the livestock, over all the Earth, and over all the creatures that move along the ground."

However, this verse does not allow us to dismiss the animal's viability and importance. This verse is left to opinion and agendas, as with all religious texts. We also have dominion over our children, but that does not give us the liberty to dismiss their importance or slaughter them.

Well, some Bible verses do.

The Bible defines "dominion" as the task of a righteous king: to be the caretaker, helping the poor and weak, and creating an environment of safety and security. The Bible gives us the job description in Psalms 72, specifically verses 11-14.

"For he will deliver the needy who cry out, the afflicted who have no one to help. He will take pity on the weak and the needy and save the needy from death. He will rescue them from oppression and violence, for precious is their blood in his sight."

We have only focused on our supremacy, not that we are supposed to be caretakers.

An example of treating animals as property is most zoos and all marine entertainment parks. These parks show our ability to inflict emotional pain and how they grieve after we have imprisoned them. The documentary "Blackfish" details the horror inflicted on orcas in the water parks. Their social bonds equal or exceed that of humans, and we kill and capture these amazing creatures for entertainment.

One orca, in the first hunt, fathered over 40% of all orcas now in captivity. Dozens of animals, never able to realize their innate desire to swim vast distances and form familial bonds, are living their entire lives confined to the equivalent of a bathtub. They are our slaves.

Entire pods of marine mammals beach themselves, refusing to leave their sick or dying friends. Humans will walk by a dead person on the sidewalk, pretending not to see the corpse. Blackfish documented these mammals mourning, screaming in angst, and shaking violently when one of their own was taken. We consider achieving such bonds fortunate, but we ignore entirely their goals for the same thing.

"Animals are more than ever a test of our character, of mankind's capacity for empathy and for decent, honorable conduct and faithful stewardship. We are called to treat them with kindness, not because they have rights or power or some claim to equality, but in a sense, because they don't; because they all stand unequal and powerless before us."
~ Matthew Scully

We've long known elephants are intelligent, but through research, we realize it goes beyond memory. They are also emotional. Elephants experience grief, selflessness, kindness, and creativity. They have documented that elephants protect other elephants from scavengers, wrap their trunks around their fallen friends, and cry for hours, even days.

Elephants have painted beautiful pieces of art. Their paintings detail other elephants or their surroundings with extraordinary detail. I can barely draw stick figures, and they are creating actual artwork. They hold the brush with their trunk, pick colors from a painter's pallet, and create masterpieces Picasso would have envied. Elephants have played a piano, music on a tablet computer, and danced—a few leg kicks and head bobs.

In many ways, animals are superior to us. Animals take as much as they need; people take as much as they can carry. Animals kill to survive; humans murder for a plethora of reasons. An animal's life includes survival, play, and companionship. Human lives consist of possessions, pride, and domination.

And because of this, we annihilate species, destroy the land, and consume more than we would ever need. All to the detriment of every other species, and often claiming God's blessing and appointment.

Only recently has science started studying animal's capabilities. But Eastern religions have long exalted and respected animals far more than the West. As world leaders, our lack of respect, yet complete authority, has led to brutality in breeding and horrific living conditions for animals just trying to survive. This only contributes to the demise of our planet, and all because we lack any restraint for the lust of our every whim.

Buddhism, Hinduism, Jainism, and the pagan religions have always considered animals sentient beings. These belief systems honor and exalt "God's creation." Islam believes,

> "All creatures on Earth are sentient beings. There is not an animal on Earth, nor a bird that flies on its wings—but they are communities like you." (Qur'an, 6:38)

The biblical authors of the O.T. used animals as proof of God's love for us. They surmised that if God met the animal's needs, surely ours would be too. In times of trouble and crisis, I rested my faith on the fact that if the squirrels ate daily, so would I. Throughout the Bible, it says God takes care of the animals.

> "He provides food for the cattle and for the young ravens when they call." (Psalm 147:9)

> "Consider the ravens: They do not sow or reap, they have no storeroom or barn; yet God feeds them. And how much more valuable you are than birds!" (Luke 12:24 and Matthew 6:26)

> "The Earth is the Lord's, and everything in it, the world, and all who live in it." (Psalm 24:1)

If all creatures are loved and cared for by God, why do some assume they do not have souls?

> Psalm 50:11 states, "I know every bird in the mountains, and the creatures of the field are mine."

Believing that only we have souls makes us feel like the greatest beings on Earth. But that is not true. The Bible insomuch says they have souls: "Let everything that has breath praise the Lord." (Psalm150:6)

These verses get ignored because they do not feed our ego.

We gave up our connection with nature, creating a world that caters only to our desires and disregarding everything else within the ecological system. We destroy the planet, ruin countless habitats, and dismantle what keeps us alive. We use "God" to justify our supremacy, resulting in a trail of devastation only previously seen with the extinction of the dinosaurs.

If humans were to become extinct, the planet would thrive. But a frog, bird, or fish becoming extinct could collapse entire ecosystems and cause thousands of other creatures to become extinct. Our behavior shows us to be a virus when we should be assets and guardians.

Animal sacrifices show the importance of animals throughout history and the Bible. Before Jesus, millions of animals were slaughtered on the sacrificial table. Jesus did more for them than man. His death ended the need for sacrifices, saving millions of animals.

> *"But ask the animals, and they will teach you, or the birds in the sky, and they will tell you; or speak to the Earth, and it will teach you, or let the fish in the sea inform you. Which of all these does not know that the hand of the Lord has done this? In his hand is the life of every creature and the breath of all mankind." (Job 12:7-10)*

> *"Who teaches more to us than to the beasts of the Earth and makes us wiser than the birds of the air?" (Job 35:11)*

Isaiah 11:6-9 states there are animals in Heaven:

> *The wolf will live with the lamb, the leopard will lie down with the goat, the calf and the lion and the yearling together; and a little child will lead them. The cow will feed with the bear, their young will lie down together, and the lion will eat straw like the ox. The infant will play near the cobra's den, and the young child will put its hand into the viper's nest. They will neither harm nor destroy on all my holy mountains, for the Earth will be filled with the knowledge of the Lord as the waters cover the sea.*

For me, there can be no paradise without animals.

Historically, we just needed to ask questions or study them. For most of civilization, we were trying to survive, not contemplate if Betsy the cow was happy. We saw animals as food, tools, or status, not considering their existence. We forget everything is just trying to make it through another day with food and shelter.

Technological advances are allowing us to "see" their voices. Our hearing only detects specific wavelengths, so most of their vocalizations are muted to us. Our ego assures us that if we cannot see it or feel it, it does not exist. But through testing frequencies and sound patterns, we can now see what we cannot hear. These advances enable us to understand animal motives, coordination, and familial structures.

We can now "hear" them communicate in ways we never imagined:

- Lower and higher sound waves.
- Communication over vast distances.
- Alerting each other.
- Organizing between pods, packs, and herds.
- We see entire groups uniting to save junior members from a predator.

But we are told not to anthropomorphize them.

What would happen if we measured humans against animals? They would give us character, loyalty, and ambition for which to strive. Mark Twain said, "I have been studying the traits and dispositions of the so called, 'lower animals' and contrasting them with the traits and dispositions of man. I find the result humiliating to me."

Even when we can hear them, like birds, we still diminish their sounds to mindless whistles, not correspondence and culture. We see their organized flight patterns and ask if they use sonar to accomplish such a feat—silencing their communication to just chirps and songs.

A study led by Ron Douglas, a biologist at City University London, found that insects, fish, birds, reptiles, cats, and dogs can see ultraviolet light. We lack this ability, so his research hopes to broaden our understanding of how vision affects animal's lives.

Animals have superior sight, hearing, agility, strength, and speed; some even have shape-shifting abilities. Our only advantage is our ability to build and use weaponry.

Despite all this evidence, our ego tells us they are lesser because (supposedly) God told us so. Maintaining the premise that everything doesn't feel pain and pleasure enables us to diminish their existence and justify our actions. If they are soulless, mindless animals, then we can own them, often resulting in neglect, abuse, and murder. Instead of embracing and accepting these magnificent creatures, our out-of-control egos claim they are worthless and at our disposal.

Jane Goodall opened our eyes to the impressiveness of gorillas. Her studies showed their family bonds, hierarchy, communication, and internal struggles to maintain their community. Before Goodall's research, they were viewed as vicious creatures who could easily tear us limb from limb. Her research forced us to redefine the human animal. Before her exploration, our use of tools set us apart from primates. After Goodall's studies and years of seeing chimps using tools, the definition was changed to: "consciousness."

Biologists theorize that the most intelligent creature on the planet is the octopus. The octopus is a rapid learner who can predict outcomes based on experiences and apply this knowledge to new challenges. They can complete exceedingly complex tasks, and some believe they can predict the World Cup or Super Bowl results.

Octopuses sense earthquakes and volcanic eruptions and flee before an event. Despite all this mental power, since they live in solitude, they do not learn from each other. Each octopus must learn everything without guidance or instruction, only instinct. If they ever evolved to live in communities and learn from each other, they could easily take over the planet—to the amusement of every science-fiction fan.

Pigs, chimps, dogs, and birds have problem-solving skills and memory. They remember what they have learned, which shows abstract thinking. They are also capable of lateral learning, which is learning new behaviors by sensing potential hazards and planning to avoid them. Pigs do this faster than most chimps and significantly quicker than dogs.

Scientists are just now grasping the higher levels of intelligence in animals. We have learned that crows can master 8-step sequences and solve puzzles after previously thinking only humans and octopuses could accomplish such complex tasks.

Crows were seen using cardboard to sled down snow-covered roofs. Scientists worldwide are discovering animals using tools, most often to get food but sometimes for pleasure, as noted by the bobsledding crow.

A pig's anatomy is almost identical to ours. A pig's blood and oxygen levels and internal organs are the second closest thing to humans, next to primates. Pig's skin is used for burn victims. Their brain cells can treat Parkinson's disease, and their pancreatic cells treat diabetes. Their eyes are used for cornea replacements.

Since video is now widely available, we are discovering interspecies friendships. Stories include a blind horse and a goat becoming friends. Best friends include a deer and dogs, a dog and a kangaroo, cats and birds, dogs and cats. It goes beyond animals coming together as friends; there's evidence of compassion in the wild, too. Lions acted as surrogate mothers to deer, and a tiger nursed piglets.

Regularly, there are reports of dogs saving their owner from a pending disaster. They credited two dogs with leading their blind owners down the stairs and out of the World Trade Center before it collapsed. Stories have been told since ancient times of dolphins saving men by warding off sharks.

There is even a story of a lion, a tiger, and a bear living in a rescue reserve as a family unit. The cub trio was found in the basement of an Atlanta drug dealer. The rescue organization quickly noticed their bond, so they kept them together. Today, they have their own giant "dog" house and are inseparable. They are living their best life and are no longer trophies.

When we humanize or anthropomorphize these animals, we can see their soul, motives, and purposes because we understand them from our perspective. While we continue to study them, we will see their souls just by opening our eyes to their reality, not just our desires.

We should cherish, honor, and respect other creatures. Not own, hunt for sport, terrorize and imprison for our entertainment.

Chapter 20: The Birds and The Bees

Many creatures mate for life. We still debate if monogamy is natural, but many examples exist. We find social monogamy in 90% of birds, 15% of primates, and 3% of all mammal species. Cockroaches and a parasite, the Schistosome Mansoni worm, are also monogamous.

Dolphins, pigs, horses, rats, primates, cats, and almost all birds have sex for pleasure. Dolphins have a neocortex associated with higher consciousness and sexual desires in humans. Casual sex between these animals increases social bonds, which are crucial in their societies.

Many animals masturbate, but they rarely reach climax. Scientists believe it is because they lack the mental capacity for fantasy or eroticism. Animals do what feels good and use tools like rocks, blades of grass, sticks, or, in a dog's case, their human's leg. Bears, dogs, squirrels, birds, penguins, deer, porcupines, orcas, and turtles use masturbation tools.

If sex is so disgusting and needs to be controlled, as Western religions assert, then God is constantly appalled and disgusted over most of his creation because animals are wild!

Animals experience fear, pain, grief, attachment, jealousy, and organization, and they use tools, problem-solve, play, learn, and organize in vast numbers to carry out their goals. All animals run from fear, except for humans. We walk right into it, another example of our ego acting against our best interest and animals being more intuitive.

Without thought, we destroy other species' families, societies, and often their very existence. Tragically, the animals we hold to our every whim, own, and slaughter are often kinder, more loyal, and more loving than us.

Based on all this evidence, how can we claim they are lesser, soulless beings?

How can we claim animals are unaffected by our ego-driven commercialism, gluttony, and selfishness?

How can we argue that humans are more important to God than all the other creatures?

I cannot.

"I want to realize brotherhood or identity not merely with the beings called human, but I want to realize identity with all life, even with such beings as crawl on Earth." ~ Mahatma Gandhi

Section V: God Loves the Gay

"Nature loves diversity; society hates it."
~ **Dr. Milton Diamond**

Please note that my use of "Gay," "Homosexual," or "Trans" are intended to be all-encompassing terms that include all spectrums of the LGBTQ+ (Lesbian, Gay, Bisexual, Transgender, Queer/Questioning plus all other identities and orientations). While I understand there are differences, these words are the most concise way to describe someone who is not cisgender or heterosexual. Enough divisions surround the gay community; it is not my intention to create any within it.

Section V: God Loves the Gay

Chapter 21: But, the Bible Says...!

Growing up, I was not exposed to the church's abuse against the gay community that we now see. I was aware of their societal degradation, but I saw none. I grew up in the San Francisco Bay Area in the 1970s and 80s, and the gay community was part of the culture.

As a child, whenever we would go to "The City," I would ask to go to the gay section. I loved their flamboyance, freedom, and rebellion against the "norm." I admired their bravery, boldness, affection for each other, and camaraderie as a community. They were outcasts, just like me, trying to find their way in this mad world.

I started attending a public school in the tenth grade, and like most high schools, we had jocks, nerds, cool kids, partiers, and prudes. But unlike most schools (back then), our gay students were a prominent group. They were not labeled "LGBTQ+". They were primarily the "punkers" or the self-inflicted recluses. Each clique had its section on campus, and theirs was "the stairs."

One day, while walking by them, a friend said his dad called them sinners. I said, "We're all looking for love. You should never look down on someone who has found it." Nothing more was said.

The gay kids were not quiet nor kept to themselves. Their break-ups and love affairs were as public as ours, and we joked about them, just like we did with everyone. They were just another group.

My high school was so diverse; if there were anything other than tolerance and acceptance, the campus would have been a war zone. There were a few times it nearly was.

We tend to distrust or even dislike those that differ from us. It is part of our evolutionary process. Historically, we needed to detect a friend or foe. Our brains seek to establish what someone is, and if no answer arises, confusion and fear ensue. Our minds cramp, looking for a definition and what box to place them. Our psyche runs through the drills: male or female, old or young, ally or enemy? When these answers are not readily available, the result is panic.

To which degree the panic sets in depends on how much the definition matters. The first response is fear of the unknown, which invokes an instinctual fight or flight response. Any other response is a choice of consciousness. You can be kind, or you can be afraid. The more we override our flight or fight instinct, the less power it has.

I have been there. I have been in many situations where someone was standing before me, and I did not know what they were. They could have been a boy or a girl. My brain strained to understand the human in front of me. Knowing what was happening inside my head, I took a breath, realized that what they were was none of my business, and opened my heart to learn who they were.

What someone is, is what they were born as. Who they are is what they have done with their life since birth. It is the "who" that matters. Not the "what." We must remind our ancient minds of this.

Without religion's input on homosexuality, most phobias would not be associated with it. Whether they present it as disgust or blatant fear, little incites a devoutly religious person like a gay person. Homosexuality is a crime in seventy countries, and ten of those countries execute gay people—all based on "God." Ironically, religions prove to be far more dangerous and detrimental to society than same-sex relationships.

Bigotry and ignorance cause some to attribute the worst atrocities to the gay community, like molestation and rape. However, statistics prove that White cisgender, heterosexual men commit an overwhelming majority of all sexual assaults, not homosexuals or transgender people. Sexual assaults are linked to emotional and/or mental defects; homosexuality is neither of those.

Homosexuality was not always an "abomination." Most of the "biblical evidence" is just more examples of us warping "God's will" to our hatred and ignorance. The scriptures currently used were referring to sexual shrine worship, pederasty, and temple prostitution, not same-gender relationships.

"Do not have sexual relations with a man as one does with a woman; that is detestable." (Leviticus 18:22)

The problem with this verse is that most ignore the preceding verse, 21: *"Do not give any of your children to be sacrificed to Molek, for you must not profane the name of your God. I am the Lord."*

Read together; it means sex with temple shrines and child prostitutes, not same-sex unions of love.

Sodom and Gomorrah were changed from a story about cruelty to migrants and rape to homosexuality. The destruction of the twin cities is often told through the tainted lenses of the storyteller. We never hear about the incest between Lot and his daughters. Or how the municipalities were inhospitable thoroughfares full of abuse, bribery, enslavement, rape, and murdering weary travelers. The story that is now told is one of a dire warning against same-gender relationships.

Ezekiel 16:40-50 states why they were destroyed,

Now this was the sin of your sister Sodom: She and her daughters were arrogant, overfed and unconcerned; they did not help the poor and needy. They were haughty and did detestable things before me. Therefore, I did away with them, as you have seen.

Church leaders twisted a story of severe inhospitality and gang rape into an ominous precursor for an apocalyptic scenario if we allow gay people to exist.

Many Theologians speculate that the biblical Ruth and Naomi are examples of same-sex love. The book of Ruth details their passion and commitment. Ruth's vow to Naomi is often used at weddings, albeit primarily by people who do not know it is a vow between two women.

> *But Ruth said, "Do not press me to leave you or to turn back from*
> *following you! Where you go, I will go; where you lodge, I will lodge;*
> *your people shall be my people, and your God my God. Where you die,*
> *I will die—there will I be buried. May the Lord do thus and so to me,*
> *and more as well, if even death parts me from you!" (Ruth 1:16-17)*

Dissenters of this theory assert that labeling them lesbians distorts
the love between a mother-in-law and a daughter-in-law. Maybe, but
it would be abnormal for a mother-in-law to love her son's wife that
much. Ruth was an ancestor of Jesus, one of only four women listed in
his lineage, and probably a lesbian.

David (i.e., David and Goliath, aka King David) and King Saul's
eldest son, Jonathan, were biblical heroes with an extraordinary
friendship and were probably gay.

> *After David had finished talking with Saul, Jonathan became one in*
> *spirit with David, and he loved him as himself. From that day Saul*
> *kept David with him and did not let him return home to his family.*
> *And Jonathan made a covenant with David because he loved him*
> *as himself. Jonathan took off the robe he was wearing and gave it to*
> *David, along with his tunic, and even his sword, his bow, and his*
> *belt. (I Samuel 18:1-4)*

> *After Jonathon was killed in battle, David cries out, "I grieve for you,*
> *Jonathan, my brother; you were very dear to me. Your love for me was*
> *wonderful, more wonderful than that of women." (II Samuel 1:26)*

Again, some claim this was just a story about best friends, but
friends rarely get naked together.

Jesus said nothing about homosexuality, but there are stories
of how he treated them. Matthew 8 says Jesus healed a centurion's
servant, who was probably the officer's lover. Texts state the officer
initially said the servant was "at home," which is innocuous. But
when Jesus asks to go there, the centurion admits it is his house. Staff
rarely lived in private residences, especially those in government. At
the time, this was common knowledge. So, claiming it was a servant

provided cover for their relationship.

What did Jesus do? Jesus used him as an example of great faith:

> *When Jesus had entered Capernaum, a centurion came to him, asking*
> *for help. "Lord," he said, "my servant lies at home paralyzed, suffering*
> *terribly." Jesus said to him, "Shall I come and heal him?" The*
> *centurion replied, "Lord, I do not deserve to have you come under my*
> *roof. But just say the word, and my servant will be healed. For I myself*
> *am a man under authority, with soldiers under me. I tell this one, 'Go,'*
> *and he goes; and that one, 'Come,' and he comes. I say to my servant,*
> *'Do this,' and he does it." When Jesus heard this, he was amazed and*
> *said to those following him, "Truly I tell you, I have not found anyone*
> *in Israel with such great faith." (Matt 8:5-13)*

Imagine this officer's bravery, potentially exposing himself and being vulnerable to Jesus. This story is a historical account of an officer "coming out of the closet" because of his love for his "servant." Jesus did not inquire about their relationship or ask if they were living an "abomination." Even though the officer said his home was not worthy of Jesus. Instead, Jesus used the centurion's faith as an example. Jesus' silence on the matter of their relationship speaks volumes.

The modern-day equivalents to eunuchs are trans people, and they are mentioned a few times in the Bible. They oversaw domestic duties for the wealthy and were also singers, royal soldiers and guards, and even religious sages. They were afforded access to the most personal aspects of royal life because they posed no threats to their husbands.

Jesus mentioned them.

> *Jesus replied, "Not everyone can accept this word, but only those to*
> *whom it has been given. For there are eunuchs who were born that*
> *way, and there are eunuchs who have been made eunuchs by others —*
> *and there are those who choose to live like eunuchs for the sake of*
> *the kingdom of Heaven. The one who can accept this should accept*
> *it." (Matthew 19:11-12)*

The word "homosexual" was only added to the Bible in 1946

in the Revised Standard Version. The original words used in the scriptures were "malakoi" and "arsenokoites," which most scholars believe meant effeminate and pederasty, respectively. Jesus used malakoi to describe a soft, delicate fabric (Matthew 11:8, Luke 7:25).

The biblical authors condemned men acting subservient like women were ordered to be. Paul told men to remain strong, masculine, and, therefore, righteous. Paul had issues with all forms of relationships and his own distorted ego.

The word "Arsenokoites" only appears in the Bible, so Paul's meaning is debatable. He made up the word. In Greek, "areseno" means "male" and "koites" means "bed, to lay, sex." So, when the LGBTQ+ community became the church's target, it was an easy change.

There were already terms for adult, male and male relationships. The most widely used was andro koites. There were terms for sex with slaves, promiscuity, and multiple partners. The Greeks and Romans were prolific and detailed in their sexual escapades.

To decipher Paul's intent, we must look at his concerns. They believed women were weak, so acting feminine was horrible. However, they did not have the same problems with masculine or dominant same-sex relationships.

What fueled Paul's rage was pederasty: adults having sex with children. The Pagans were practicing temple prostitution in Corinth, so Paul addressed that in his letters. It is safe to say that most people are against pederasty. Anytime a child is used for an adult's sexual gratification, it is an abomination.

Pederasty was a problem throughout the ages and maintained its presence in organizations like NAMBLA (North American Man-Boy Love Association). Or the issues in the Catholic Church, Islam, and Asia. But pederasty and same-gender relationships are different.

Pederasty is molestation and about control and domination through sex; it is an act. A gay person is who a person is. To compare pederasty to homosexuality is like comparing intimacy to rape. The comparison is based on apathy and ignorance, resulting in bigotry.

The Bible does not address lesbianism, making homosexuality a sin only for men. Because it was never about same-sex love; it was about maintaining the Patriarchy's power.

Chapter 22: Saints, Not Sinners

In the third and fourth centuries, there were three sets of same-sex Saints: Perpetua and Felicity, Polyeuct and Nearchus, and Sergius and Bacchus.

Perpetua and Felicity were from Northern Africa and were imprisoned because of their Christianity. Early Christianity noted Perpetua's diary (Passion of St. Perpetua, St. Felicitas, and their Companions) as the first document written by a woman. In the fourth century, its popularity caused Augustine to warn that it was not divine and should not be more revered than the Bible. Catholicism values the two women, and they are pictured together as saints. Their feast day is March 7th. An inspiration for the gay community, they are included in their list of LGBTQ Saints.

In the third century, Armenians Polyeuct and Nearchus were Roman soldiers. A fourth-century biographer said they were "brothers, not by birth, but by affection" and shared "the closest possible relationship, being both comrades and fellow soldiers." Polyeuct converted to Christianity, believing they would spend eternity together. Shortly after, Polyeuct attacked a pagan procession and was beheaded for his crime. He is considered a martyr, and they are always pictured together as saints.

And the fourth-century Roman soldiers Sergius and Bacchus.

They were high-ranking officers: a commander and a second lieutenant, respectively. They were martyred sometime between 303 and 311 for refusing to perform pagan sacrifices. The legend states that Bacchus was killed first. After his death, he appeared to Sergius as a soldier with the illuminated face of an angel. Bacchus assured Sergius they would indeed spend eternity together in Heaven. Sergius' tomb is a shrine, and many Byzantine-era churches are named after him. They are venerated saints in the Assyrian Church of the East and Roman Catholic, Coptic, Eastern, and Oriental Orthodox Churches.

Religion's judgment, division, and superiority—often resulting in death—is ancient, but their condemnation of same-sex relationships is not.

We Have Ruined God

Chapter 23: Natural Or Unnatural?

The Church uses Saint Thomas Aquinas' theories on Eternal and Natural Law as their argument against homosexuality. Ironically, I use it to support it.

Aquinas's theory states:

> In the case of the Eternal Law, the things of creation that are ruled by that law have it imprinted on them through their nature or essence. Since things act according to their nature, they derive their proper acts and ends (final cause) according to the law that is written into their nature. Everything in nature, insofar as they reflect the order by which God directs them through their nature for their own benefit, reflects the Eternal Law in their own natures.

The problem with using nature as your argument against homosexuality is that virtually all living creatures (mammals, birds, fish, reptiles, and insects) have segments of homosexuality. Same-sex unions have been scientifically observed in over 1500 species and are well-documented in over five hundred species. Several books detail and document this natural occurrence. Echoing Saint Thomas Aquinas' sentiments, Albert Einstein said, "Look deep into nature, and you will understand everything."

The opposite sex's availability has no impact on gay behavior in these species. So, regardless of the opportunity to have heterosexual mates, some still prefer same-gender sex and companionship: a homosexual relationship. The behavior is not limited to penetration but includes all sexual conduct, such as genital stimulation, copulation, and mating games.

In nature, gender and sexuality are mutable. Our Universe is continuously displaying the beauty of diversity. It is only in our minds (often derived from religion) that everything must be black and white. Without variations, we would not have the beautiful colors, balance, and lives that shape our wondrous existence.

Scientists dismiss religious criticism trying to disprove these facts because it is human judgment, not "Natural Law." The vast amount of wildlife exhibiting gay behavior proves it is entirely natural. The issue is ours, and that is unnatural. Animals lack our inhibitions and thoroughly enjoy every aspect of their sexuality. Animals "get freaky" and have beautiful lives.

If homosexuality goes against God's will, then why doesn't he stop creating them?

Are gay animals going to Hell with gay humans?

Religion claims that between three and twenty percent of the Omnipotent Being's creation are entirely flawed by design.

This belief is an abomination, not same-gender relationships.

No life is flawed, just our judgments of them. We do not understand everything "God" does, but nothing created is loathed or unloved. (Although, I seriously question mosquitoes, red ants, and fleas.)

How can one say that God's creations are perfect, then curse them and call them an imperfection? Homosexuality is not a sin. The sin is how poorly they are treated in the name of God.

I have had many gay friends, and none of them would have chosen to be gay. They have grown to embrace, accept, and love who they are, but they would not have chosen such a tough life—because of society's condemnation of who they are.

It is impossible to demand that a person of color become White.

Sexual orientation and gender identity are the same as race—it is how someone is born. It is our obligation to love, not to judge; it is what Jesus would do.

With scientific revelations, the Church's stance against homosexuality as "unnatural" must now cease—along with the flat Earth theories, and we are the center of the Universe.

Since science expounded on the laws of nature, the Church must renounce their bigotry and stop using mistranslated texts for their condemnation.

"When we know better, we do better." ~ *Maya Angelou*

Chapter 24: Love the Sinner. Hate the Sin

The day "Don't Ask. Don't Tell" was repealed, a U.S. soldier serving in Iraq "came out" to his parents on Skype. His fear was unmistakable. He tried to be strong, but his voice still cracked.

As he finished his confession, his mother sobbed. His father sat there silently and stoically. She tried to speak through her tears. She genuinely feared for his soul. His mother cried out, begging for God's forgiveness and mercy on her son. She wailed as if her child had just died, and she was seeing him burning in Hell.

When parents believe their child's soul will burn for eternity, it is consumptive and terrifying. A parent's job is to protect and guide their kids, and when they fear eternal damnation, it can be overwhelming. The fear engulfed them.

But their concerns were based on bullshit, not love or guidance, but mistranslations and agenda-driven dogma. Their son suffered, and they shattered their relationship because of fear and indoctrination based on false premises.

Another mother posted an obituary in the local newspaper after her son told her he was gay. Because to her, he was dead. In a follow-up blog, she bemoaned his "sinful" life and how she considered his "lifestyle" a personal attack. She said being anywhere near him would cause her damnation.

She rejected and disowned her son because "God told her to." Religion's twisted dogma of fear and damnation creates a hell here on Earth. Our lives are full of fear of the hereafter. We forget about the present and ignore the anguish inflicted on those we claim to love.

Feeling isolated and hopeless because of society's judgment has driven many kids to commit suicide, and the Church is the biggest promoter of this hate. Religion's shame has permeated so profoundly that children think they are an abomination. They are told to despise what they are. They would not feel so hopeless if they were not born this way.

Kids are killing themselves over flawed, heartless ideologies. They would if they could choose a different identity and who they love. They want to be accepted and loved, but the same people representing God say they are trash. These are not isolated incidents. We see it worldwide. These beautiful people's lives are full of prejudice, discrimination, ridicule, and isolation, all because of our judgment of "God's" creation.

What could be godlier than "God's" creation? What could be more ungodly than turning your back on your fellow man? Jesus asked us to love everyone, not just the ones who agree with us, are like us, and have the same goals. Jesus demanded just the opposite. Yet today, the Church condones and justifies this hate and isolation in God's name.

People, children, are dying over this bigoted indoctrination. Mother Teresa said, "Being unwanted, unloved, uncared for, forgotten by everybody, I think that is a much greater hunger, a much greater poverty than the person who has nothing to eat."

A life without love is no life at all.

No one taught me who to love. Well, I choose completely dysfunctional men because of my parents and all the Freudian issues that go along with that. But no one ever said, eluded, or prescribed to me, "You will be attracted to tall men with dark hair and bright eyes, who are funny and driven...." The fact that I am still attracted to men proves it is not a choice. I have no control over my attractions or lack thereof, and to imply, suggest, or demand that others do is cold and inhumane.

The catchphrase for many believers is "Love the sinner, hate the sin!" It is challenging to find a more judgmental, egotistical statement. Let alone the atrocity of it being said "in the name of God."

Saying it implies you alone know how God will judge us and are holy enough to make that judgment. It also claims that while you claim to love this person, you do not. At least, not the parts you consider yucky.

I love the way John Pavlovitz, pastor and author, said it,

> To say to a LGBTQ person, 'I love you but I hate your sexuality,' is the same as saying to someone, 'I love you, but the color of your eyes disgusts me,' or 'I love you, but I hate the way you laugh,' or 'I love you, but God believes that the freckles on your shoulders and cheeks are an abomination.' (2015)

In 2015, the Evangelical Covenant Church asked Pastor Adam Phillips to lead an Oregon congregation but then fired him because he supported the LGBTQ+ community. They tried to silence Phillips's "liberal views." So, after he published a blog and met with other affirming pastors, they terminated him. When church leadership exiles its pastors because they are too loving and accepting, we have a problem.

Dr. Thomas J. Oord is a theologian, philosopher, and scholar who directs Northwind Theological Seminary doctoral programs in Open and Relational Theology. He was an ordained minister with the Church of the Nazarene for over 30 years until the summer of 2024 when Oord was officially tried for heresy. His crime was teaching against church doctrine on human sexuality (he is queer-affirming) and misconduct for advocating for changes on queer issues. He wanted the Church of the Nazarene to be LGBTQ+-affirming. The church found him guilty and revoked his ministerial license and membership. In their decision, the church said, "The seriousness of offenses cannot be overstated. Only eternity will show how many souls have been led astray through his false teaching" (Newsweek, Sept. 2024). Dr. Oord was declared a heretic for loving his neighbor. The Church of the Nazarene proved its alliance with the Pharisees, not Jesus.

We are commanded to love, no exceptions. Nothing has ever more discussed than love. But we must understand what love *should be.*

There are many types of love (platonic, familial, romantic, etc.), but they all intersect at empathy. Empathy is kindness, compassion, and unity, and it prioritizes the well-being of others over beliefs, race, or identity. Empathy demands social justice, equity, and inclusion, while its opposite, apathy, has allowed every atrocity.

"Love your neighbor" is empathizing with them, acknowledging their humanity regardless of their race, religion, culture, or status and caring if they are fed, clothed, healthy, and safe. Empathy does not care about the afterlife, focusing instead on how individuals are treated in the present. Empathy is present tense: presence and concern. Love is action, not words.

When we separate "the sin" from the "sinner," we remove their divine motivation to love. We ask them to deny who they are so we will be comfortable. We are silencing them and asking them to be alone. The Bible was used to justify slavery, ban interracial marriage, and, frankly, kill anyone outside of your social circle. Same-gender relationships are the "abomination" of today, and I hope it goes the way of potatoes, tomatoes, and being outside while menstruating.

Condemning love is reprehensible. Oppressing someone because of the way they were born is an abomination. The actual sin is the censure of God's children—His creation and people He loves. The genuine horror is using "God" to justify discrimination, judgment, and shame.

Everyone deserves love.

Section VI: The Evolution of Christianity

"However many holy words you read, however many you speak, what good will they do you if you do not act on upon them?"
~ Siddhartha Gautama

Chapter 25: Flawless Texts, Dogma and Doctrine?

I was taught that the Bible was God's spoken word, ordained by God, immutable, indisputable, and divine. The Bible was our guidebook for living the ideal life and our history book. The Bible's continuity of content and its longevity in circulation and worldwide acceptance helped to confirm these conclusions. My belief in these things was not solely based on faith, but also facts.

Or so I thought.

A few months after my mom passed away, I learned that Mary Magdalene was not a prostitute. Mary was one of Jesus' closest disciples. Because of other's jealousy and the Church's degradation of women, she mistakenly received the title of whore. The disciples disregarded her, and then in 591 C.E., Pope Gregory the Great (his greatness is debatable) grouped her with another Mary (of Bethany) and an unnamed sinner, claiming they were all one.

Pope Gregory claimed all three women were Mary Magdalene, and she was a whore. In 1969, the Second Vatican Council announced the error and "corrected the record." The Vatican must have whispered their mistake. I was born in 1970. This revision was obviously never formally announced, leaving churches to continue teaching an incorrect and slanderous doctrine.

I vividly remember the moment I learned of this modification.

It was a lazy Sunday afternoon, and I was relaxing watching documentaries on TV. As the narrative about Mary's misidentification unfolded, I sat on the edge of my seat, my mouth agape, my hands nervously on my chin. Once it concluded, I became flush and disoriented. I got up for a drink and began pacing through my apartment. Freaking out, I started flailing my arms and shouted, "Mary wasn't a whore? She was not a whore!"

The same halls that I walked to take care of my dying mother were now my pathway through an existential crisis.

My mom questioned everything before she died, and I assured her that her beliefs were correct. Then, I discovered that a fundamental part of the story of Jesus and his followers was false. False! Growing up, I was Mary Magdalene in the Church's Easter productions. She symbolized Christ's tolerance, forgiveness, and ability to restore purity. And I was learning it was all a fabrication of the early Church. A man's ego was shaming a mighty woman of Christ. The revelation was earth-shattering news; it rocked everything I believed.

I had always taken pride in my knowledge of the Bible and the "truths" it represented. The Bible was my history book, my rulebook, the answer to every question.

Was it full of lies, or were the teachings and interpretations wrong?

Whose fault was this?

Who could I blame for this betrayal?

I was oscillating between confusion and rage. It was one of those earth-shattering, pivotal moments, but it was without my mom this time. I wished she were there to guide me.

How would she feel about this massive revelation?

How would she justify it?

I could not get my head around it and how the revelation affected my belief system. It affected me so profoundly that I brought it up over a business lunch with a client. Her response was perfect and relieved so much anxiety about my mom not being here to help.

My client said compassionately, "Sheri, just think if this question arose before she died. Your mother was already questioning her entire existence. I am sure this would have been a traumatic revelation for her like it is for you. I'm sure this information is timely. You would not want your mother further questioning her religion and the decisions she made. This is truly an example of ignorance, is bliss."

After discovering the distortion, I became intrigued and soaked up all the information I could get. The Dead Sea Scrolls fascinated me. All the information coming forth, texts ordered to be destroyed and lost to history. It felt like I could finally see Jesus' life through something other than the Church's eyes. These texts add to, and sometimes contradict, what we were taught and have believed in the Bible. Of course, for thousands of years, the Church condemned and dismissed them as heretical. These scriptures were from the "losers" of their time. Winners make history, and they banish the losers from it.

My mom always said that Catholicism was primarily a political religion: controlled by politics, built on politics, and often pagan foundations. My pastor would shout from the pulpit, "Why do Catholics still have Jesus hanging from the cross? He has risen! He's no longer there!" and we would all stand and applaud. That was the extent of my knowledge of Catholicism.

As a teenager, I attended a quinceañera (a Latina's coming of age celebration) in a Catholic church. I remember being exhausted from all the standing, kneeling, then sitting, and repeat! Now, whenever I enter a Catholic church (or resembling), I am in awe of the pomp and circumstance: the rituals, the robes, and the gold.

Our churches were informal. We passed around giant trays of tiny plastic cups of grape juice and broken saltine crackers for communion. However, some churches had fantastic wafers. Taking my first communion at a Catholic church (yes, I am sure I broke all kinds of rules in doing so) was more nerve-wracking than spiritual. It was as if I was in front of nobility and afraid of doing something wrong. I focused more on the procedure than I did on remembrance and gratitude.

Jesus was not wealthy. He was humble and said it was easier for a camel to get through the eye of a needle than for a rich man to go to Heaven. I often wonder what Jesus would say about drinking from golden chalices or walking into the Vatican. I have a feeling it would be like, "What the.... How did you get this from what I said?"

My Christian school never discussed the Reformation, so I did not know that the entire basis of "our" religion was Catholicism, which evolved from Judaism—all of which have pagan myths, symbolism, holidays, and practices intertwined. I always thought they were separate. My mom used to say they were "a political movement," and we were about Jesus!

I thought it started with the Torah, then the Catholic version, and then the revised and "better" version: the Protestant editions! Imagine my dismay when I discovered that not only does the Bible lack continuity across the scriptures, but it also lacks consistency in the books represented in each Bible. There are many Bibles, not just translations.

Bibles with different books!

Here is the breakdown…

The Old Testament:

The Hebrew Bible (or Tanakh): The Biblical Canon commonly used in Judaism, Christianity, and Samaritanism, but not the Protestant "New Testament Only Christians" who reject the O.T.:

Genesis	Exodus	Leviticus	Numbers

Biblical Canon in Judaism and Christianity, but excluded by the Samaritans:

*Hosea	*Joel	*Amos	*Obadiah
*Jonah	*Micah	*Nahum	*Habakkuk
*Zephaniah	*Haggai	*Zechariah	*Malachi

Considered "Minor Prophets." These books form a single book in the Jewish Bible, called "Trei Asar" or "Twelve."

Included by Roman Catholics and the Orthodox Church, but excluded by Jews, most Protestants, and Samaritans:

Tobit	Judith	Wisdom (Of Solomon) Ben Sira
Additions to Daniel	Additions to Esther	

Included by the Orthodox Church:

1st Ezra	Prayer of Manasseh
	4th Maccabees
3rd Maccabees	(in the appendix but is not canonical)

Included By Russian and Ethiopian Orthodox Churches:

2nd Ezra

Included By the Ethiopian Orthodox Church:

Jubilees	Enoch

Included by the Syrian church:

Psalms 152-155	2nd Baruch

The Books of The New Testament are consistent across all versions.

After Jesus was crucified, factions developed between his followers. Since then, everything has been subjected to the political environment, interpretations, and eras. Jesus was a Jew, so the founding philosophy of Christianity is Judaism. However, the divide between them continues to grow. The ideologies of Christianity experienced a massive evolution, as have the religious texts. All teachings, interpretations, writings, and beliefs depended on who was in control.

Learning this shattered the belief that "The Bible has been consistent for 2000 years!" It was hard enough grappling with the alterations of what was sinful. Still, this revelation rocked the foundation of my education and belief system.

Primarily, we only focus on the central characters in the Bible. Their stories are taught through the teacher's lens and compartmentalized to one verse at a time. I wanted a bigger picture of the people who shaped the Faith and to discover what was not being taught. It did not matter if I agreed with their impact and influence. I wanted to connect the dots and see how we got to the Christianity we see today.

Chapter 26: The Women

Jesus' female followers are rarely mentioned in the Bible. They included his mother, Mary; the "Apostle to the Apostles," Mary Magdalene; Zebedee's wife, Mary Salome; Lazarus' sister, Martha; Chuza's wife, Joanna; and the Apostle Phillip's sister, Mariamne. Most of what we know about them comes from the non-canonical gospels: the apocryphal texts.

Information on these women is minimal. We usually only know their names because of their association with a man. There is a ton of conjecture but minimal evidence to support it. The Bible does not hide its disregard for women and ordains women as lesser. So, giving women any power within the spiritual movement is purposefully absent.

Women were not allowed to be in positions of power, which prevented their teachings from being included in the transcripts of history. Western Religions labeled women as inferior and perpetuated that ideology through the degradation of their societal influence. However, Jesus' life and teachings were contrary to that misogynistic dogma. The women remained by Jesus' side when he was arrested and crucified, while all the men abandoned him out of fear. But that fact tends to be a PostScript.

Chapter 27: Mary, Jesus' Mother

Catholicism considers Mary the mother of God. They believe she was miraculously conceived: the Immaculate Conception. I always assumed the term referred to Jesus' conception. However, Catholics believe God selected her in the womb, and she was conceived without the "original sin." They believe that only she and Jesus were "never touched by Satan," meaning through sex. They also think that she stayed a virgin, even after giving birth to Jesus, and was celibate for the rest of her life—the perpetual virgin. Catholicism asserts that Mary's body and soul went directly to Heaven—the Assumption.

Mary did not always have these sacred designations. For over 300 years, Christianity lacked a feminine deity, which was present in all the pagan faiths. To assimilate the belief systems, Christianity needed a female presence. Because of a lack of biblical information, they easily molded her into whatever the Church needed her to be.

Mary's transformation from human mother to holy intercessor and Mother of God took over 1500 years. The earliest known prayer to Mary is from the late third century. The "virgin birth" of Jesus was not established until the Council of Nicaea in 325.

Artwork of her appeared in the fourth century. The Council of Ephesus in 431 labeled her the "Mother of God." Around the same time, they gave her the title of "Mediatrix," or mediator between Jesus and us. The Second Ecumenical Council at Constantinople in 553 and then again in 1537 proclaimed her the "Perpetual Virgin."

In 1834, Pope Pius IX declared her Immaculate Conception. And in 1950, Pope Pius XII affirmed the Assumption. Practices, feasts, and venerations were present in certain cultures and Christian denominations but were not dogmatically defined for centuries.

Islam also venerates Mary. The Qur'an mentions her significantly more often than the Bible. An entire chapter is dedicated to her; she is the only woman named in the Qur'an. She is considered the most magnificent woman that has ever lived. The Qur'an states, *"Mary! God has chosen thee and purified thee; He hath chosen thee above all the women of creation"* (3:42).

The stories of Mary in the Qur'an (Suras 3 and 19) mirror the Gospel of Luke. They echo beliefs about the Immaculate Conception, Annunciation, and virgin birth of Jesus. Islam calls Mary the Purified, Chosen, and Truthful One. But they do not pray to or worship her. Muslims are devout about praying to and serving only God.

Most scholars assert that Mary was a teenager when she birthed Jesus. She was betrothed but not yet married. So, she would have been 12-14 years old for that time and culture. Most scholars agree Joseph was much older, some claiming he was 90 when they married. However, the consensus is that he was in his late 40s, possibly 50s.

The Catholic Encyclopedia addresses the apocryphal texts that perpetuate these theories:

> It will not be without interest to recall here, unreliable though they are, the lengthy stories concerning St. Joseph's marriage contained in the apocryphal writings. When 40 years of age, Joseph married a woman called Melcha or Escha by some, Salome by others; they lived 49 years together and had six children, two daughters, and four sons, the youngest of whom was James (the Less, "the Lord's brother"). A year after his wife's death, as the priests announced through Judea that they wished to find in the tribe of Juda, a respectable man to espouse Mary, then twelve to fourteen years of age. Joseph, who was at the time 90 years old, went up to Jerusalem among

the candidates; a miracle manifested the choice God had made of Joseph, and two years later the Annunciation took place. (Souvay, 1910)

The apocryphal texts referenced are the Gospel of James (second century) and the Infancy Gospel of Matthew (seventh century). The texts also claim Mary was a Consecrated Temple Virgin, like the Vestal Virgins of Ancient Rome. Pope Innocent 1, in 405, and Saint Thomas Aquinas in the 13th century disputed the apocryphal claims about Mary.

As a mother, I always felt kinship with Mary. Experiencing her pain was always my greatest fear. She was a woman of tremendous strength, and she has my admiration for that. But for the patriarchy to recognize her, she had to be more than human. She had to be untouched and flawless.

Some scholars contend that Jesus' brothers and sisters could not be his blood relatives because they were not mentioned when Jesus was a child at the temple or the crucifixion. These assertions are weak and are molding the text to fit the agenda. Hypocritically, the Church uses apocryphal books to justify their claim that Jesus was an only child. They use what they label as forbidden to justify their dogma.

I took issue with the procession to God. Mary intercedes to Jesus, and Jesus intercedes to God. What about the first commandment? By appointing Mary as a go-between, it literally placed her before God. The Orthodox believe the line of Saints is long: Mary and the angels, prophets, apostles, Fathers, Martyrs, etc. God has an entire posse preceding him.

Catholicism defends this, claiming that they venerate her, not worship her—they revere her. They also believe she is superior to all "created beings." Catholics claim all prayers to her are answered by God, and all worship of her is ultimately for God.

This is where the technicalities of manufactured religions rear an ugly head. Fundamental commandments, philosophies, and teachings are acceptable to ignore if it suits the religious leaders of the time. Christianity took a monotheistic religion and turned it into a polytheistic belief system—resembling the ancient pagans much more than Abraham's faith.

Mary is not the mother of God because Jesus said he was not God:

> *"'Why do you ask me about what is good?' Jesus replied. 'There is only One who is good. If you want to enter life, keep the commandments.'" (Matthew 19:17)*

She and Jesus were not very close. The Gospels of Mark and Luke claim he rejected her.

> *"Your mother and brothers are standing outside, wanting to see you."* *He replied, "My mother and brothers are those who hear God's word and put it into practice." (Luke 18-:20-21)*

His family thought Jesus was nuts:

> *"When his family heard about this, they went to take charge of him, for they said, 'He is out of his mind." (Mark 3:21)*

But the Church says Jesus is God, and Mary has intercessory power with Jesus. We not only ruined God, but we did a number on Jesus and Mary, too.

Chapter 28: Mary Magdalene

Mary from Magdala (meaning tower) was the epitome of feminine strength. But for 2000 years, because of the twisting of translations and blatant misogyny, she was undermined and silenced. She is shrouded in mystery and controversy, but there is one thing we conclusively know about her: she was special to Jesus.

The Gospels state that Mary is the only person to see all three of Jesus' key events: crucifixion, burial, and the first to see him resurrected. She had to be mentioned because of her prominence in these noteworthy events. Still, the Christian founders tried to silence her. At one point, they erased her from witnessing the resurrection. Paul disregarded her from his list of apostles. Except for one verse in Luke (8:2), saying Jesus cast out seven demons from Mary, they do not mention her before the crucifixion.

The early Church called her "The Apostle to the Apostles." They based this title on biblical qualifications. The requirements, detailed in the book of Acts, were someone who accompanied Jesus during his earthly ministry and witnessed his resurrection. Or Paul's version (because he did not qualify), someone who saw the appearance of the risen Christ and received a divine calling to spread Christ's message. Based on all the benchmarks, Mary qualified for apostleship. If Paul had not changed the criteria, he would have been ineligible to be a disciple. Paul's tantrum about this is noted in 1 Corinthians, specifically chapters 9 and 15.

Whether officially declared a disciple, Mary's status within the discipleship infuriated the men. Especially Peter. The Gospels of Mark (16:11) and Luke (24:6) contend that the disciples did not believe Mary when she told them of Jesus' resurrection. And they completely dismissed what she claimed Jesus said.

The "Gospel of Mary" (The Gnostic Society Library), an apocryphal text, says Peter asked her:

> Sister, we know the Savior loved you more than the rest of the woman. Tell us the words of the Savior which you remember, which you know, but we do not, nor have we heard them." Mary answered and said, "What is hidden from you I will proclaim to you." And she began to speak to them these words: "I, she said, I saw the Lord in a vision, and I said to Him, Lord I saw you today in a vision.

Unfortunately, what follows this text is missing, but we know it upset most of the men. Andrew and Peter dismissed her because she was just a woman. The next legible texts state:

> Did he then speak secretly with a woman, in preference to us, and not openly? Are we to turn back and all listen to her? Did he prefer her to us?" Then Mary grieved and said to Peter, "My brother Peter, what do you think? Do you think that I thought this up myself in my heart or that I am lying concerning the Savior? (9:4-5)

Levi jumps in to defend Mary, proclaiming:

> Peter, you have always been hot-tempered. Now I see you contending against the woman like the adversaries. But if the Savior made her worthy, who are you indeed to reject her? Surely the Savior knows her very well. That is why He loved her more than us. Rather, let us be ashamed and put on the perfect man, and separate as He commanded us and preach the gospel, not laying down any other rule or other law beyond what the Savior said. (9:6-8)

Another apocryphal text, the "Gospel of Phillip," labels Mary as Jesus' "koinônos," which means associate, companion, or partner in

Greek. Some scholars believe this text reveals that Jesus kissed Mary
on the mouth, but since there are missing pieces, no one conclusively
knows. The assumption is:

> And the companion of [the Savior was Mar]y Ma[gda]llene. [Christ
> loved] M[ary] more than [all] the disci[ples and used to] kiss her
> [often] on her [mouth]. The rest of [the disciples were offended by it
> and expressed disapproval]. They said to him, "Why do you love her
> more than all of us?" The Savior answered and said to them, "Why do
> I not love you like her?"

The treatment of Mary epitomizes the Church's misogyny and
reveals that she always posed a threat to their sexist ideologies. If she
and Jesus were married, it would contradict the Church's stance on
celibacy. If she was the mother of his child(ren), then his offspring
could have an advantage, and therefore control, over the Church.
If she were an influential leader, their ban on women in leadership
would reveal their sexism. Some scholars believe Mary was wealthy
and was Jesus' benefactor, which could damage the patriarchal image
of manliness. If Jesus favored her above the rest, then how does the
Church justify their belittlement of women? Mary created too many
problems for the Church. It was better to keep references to her at a
minimum, not to contradict their entire doctrine.

What happened to Mary after Jesus' ascension is lost to history.
Most scholars believe she went to France and lived in a cave for the
rest of her life. For centuries, Mary was just a whore who followed
Jesus and was there at all the correct times.

Since she is no longer considered a prostitute, people care about
her and wonder what we missed because of her suppression.

What could we have learned from her? What made her so special
to Jesus and loathed by so many men?

The apocryphal texts detail her influence. The "Gospel of
Thomas" is enlightening and worth the quick read. It paints Jesus in
a mystical light and documents women asking him questions, which
was unseemly.

The last verse is particularly interesting and highlights the sexism.
It is believed to be a later addition to the text, but that is still up for

debate.

> *"Simon Peter said to them, 'Make Mary leave us, for females don't deserve life.' Jesus said, 'Look, I will guide her to make her male, so that she too may become a living spirit resembling you males. For every female who makes herself male will enter the kingdom of Heaven."*
> *(Verse 114)*

I think it was a later addition because the gospel revealed that women were speaking publicly and directly to Jesus. The Gospel of Thomas shows that Jesus gave women a voice, which had to be corrected. The addition contradicts the Gospel, but consistency was rarely the editor's goal.

Dan Brown's The DaVinci Code highlighted a theory about Mary being "the Beloved Disciple," meaning she was responsible for the Gospel of John and Acts. Dan Brown did not start this concept; he merely gave it a nice wrapper and a path out of the shadows. One believer could have been Leonardo DaVinci since the person sitting next to Jesus in The Last Supper is remarkably feminine.

The Church turned one of Jesus' closest followers into a Devil-possessed whore just because she was a woman. It would be typical of them to deny her credit for authorship, marital status, or anything jeopardizing the patriarchy and their fragile egos. But for now, we can only speculate.

Chapter 29: The Rock

Peter was named Simon before becoming an apostle of Jesus. Jesus gave him the name of Cephas, which translates to Peter and means "The Rock."

> *I tell you that you are Peter and on this rock I will build my Church, and the gates of Hell will not overcome it. I will give you the keys of the kingdom of Heaven; whatever you bind on Earth will be bound in Heaven and whatever you loose on Earth will be loosed in Heaven. (Matthew 16:17-20)*

Stories of Peter show his humility, temper, and impulsivity. But Jesus saw beyond Peter's self-perceptions and insecurities. Jesus did not focus on Peter's humanity; he saw Peter's soul. Jesus valued Peter's stability, strength, faith, loyalty, and leadership skills.

Peter is an excellent example of the struggles we all go through and how to relate to the spiritual world. Our ego always leads to spiritual failure, and Peter shows us how he stayed humble through his struggles and apprenticeship. Peter's vulnerability is inspiring.

Peter was an angler by trade, and most of his business partners, including family, also became apostles. Peter was not wealthy. He would be poor by today's standards.

We can assume Jesus knew Peter and Andrew before they became his disciples. According to scripture, they dropped everything and followed him. However, it is often taught that since the scriptures do not detail a past friendship, Jesus' spiritual stature was so grand that it caused people, upon first sight, to abandon everything and accompany him. But that is not logical, or it sounds more like a cult.

The Gospels show that Jesus built his following through words, actions, and miracles. Religion likes to turn him into a magician who captured everyone he met, but that is untrue. Many people despised Jesus, and proof of that is in his crucifixion. The Gospel of John (8 and 10) says people threw rocks at Jesus.

Jesus used Peter's boat to preach to the masses. When Jesus walked on water, Peter wanted to, too. Peter labeled Jesus as the Messiah.

Peter offered his life so that Jesus would be spared. He helped prepare the Last Supper, drew his sword when Jesus was arrested, and denied Jesus three times. Peter was the last person to see Jesus before the Ascension. The Gospels clearly state that Jesus intended for Peter to continue the ministry.

The Gospel of Mark is believed to be based on Peter's teachings. The books, 1st and 2nd Peter, are attributed to him, but most of what we know of him is only in the first four books of the N.T. Most works from or about Peter were discarded or considered apocryphal.

Peter's books included The Gospel of Peter, The Acts of Peter, The Acts of Peter and Paul, The Acts of Peter and Andrew, The Acts of Peter and the Twelve, The Gnostic Apocalypse of Peter, A Letter of Peter to Philip, The Apocalypse of Peter, and The Epistula Petri.

In the early fourth century, Emperor Constantine silenced Peter. Archeologists only discovered most texts in the last 200 years—silencing Peter for almost 1500 years. Possibly as an act of contrition, Constantine constructed St. Peter's Basilica and posthumously named Peter as the first Pope.

Whatta guy!

Peter believed that Jesus' message applied to everyone, but he thought the disciple's objective was to preach to the Jews. With Peter's anointing, Paul was established as the "Apostle to the Gentiles," or non-Jews. Paul considered Peter the "Pillar" of the movement but not the "Rock" that Jesus declared. Peter was dogmatic in his belief that any follower of Jesus must adhere to Jewish law, and Paul disregarded it.

Although contrary to Jesus' directives, the current Christian doctrine is primarily based on Paul's epistles. When the political and religious leaders aimed to make Christianity a world religion, they chose the doctrine that furthered their agenda: Paul's. Mass appeal and application meant more than intention and accuracy.

Chapter 30: Paul, the Pharisee

Paul of Tarsus, or Saul, was an integral part of the propagation of
Christianity. He was also a proponent of the persecution of Christians
before his conversion. Paul's abuse of the Jews was primarily about
nationality, not religion. He was born a Jew, but he preferred a more
liberal version of Judaism, Hellenism.

Paul was a Greek Jew who disregarded Mosaic laws, customs,
and cultures. Initially, Hellenism was the Greek religion that included
the twelve gods of the Olympiad. Wars and conquests of Jerusalem in
the fourth and fifth centuries B.C.E. caused Hellenism and Judaism
to merge. It was an established, well-known, upper sect of Judaism
by Paul's time. Hellenism sharply declined in the second and third
centuries (C.E.). Many scholars see the drop in Hellenism and the
emergence of Christianity as symbiotic.

Paul was a Pharisee, the era's political, religious, and social
leaders. Jesus spoke about them and viewed them as utterly corrupt.

> "For I tell you that unless your righteousness surpasses that of the
> Pharisees and the teachers of the law, you will certainly not enter the
> kingdom of Heaven." (Mathew 5:20)

> Woe to you, teachers of the law and Pharisees, you hypocrites! You
> give a tenth of your spices—mint, dill, and cumin. But you have
> neglected the more important matters of the law—justice, mercy, and

faithfulness. You should have practiced the latter, without neglecting the former. You blind guides! You strain out a gnat but swallow a camel. (Mathew 23:23-24)

Because of outbursts like these, the Pharisees plotted against Jesus. They found the opportunity when he healed a disabled man on the Sabbath, a crime punishable by death.

Ironically, Jesus warned of the hypocrisy of the Pharisees, and they started his persecution. Yet, a Pharisee became a primary reason Christianity became a worldwide religion. Besides Paul's hallucination, historical records, including scripture, state that Paul and Jesus never met. Paul even boasted about never knowing him. (Galatians 1)

As detailed in Acts, Saul was going to Jerusalem from Damascus. He was going to *"bring these people as prisoners to Jerusalem to be punished,"* which was a quest for more brutality against the "lost" Christians. During this trip, Saul had a vision that altered all of Christianity. Saul's apparition was of the resurrected Christ within a bright light. He said Jesus came to him as the "Heavenly Adam," and they went to a third heaven. Saul was told things he could never repeat in this third Heaven: "Only God knows."

After this vision, Saul was blinded for three days. When he regained sight, they baptized him and changed his name to Paul. He then began what he believed was his duty to spread his message and his views of Jesus' philosophies.

Paul believed this event was a gift from God. And "God" gave him the power to convert people to Christianity and issue laws, covenants, and commands. Paul based all his teachings and edicts on this "divine gift," and it was not up for debate, doubt, or disagreement. Paul perceived his message as Divine Law, therefore infallible.

I am astonished that you are so quickly deserting the one who called you to live in the grace of Christ and are turning to a different gospel—which is really no gospel at all. Evidently, some people are throwing you into confusion and are trying to pervert the gospel of Christ. But even if we or an angel from Heaven should preach a gospel

Chapter 30: Paul, the Pharisee

other than the one we preached to you, let them be under God's curse!
As we have already said, so now I say again: If anybody is preaching
to you a gospel other than what you accepted, let them be under God's
curse! (Galatians 1:6-9)

Even though he refused to disclose his message, he adamantly
preached that we only had to trust and believe in God and Paul's
vision. He spent the rest of his life trying to prove, establish, and
maintain its validity.

Although Paul had literally "seen the light," he remained firm in
Hellenistic and Pharisaical beliefs. Paul did not believe that learning
from Jesus' disciples or studying Jesus' teachings was necessary.
Instead, he continuously fought with the apostles. James (Jesus'
brother) and Peter clashed with Paul over what Jesus taught and the
contradictions Paul received in his vision. (Galatians and Acts)

Paul did not think Jesus' teachings were necessary. Instead, Paul
believed he was called to expand on what Christianity meant since
Christ was resurrected. I imagine James and Peter, Jesus' closest
confidants, looking at Paul and thinking, "Seriously? Who do you
think you are? You never met Jesus, and you are not willing to learn
from us? Who knew him best?" Paul's audacity is mind-blowing.

Paul is credited with 13 of the 27 books of the N.T.: Romans,
1&2 Corinthians, Galatians, Ephesians, Colossians, Philippians,
1&2 Thessalonians, 1&2 Timothy, Titus, and Philemon. The book of
Hebrews is presumed to be written by Paul because of its writing
style, but that is debatable.

Almost half of the Christian texts are based on Paul, whose
beliefs were solely from a vision, not physically meeting Jesus or any
education about Jesus' life and works. Paul appears to be the ultimate
narcissistic "know-it-all."

He has been compared to Mohammad in Islam or Joseph Smith
of the Mormons because their faith was also based on visions. The
Church obviously has issues with these comparisons.

The Pharisee's agendas were never about morality. They were

about control, which is why Jesus called out their hypocrisy. Paul's perceived ordination gave him the power to pick and parse what he felt was relevant from the Torah.

He believed that without the laws, there would be no sin. (Romans 4:14-15, 5:13, 7:6) The rationale was that without laws, there would be no crime. While technically a correct statement, it is an illogical way to run a functioning society. Paul's contempt for Mosaic law understandably created an enormous problem with Jesus' disciples, who were Jewish.

Because of Paul's arrogance and refusal to learn from the disciples, he could not spread Jesus' teachings. Paul taught his view of Jesus, which resulted in Jesus' compassion, tolerance, acceptance, and forgiveness being considered unimportant or secondary. Jesus' warning about the Pharisees appears to be prophetic, not ironic.

Paul saw everything as black and white, good or evil. He taught that Heaven's only requirement was faith in Jesus. There were no longer any sins because Jesus' crucifixion gave us immediate forgiveness. The one concept the Church could not adapt, or they would become obsolete.

Paul did not disregard all religious laws, just the laws of Moses. Paul had his own laws, which he thought superseded everything else, even Jesus.

Paul believed his responsibility was spreading Christ's message to the Gentiles. Circumcision was a volatile issue between Paul and the Jews. Jewish law dictated that an uncircumcised male could not enter Heaven. Since Paul's audience was predominantly uncircumcised (it was solely a Jewish custom), his message had to be reconciled to appeal to his crowd.

Circumcision was often fatal because of disease and unsanitary conditions. At best, it was excruciatingly painful. However, tradition and Mosaic law demanded circumcision, and it was a prerequisite to Heaven.

If Paul's ego did not cause him to disregard Jesus' teachings, he would have learned that he and Jesus were in relative alignment with this. The "Gospel of Thomas" is the only source that addresses Jesus' opinion on circumcision.

> *His disciples said to him, 'Is circumcision useful or not?' He said to*
> *them, 'If it were useful, their father would produce children already*
> *circumcised from their mother. Rather, the true circumcision in spirit*
> *has become profitable in every respect.' (verse 53)*

The Jewish law remained, as circumcisions are still performed throughout the West.

When Joey was born, my mom was totally stressed that the hospital would not wait eight days to circumcise him. Her concern was maddening and caused stress I did not need over something I did not care about. I was more worried about the pain it was inflicting on him. Not when the Bible said to do it.

I never understood how circumcision was "godly." It is claiming an error by "God" by leaving an extra piece of skin that needs to be removed. Or men must prove their loyalty by cutting off the most sensitive part of their body.

We conceive of such a fallible and sadistic god.

I understand Paul's logic behind disregarding the ancient law of circumcision, but how does one reconcile the complete defiance and new philosophy? Were Jesus' religion and teachings no longer significant and could be disregarded? Jesus' entire life and teachings were based on his faith in the Torah. He was a devout Jew, and through the Jewish prophecies about an upcoming Messiah, Jesus satisfied the requirements that fulfilled those predictions.

Jesus would not have been labeled divine without the existence of Jewish law. The primary reason for the separation between Jews and Christians is that Jews are still waiting for the Messiah. Judaism believes Jesus was only a righteous man, not the real Messiah. However, if Christians are to worship and follow Jesus, his religion must be considered. Christianity is not supposed to be about Paul; it was supposed to be based on Christ.

Several books in the N.T. detail the debate between the proclaimed divine knowledge of Paul and Jewish history, tradition, and laws. Like Jesus, Paul fought religious doctrine, but unlike Jesus, Paul made his requirements paramount to love. Paul was under constant scrutiny from Jesus' followers, so he just touted the supremacy (he believed) his vision gave him.

Paul's ego and arrogance are apparent throughout his books— Galatians chapters 1 and 2 detail his rebellion against anything not Paulinian. Biblical scriptures, supposed holy books, are more about Paul's legacy and his authority to spread Jesus' "real" desires, not the dissemination of Jesus' teachings, message, and purpose.

Hundreds of people, and especially the disciples, spent years learning from Jesus, and they still grappled with his concepts. Paul had a vision and swore he knew it all. Paul's dissertations are often more like political campaigns, not spiritual movements.

His writings reiterate his supremacy and scold the original apostles, angels, and any text he did not issue. Paul argued that before his vision, he was the persecutor-in-chief of the Christians. Because of that radical conversion, he knew more than anyone else. Paul thought he had all the wisdom, so consulting anyone was unnecessary. What an ego!

Paul said that James, Peter, and John rebuffed him with an "agree to disagree" attitude. I am sure they were kind but dismissive, thinking Paul would eventually burn out and go away. Having no foresight into the influence he would have over Jesus' message.

He boasted about his lack of learning and unity with Jesus' original followers. Then, he condemned anything that he was not told in his vision. His arrogance elevated himself above Christ by diminishing Jesus' life and teachings.

I used to tell my son, when at four, he said he knew more than me, "You only know something when you realize you know nothing." Paul was acting like a four-year-old child, pouting and throwing a tantrum because he wasn't getting the deserved attention. All while claiming to be "Dad's" favorite.

Paul belittled any oppressor and biblical law and insinuated that only he had the truth, again, solely because of his vision.

"But when Cephas (Peter) came to Antioch, I opposed him to his face, because he stood condemned. (Galatians 2:11).

Paul's stories assert that Jesus was fallible or forgetful. Jesus had to come back and set the record straight.

> *"Oh yeah, I forgot to mention this… And now you can disregard this… I said that while I was alive, but things are different now."*

Or

> *"I know I'm supposed to be God and all, but since I ascended to Heaven, I've learned a ton and changed my mind about many things! Talk to Paul…"*

The struggle between Paul, and Peter and James continued for the rest of their lives, but with Rome backing Paul, it was an impossible fight. The divide between pagan philosophies and Paul's Christianity was minimal. This assimilation corresponded with Roman culture significantly more than James and Peter's Jewish version of Christianity.

So, Paul's adaptation spread quickly across Rome's control. Hebrew was the language of the Jews and Jerusalem, and Paul's was Greek, further elevating his reach and power.

Before Rome's conversion to Christianity, it was the principal oppressor of the Jews. So, their alignment with a (former) anti-Semitic Paul was a natural one. Rome was in charge, and what they believed became law. With Rome's power, Jewish philosophy and Mosaic laws diminished, and Paul's version became Christianity.

The worst part of Paul's legacy was his antisemitism and its immense influence on the West. Paul's doctrine has resulted in massive bloodshed: The Crusades, the Holocaust, and the continuing antisemitism within Christianity can all be linked to Paul.

Jesus was "The King of the Jews," so I can only imagine how heartbroken he would be at the atrocities done in his name to his people. Jesus taught peace, love, and forgiveness; historically, the Church was the antithesis of this philosophy.

Some people claim that the progress of the Church, through Paul, was divine. Thomas Jefferson said that Paul was "the first corrupter of the doctrines of Jesus." (Augustine, 1853) Regardless of one's personal beliefs, Paul made history, and millions cherish his philosophies. Paul was imprisoned for his teachings and declared a heretic, but his message is in more books in the Bible than any other author.

Millions died because they trusted their beliefs to be facts and infallible. In reality, religions are like government: full of personal agendas, feelings of superiority, and a need for control. What they teach about "God" and Jesus resulted from many councils, where a consensus was obtained, debated, and voted on. The most votes won, and HIStory was adjusted to fit the agenda and philosophies. And then it was labeled "God's will."

Chapter 31: The Acts of Paul and Thecla

Thecla lived approximately 30 to 120 C.E. and was raised in Iconium, now central Turkey. The book was considered apocryphal but was so popular in the early Church that they translated it from Greek into five separate Latin translations, as well as Syriac, Armenian, Slavonic, and Arabic. This gospel provided an apostolic blessing for women's leadership in the Church.

Which is why most people have never heard of it.

Thecla's story begins with Paul arriving to preach in Iconium. As a young pagan virgin, she was prohibited from joining the crowds gathered to hear Paul, so she sat in her bedroom window to listen. She went days without eating, so she missed nothing.

She was engaged to a pagan man who had enlisted and aligned with her mother. The two forced Thecla into marriage and the pagan culture. She rejected her fiancé and his beliefs and committed her life and virginity to Christ.

Thecla was from an influential, wealthy family whose power of influence included the Governor. After her rebellion, Paul was jailed to control his impact on her. She refused to stop seeing him, so they condemned her to death. Paul was stoned and exiled, and she was to be burned at the stake.

While she was tied to the stake, a sudden and unexpected

thunderstorm appeared, causing a torrential downpour and extinguishing the flames. Embarrassed by the failure, the Governor set her free, banishing her forever. Upon her release, she promptly rejoined Paul.

Thecla believed her purpose was to be a servant of God, so after she rejected a young aristocrat's advances, she was (again) sentenced to death. The Governor ordered her to face the wild beasts in the arena. She was taken into the stadium, and a lioness was released. It tamely approached her, laid at her feet, and licked her toes. They then released a bear, and the lioness killed it. Finally, they released a larger lion, and the lioness died protecting Thecla.

After realizing the animals could not harm her, the Governor had each of her arms tied to a different bull, hoping they would tear her apart. The beasts charged in opposite directions, but the rope miraculously untied, and she was spared again. Finally realizing his efforts were futile, the Governor released her, and she promptly rejoined Paul. Paul gave her his blessing, and she began a life of servitude to the Church and an apostle of Paul.

Many years later, while praying in a deserted canyon, a young pagan boy tried to rape her and claim "the prize of her virginity." Backed into a corner, Thecla prayed, and the canyon wall miraculously cracked open, allowing her to escape through the narrow crack. It quickly closed behind her so the boy could not follow.

"The Acts of Thecla and Paul" is a remarkable story. Many have labeled it a love story between Paul and Thecla, but it was more about her love of Paul's God, not Paul.

Then said Thecla to Paul, "If you are pleased with it, I will follow you wherever you go." He replied to her, "Persons are now much given to fornication, and you being handsome, I am afraid you might meet with greater temptation than the former one, and would not withstand it, but be overcome." (Chapter 6:12-13)

This text is a prime example of Paul's narcissism. It is like saying, "You're too hot to be an apostle!" and "Don't do this because you want me." Oh, his ego!

Thecla again showed her commitment and dedication to Christ and reassured Paul that it was not about him. "Grant me only the seal of Christ, and no temptation shall affect me."

As a man driven by his ego, it must have crushed Paul, especially since, according to him, women were to be seen and not heard. A "lesser being" rejected him personally while assuring him that her mission was to God, not to him.

Thecla was a mighty woman of faith and caused many to become Christians. The scholars and leaders of her time declared her "equal to the apostles." Her life story is full of miracles and many intercessions from God. She was a faithful disciple of Paul, but he never mentioned her in the Bible.

In the second century, her life of abstinence caused disruptions because women began leaving their husbands for a religious marriage with their new bridegroom, Jesus. Church leaders used 1 Timothy 2: 11–15 to dismiss Thecla's followers.

A woman should learn in quietness and full submission. I do not permit a woman to teach or to assume authority over a man; she must be quiet. For Adam was formed first, then Eve. And Adam was not the one deceived; it was the woman who was deceived and became a sinner. But women will be saved through childbearing—if they continue in faith, love, and holiness with propriety.

Paul is attributed to 1st Timothy. His views on women are abundantly clear. Any role other than submission and silence was unacceptable. It is not shocking that Thecla does not appear in any of his books.

Like most men of that era, Peter was misogynistic, but Paul made it religious law. Besides the references in 1st Timothy, it continues in 1st Corinthians 11:4-9:

Every man who prays or prophesies with his head covered dishonors his head. But every woman who prays or prophesies with her head uncovered dishonors her head—it is the same as having her head shaved. For if a woman does not cover her head, she might as well have her hair cut off; but if it is a disgrace for a woman to have her hair cut off or her head shaved, then she should cover her head. A man ought not to cover his head since he is the image and glory of God, but a woman is the glory of man. For man did not come from woman, but woman from man; neither was man created for woman, but woman for man.

And 1 Corinthians 14:34;
"Let your women keep silence in the churches: for it's not permitted unto them to speak, but they are commanded to be under obedience as also saith the law."

These are merely examples of a man's ego instituting laws and trying to reinforce them by claiming it is God's will.

Thecla is a saint according to the Catholic Church, but more for the miraculous events that happened to her rather than her ministry. Thecla with Paul, Mary Magdalene with Peter, and thousands of other influential, godly women were erased, disgraced, ignored, and dismissed by the Church because they contradicted and diminished the male superiority complex.

I am so grateful for all the women that preceded me. They paved the path for me. At any other time in our history, I, too, would be silenced or burned at the stake.

Chapter 32: Build It, and They Will Come

From 50 to 150 C.E., many religious texts were circulating. There were epistles, gospels, sermons, memoirs, apocalypses, and teachings. Most were centered on local beliefs and specific churches. Their purpose was to extend, interpret, and apply Jesus' and the apostle's teachings to meet particular needs.

A common misconception is that the N.T. was authored hundreds of years after Jesus. Canon law asserts that all the scriptures must predate 70 C.E. However, it is debatable if that is true. For example, Revelation is believed to have been written in 96. But the four Gospels (Matthew, Mark, Luke, and John) were reportedly written before 70 C.E., composed and distributed less than 40 years after Jesus' death. As early as 200 C.E., the books that we now use, the 27 books of the N.T., were used by early Christians.

It took hundreds of years to debate, decide, and canonize the books, but not hundreds of years for them to be written, collected and distributed. Studies of The Dead Sea Scrolls confirmed that the content of the scriptures had changed little over the millennia. The most significant dichotomy was seen in which books were accepted and which were banished from the Church and history.

Chapter 33: The Gospels According to Marcion

Marcion of Sinope (85 -160 C.E.) was a consecrated bishop and one of the first collectors of the Gospels. Marcion believed the God of the O.T. was inferior and utterly incompatible with the God that Jesus said was his Father.

Marcion believed Jesus liberated humanity from the O.T. God and delivered a superior God encompassing goodness and mercy. Theologians assert that Marcion was the first collector of Paul's epistles. If this is true, then Marcion's role in the church was pivotal. Marcion highlighted Paul's teachings and labeled him as the proper interpreter and communicator of Jesus.

Paul and Marcion dismissed Jewish laws, so they made perfect theological allies. Marcion wanted to separate the Old and New Testament but lacked the authority. In the end, even as an apostle of Paul and agreeing with Paul's attempts to subvert the O.T., the church labeled Marcion a heretic.

Throughout history, Marcion's teachings forced many Christians to ask why the texts were authorized and chosen. In response, the Catholic Church labeled Marcion "Perhaps the most dangerous foe Christianity has ever known." But his support of Paul's doctrine added to its prominence.

Chapter 34: Origen: The Fanatic and Equalizer

Another significant contributor to the early Church was Origen Adamantius. The years vary, plus or minus a year of his birth and death, but are roughly 184-253 C.E. He was raised near Alexandria, Egypt, and some labeled him the original religious fanatic.

He slept on the floor, fasted two times a week, did not eat meat, drink wine, nor own any shoes, and castrated himself. He defended his self-mutilation based on Matthew 19:12, "For some are eunuchs because they were born that way; others were made that way by men..."

Origen is noted as the first biblical scholar. He analyzed the scriptures based on three categories: the moral, the divine, and the allegorical. He believed, "For just as man consists of body, soul, and spirit, so, in the same way, does the scripture." (Adamantius, 275) He preferred the symbolic texts because of the difficulties he saw in the literal translations. He questioned the creation story. "Now, what man of intelligence will believe that the first and the second and the third day...existed without the Sun and moon and stars?"

He taught that God created all souls equally, and they existed before life on Earth and fell from grace. Origen believed that initially, God created many souls for his enjoyment. Eventually, these spirits became bored with God. Because of their disrespect, God judged them according to their amount of love. Those who lost the most became demons. Those who lost a moderate amount became humans. And the ones who lost the least love for God became angels.

Origen also taught that all souls, even Satan, were redeemable. He declared, "Those rational beings who sinned and on account fell from the state in which they were, in proportion to their particular sins, were enslaved in bodies as punishment—some demons, some men, and some angels."

He concluded, "The power of choosing between good and evil is within the reach of all." (CSB Bibles by Holman, 2019)

Origen believed this explained the various conditions in which we are all born. Our earthly status depended on what our souls did in their preexistence. So, what seems unfair to us (some people are born poor and others wealthy, some sick and others healthy, etc.) are by-products of the soul's free will.

This philosophy is close to karmic reincarnation, the only difference being heavenly sins instead of earthly ones. Origen also taught that the Holy Trinity was more of a hierarchy: God is the head, Jesus is secondary, and the Holy Spirit our conscience.

They denounced Origen and declared him a heretic in 553 C.E. at the Council of Constantinople. They ordered his writings and teachings to be destroyed. What few remain are rumored to have been edited by the Church, intending to reflect their theology instead of his.

The Council said, "Whoever says or thinks that the punishment of demons and the wicked will not be eternal...let him be anathema." (Justinian, 543)

However, Origen is declared a father of the Church and, to this day, revered as a founder and the first real Christian scholar.

Chapter 35: Whoever Has the Most Votes Wins

As early as 50 C.E., assemblies were called to define Christian doctrine. These meetings were known as ecumenical councils. Ecumenical means: "activities, ideas, and movements trying to unite different Christian churches." (Collins Dictionary, 2023) There were thirteen ecumenical councils (50–314 C.E.) before Christianity became the legal religion. However, these councils were dismissed as traditional and not as establishing the fundamentals.

The Roman Emperor Constantine ordered the First Council of Nicaea in 325. They convened approximately 1800 people for this council, which included bishops and their staff. Four Bishops recorded the attendance, and none agreed on the total. The number of attending bishops ranged from 250 to 318, and the 1800 participants are also an estimate.

The Council was to establish Christian doctrine. The most significant accomplishment was the Nicaean Creed, which documented the fundamental Christian principles. The Creed is the Church's version of a constitution. Each phrase and theory were analyzed, voted on, and altered over 1500 years.

I believed the Bible was directly from God. I never thought to ask if there were objections or alternate theories. Were there dissenters? I never fathomed the Word of God up for debate, and the books were subjected to inclusion or admonishment. The Bible says several times that no text was to be added or subtracted, so I never even questioned it.

Deuteronomy 4:2, *"Do not add to what I command you and do not subtract from it, but keep the commands of the Lord your God that I give you."*

Deuteronomy 12:32: *"See that you do all I command you; do not add to it or take away from it."*

And Proverbs 30:5-6: *"Every word of God is flawless; he is a shield to those who take refuge in him. Do not add to his words, or he will rebuke you and prove you a liar."*

Ironically, most of the commandments to not add or subtract scripture were in the O.T.

The "Divine Word of God" was subjected to debate, polling, and votes. The foundation of the Christian religion was subjected to the equivalent of a Congressional hearing. The basis of centuries of wars, hate, judgment, and exclusion was based on the social constructs and political agendas in 324. Chosen words, phrases, context, and motives were all voted on by the same people who could not even agree on who was in attendance.

Constantine was active in the debates and often used his power to ensure things went his way. Constantine was the first Christian Roman Emperor, and his reign was a turning point for the religion. The power and intimidation he had over the bishops must have been palpable. They desperately needed Constantine to move their cause forward. Without political support, Christianity would not have become a world religion.

We assume that after the Resurrection, his followers did not doubt Jesus' divinity. But it was still being questioned 300 years later. An agenda item of the Council was to decide if Jesus was divine. Like today, there were many sects under the Christian banner, and the Council's purpose was to unify them under one belief in a holy Son of God.

Arianism was a critical part of the First Council and is rumored to be the principal reason the Council met. Arians (not to be confused with the ancient Indo-Iranians or the White supremacist movement, Aryans) believed that the son of God did not always exist but was created by God the Father. Jesus was a distinct and separate being. Arius, the founder of Arianism, also aligned with Origen's teachings.

They based their belief on John 14:28, "You heard me say, 'I am going away, and I am coming back to you.' If you loved me, you would be glad that I am going to the Father, for the Father is greater than I."

But the Council determined, "born of the Father before all time." The Council declared if one was present, the other must also be. They added an anathema to the Creed to discredit the Arian beliefs:

But those who say: 'There was a time when he was not,' and 'He was not before he was made;' and 'He was made out of nothing,' or 'He is of another substance' or 'essence,' or 'The son of God is created,' or 'changeable,' or 'alterable' —they are condemned by the holy Catholic and apostolic Church.

Consequently, Arius was deemed a heretic by the Council and excommunicated. He was acquitted nine years later and then relabeled as a heretic after he died in 381. They were so fickle with their damnations.

I do not believe the Council had evil intentions. I do not think Constantine attempted to fool believers and push lies. However, humans occasionally acted politically under the guise of spreading Christianity. Since its start, the Church pursued followers through laws and fear rather than emulating Jesus' works and message. The Church cared more about finding followers than filling hearts.

Over 450 years, several councils were convened to adapt, edit, and shape Christian laws. The emperor, not the Church, called the first (official) ecumenical councils to eliminate competing theories. Whenever a movement grew with conflicting dogma, the government summoned the committees.

The councils dictated levels of superiority between classes, sects, and religious governments. All dissenters were declared heretics, excommunicated, and erased from history. There were 21 ecumenical councils, but most only became significant in retrospect.

These meetings and issuance of laws were an attempt to answer every question about a god they perceived. Jesus was asked what the most important law was, and he said, "love." (Matthew 22:36-40)

Was honoring this commandment ever addressed at the councils? Love became a minimal or secondary message rather than the message.

In 381, the First Council of Constantinople debated the Trinity. They defined the divinity of the Holy Spirit and its application in the Trinity. However, there is no biblical evidence or teachings of a Trinity. Saint Theophilus of Antioch first mentioned it in the late second century, who claimed the Trinity was God, his Word, and his Wisdom. In the third century, Roman Christian author Tertullian described the Trinity as "one in essence—not one in person."

For the first three centuries after Jesus, they believed what he said: he was inferior to God, we are to worship only God, and through his message, we would see the real God. Jesus never mentioned the Trinity and never said he was equal to God. After Nicaea, he was equal to God in a Trinity of "One." The debate to justify and define this took centuries.

God's Word, Spirit, and Wisdom are closest to a Trinity in the O.T. The Trinity was seen across the ancient lands in the pagan religions, from the Roman Empire to the Egyptian Pharaohs, from Greek Mythology to Hinduism, for thousands of years before Jesus. Having one God is what set the God of Abraham apart from the rest. A significant point of contention that Islam has with Christianity is the Trinity. Islam believes in the God of Abraham, "The One True God." The Qur'an states:

> O People of the scripture, do not commit excess in your religion or say
> about Allah except the truth. The Messiah, Jesus, the son of Mary, was
> but a messenger of Allah and His word, which He directed to Mary
> and a soul [created at a command] from Him. So believe in Allah and
> His messengers. And do not say, "Three" desist-it is better for you.
> Indeed, Allah is but one God. Exalted is He above having a son. (Sura
> 4:171)

In a letter to John Adams, Thomas Jefferson wrote:

> It is too late in the day for men of sincerity to pretend they
> believe in the Platonic mysticisms that three are one, and one
> is three; and yet that the one is not three, and the three are not
> one... But this constitutes the craft, the power, and the profit of
> the priests. (Jefferson, To John Adams from Thomas Jefferson,
> 1813)

I cannot imagine a Supreme Being randomly setting and
changing rules. The god that we created is so fickle.

In 730, Emperor Leo III outlawed all pictures of Jesus and the
saints. He created the first iconoclasm using the Ten Commandments
as justification. The Second Council of Nicaea met in 731 and
reinstated the veneration of icons and holy images. Pope Adrian
argued that, according to the Bible and tradition of the Church, these
images stimulated righteousness and imitation. The Pope declared
that the poor and uneducated would learn better with pictures;
therefore, eliminating them would not help the lesser of society.

This edict contradicted the second and third commandments.
However, this was not a giant leap for the Church since Paul
disregarded Mosaic law, and the Ten Commandments were the
foundation of those laws. At that moment, "religion" created an
indecisive god who continually changes his mind and priorities.

In 1139, the Second Council of the Lantern established celibacy
within church leadership. Because of this, 1139 monks and priests
were declared invalid and nonexistent. (The correlation between the
Council's year and number of discredited leaders is coincidental.)

In 1274, the second Council of Lyons regulated papal conclaves.
Pope Gregory X mandated that the cardinals "must be locked up." If
they could not agree on a pope within eight days, they would only
receive water and bread. (Encyclopedia Britannica, 2015)

If God assigns the Pope, and conclaves are linked to God, why
would it take so much time and require a two-thirds majority vote?

They vote and debate and then claim divine intervention. The Church is asking for faith in them, not God.

In 1415, the Council of Constance made history with the infamous declaration of Sacrosanct, ordaining the ecumenical Council superior to all popes. There were three popes, and after a debate and votes, the Council appointed one. This stance declared the Council's absolute superiority. Contradicting its current position (established in 1870) that the Pope is infallible.

Six months after the Fifth Council of Lanterns in 1512, Martin Luther issued his "95 Theses"—the start of the Protestant Reformation.

The Council of Trent covered three separate councils between 1545 and 1563. The councils were riddled with wars, reformations, and disagreements. However, the Catholic Church labels it the most successful ecumenical Council.

In 1546, the Council of Trent defined the Holy Scriptures and the Original Sin. In 1547, Justification (entrance into Heaven is obtained through faith alone), the holy sacraments, baptism, and confirmation were consecrated. The Holy Eucharist (communion), Penance (confession), and Extreme Unction (anointing of the sick) were established in 1551. Finally, in 1563, matrimony (must be performed by a priest with two witnesses), cults, saints, relic images, and indulgences (full or partial remission of temporal punishment) were decreed.

The Council of Trent reemphasized that images and relics provided a crucial education, condoning the grand cathedrals, art, and icons and contradicting the Protestant movement.

Another point of contention, furthering the schism between Catholics and Protestants, was confession. The Protestant's argument was, if God knows all, why must we confess to man? The Council reconfirmed it.

It also reaffirmed celibacy for clergy and the sin of concubinage.

They addressed divorce and agreed that the innocent party could not remarry if their spouse were still alive, even if adultery caused the divorce.

I am still not sure how any of these are godly or ungodly. However, these decrees are still used for discrimination, judgment, and exclusion. They implemented these edicts 1500 years after Jesus and have nothing to do with loving your neighbor. Such proclamations have proven only to alienate people and define the supremacy of the Church, which is entirely anti-Christ.

In 1870, the concerns over the Pope's infallibility continued to rattle the Church. The Church declared its supremacy by discrediting any misgivings, labeling them heretical, and issuing new canons. For hundreds of years, the religious leadership deliberated whether Jesus was born the Christ or became the Christ, born human and was made God or was born as God. Christian doctrine resulted from hundreds of years of debates and compromise. Claiming the Pope is infallible is a foundation for control. All humans are fallible, so this declaration made humans, in addition to Jesus, equal to God.

Despite all the scriptural warnings and prophecies, we still try to make humans into a god, and ironically, the Church is the one trumpeting this dogma.

I have no idea if my mom knew about this history. Still, she correctly assessed the Catholic Church as a political movement. Where she was incorrect is that it is not only Catholicism. All of Christianity is guilty, both in receiving and contributing to political influence.

As a Christian, I believed these things were declared and worked out during Christ's time, not through 2000 years of debate and evolution. In the name of God, people made laws and defined sin. They established social and godly superiority—dictated by the era, who was in charge, and regional beliefs.

What horrifies me the most is that hundreds of millions of people have died for this. Instead of bringing love and acceptance, the Church's history is full of devastation and destruction. Religion demands we have faith in man's interpretations of texts, which were chosen by a select few and adjusted over time. Christianity looks nothing like Jesus' Gospel, and the evolution of dogma can no longer hide in the Vatican's underground corridors.

Chapter 36: The Biggest Protest

A schism is "division or disunion, especially into mutually opposed parties." (2023). No religion has had more schisms than Christianity. Most of these divisions, or what we now call a "denomination," are ego-based because they claim they are the only true Church. All others are misguided, incomplete, or cults. It resembles the childhood debate of "My daddy is stronger and loves me more than your daddy!"

Other than the Orthodox schism, the most notable were the Protestants, whom Martin Luther started. "Protestant" is derived from "protester." Luther believed that "justification by faith alone" was the foundation on which the Church should stand. This philosophy contradicted the traditional doctrine of "faith without works is futile." The relationship between faith and good deeds remains controversial in some Protestant traditions. The Reformation caused more divisions because of different opinions on what should be highlighted or discarded.

Martin Luther saw problems with four books in the Bible: Jude, James, Hebrews, and Revelation. He felt they should be secondary and wanted them moved to the last four books or expunged. Luther believed they went against what he thought was Christ's doctrine. Sola Gratia and Sola Fide became the foundations of the Protestant doctrine. Sola Fide means "justification by faith alone," and Sola Gratia means "by grace alone." The book of James emphasizes the importance of good works, but Luther dismissed it as the "epistle of straw."

The three fundamental principles of traditional Protestantism are:

1. Scripture Alone: The Bible is the inerrant and infallible Word of God.
2. Justification by Faith Alone: Through faith alone, in the divinity of Christ and his righteousness, you are saved.
3. Universal Priesthood of Believers: The universal priesthood of believers implies the right and duty of the Christian laity not only to read the Bible in the vernacular but also to take part in the government and all the public affairs of the Church. It is opposed to the hierarchical system, which puts the essence and authority of the Church in an exclusive priesthood and makes ordained priests the necessary mediators between God and the people. (Wilhelm, 1911)

Luther believed the Church had lost its way and was corrupted by power and greed. Through his studies, he viewed penance and righteousness in new ways. He thought a sinner could become righteous by faith alone in God's grace. His message was that salvation and redemption are gifts of God's grace and only obtainable through faith in Jesus. So, the Protestant Reformation began with the belief that individuals receive the gift of salvation through faith, not the Church.

Luther defined "faith" as the knowledge and acceptance of, and the trust in, the promises of the Gospel. He believed faith was a gift from God, manifested by the Holy Spirit in the Bible and baptism. Faith was how we received salvation, not something that caused salvation. Lutherans reject the belief that people must decide to "accept" Christ or be "born again," which is a common belief among modern Evangelicals.

By eliminating works and deeds as the foundation for Christianity, it issued a blank check to be an asshole—one only had to ask for forgiveness and believe they are forgiven. This goes against any logic and Jesus' message: *"In the same way, let your light shine before others, that they may see your good deeds and glorify your Father in Heaven."* (Matthew 5:16)

We must live a loving life to be godly, and it is simply the right thing to do. No one needs religion to understand that being a compassionate person is more righteous than being an apathetic one. Your actions are who you are, not thoughts or beliefs.

Scholars in Luther's time had the same argument, and Luther's response was:

A living, creative, active, and powerful thing, this faith. Faith cannot help doing good works constantly. It does not stop to ask if good works ought to be done, but before anyone asks, it already has done them and continues to do them without ceasing. Anyone who does not do good works in this manner is an unbeliever...Thus, it is just as impossible to separate faith and works as it is to separate heat and light from fire! (Veen, 2006)

History proved Luther's assertion incorrect and showed he highly overestimated man's ability and willingness to do evil.

Luther used his interpretation of scripture to support his beliefs: *"For all have sinned and fall short of the glory of God and all are justified freely by his grace through the redemption that came by Christ Jesus."* (Romans 3:23-24)

Luther asserted, "This is necessary to believe. This cannot be otherwise acquired or grasped by any work, law, or merit. Therefore, it is clear and certain that this faith alone justifies us...Nothing of this article can be yielded or surrendered, even though Heaven and Earth and everything else falls." (Luther, The Smalcald Articles, 2005)

Making our lives solely about our faith in God and not our actions supports isolation with God, not unity with each other. Instead of the servant mentality that Jesus practiced and taught, this ideology invokes feelings of superiority, which plague religion.

Protestant scholars point out that almost two hundred statements in the N.T. substantiate the ideology that faith is sufficient for salvation. Like, John 11:25, Romans 3:28, and Romans 4:4-5.

Catholics believe faith is necessary for salvation, but it is not enough. They claim "justification" is an error because, besides faith,

God also requires obedience, acts of love, and charity to enter Heaven. Catholics still maintain this view and claim that it is in line with the traditional view of the O.T.

However, their riches contradict entirely their words and beliefs. We would not have any starving children if the Catholic Church believed "acts of love and charity" were prerequisites for Heaven.

Many verses support justification, but there are more saying we must do something; James 2:17-19 is a classic example, but Luther wanted James removed from the N.T.

The point is not which doctrine and philosophy one follows. The issue is that religious leaders created dogma according to what they wanted to do and who they wanted to control.

We must never forget that humans are entirely and utterly fallible, and anytime we put our faith in them instead of love, people die.

Chapter 37: The Church is not Perfect

Early Protestants believed the Church should constantly improve: Semper Reformanda. The first Protestant leaders realized people would naturally make God fit into their lives instead of staying within God's laws. I wholeheartedly agree, but this contradicts many people's beliefs that the Bible and religion are divine and flawless.

If something is pure and perfect, then why are reformations regularly needed?

I could not believe my faith had this edict. I had never heard of such a philosophy. I was always taught never to doubt. Always respect and believe in our Church and leaders because they were "chosen by God."

But the early fathers of Protestantism knew if left to our initiatives; we would always screw up things. When our modern-day Christian leaders declare their beliefs are the only genuine and correct ones, are they aware of the foundation of Semper Reformanda?

Do you think any of them would conclude the Church lost its way and direly needs a reformation again?

Do any of them realize their hypocrisy, judgment, and exclusivity is an anti-Christ stance?

Righteousness, or the lack thereof, is shown in how someone positively or adversely affects the lives of others. Condoning or ignoring hatred, greed, abuse, starvation, exclusion, discrimination, and war is immoral.

Generally, Christians believe that people have made mistakes throughout history but deny the truth was ever wholly lost. The Bible predicts such fallibility in Timothy 4 and Acts 20:28-29. Jesus warned us in Matthew 24:10-14.

The problem is that religions lack introspection and are consequently blinded to their own false prophets and wickedness. With our ego in total control, we still hold tightly that the doctrine we now believe is the only one that is correct and holy.

However, if it is not based on love, it is not of God.

Chapter 38: The End is Nigh?

The Book of Revelation was the most contested in the Bible. Yet today, many churches use it as the foundation of their ministry. Most people can visualize a passionate preacher pacing the stage, shouting from the pulpit so intensely that he must wipe the sweat from his brow. He emphatically and enthusiastically declares that awaiting you is a Hell full of fire and brimstone. But! You, too, can be saved if you come forward and renounce your sins! I appreciate passion and energy, but motivating people through fear is never a way to get people to love.

They did not add the Book of Revelation to the New Testament until 397 C.E. For over 200 years, the Church raised doubts about its symbolism and apostolic authorship. At one point, they considered it heretical. In 397, some argued that Revelation was challenging to understand and interpret and could lead to abuse.

In 1522, Martin Luther considered it "neither apostolic nor prophetic," citing that "Christ is neither taught nor known" and labeled it as Antilegomena or a disputed text. (Luther, 1522) But in 1530, he reversed his position and concluded that Christ was fundamental to the book. "As we see here in this book, that through and beyond all plagues, beasts, and evil angels, Christ is nonetheless with the Saints and wins the final victory." (Luther, 1530)

Thomas Jefferson labeled it as "merely the ravings of a maniac, no more worthy nor capable of explanation than the incoherence of our own nightly dreams." (Jefferson)

Over the last 1700 years, many theologians dismissed it as the author's vivid imagination or the ravings of a lunatic. The book has proven detrimental because it became the foundation of many conservative Christians and a large part of modern-day sermons.

Because of a lack of focus on love, atheists maintain the only reason Christians do good is because they are afraid. In contrast, atheists do good because it is the right thing to do. The only thing spiritual people can offer is their life by example: love, generosity, forgiveness, and charity. At a minimum, "Christians" should be the kindest, most forgiving, and genuine people. Otherwise, only through fear of eternal damnation will the Church find followers, which they realized at some point.

Chapter 39: Bringing Jesus Back

I do not believe, nor am I trying to say, that every Church is corrupt or that most of the message is a scheme. I am, however, saying that no one should offer their life or take the life of another over interpretations and social edicts in religion.

There are still churches that do good. They provide charity and teach acceptance and inclusion, but that is now more the exception than the rule. The outside world views American Christians as crazy, hypocritical, hateful people. We see examples in someone holding a sign on the street corner or at a funeral saying, "God hates..." Or the politician says "God" asked them to run for office or go to war.

The godliest hearts I have ever seen were in the Amish after the brutal slaughter of five of their children. In 2006, Charles Roberts walked into an Amish schoolhouse and shot ten Amish daughters—five fatally, and then killed himself.

Roberts' family lived in the same town and was overcome with grief and guilt. The Amish leaders asked everyone not to judge the family and to forgive the man. The same day as the slaughter, they were overheard saying:

> We must not think evil of this man... He had a mother and a wife and a soul, and now he's standing before a just God."
> Another leader in a neighboring county said, "I don't think

there's anybody here that wants to do anything but forgive, and not only reach out to those who have suffered a loss in that way but to reach out to the family of the man who committed these acts. (Jarnick, 2013)

With more than just words, the Amish community, which was so profoundly affected by the tragedy, set up a charity fund for the Roberts family and asked that all donations go to the murderer's wife and children. Members of the Amish community visited and comforted Roberts' widow, parents, and in-laws. One Amish leader held Roberts' father in his arms for an hour to comfort him while he sobbed. There were approximately 30 members of the Amish community who attended Roberts' funeral.

Marie Roberts, the widow, wrote a letter to the community, thanking them for their forgiveness, mercy, and grace. She wrote,

Your love for our family has helped to provide the healing we so desperately need. The gifts you have given have touched our hearts in a way no words can describe. Your compassion has reached beyond our family, beyond our community, and is changing our world, and for this we sincerely thank you.

This is the ultimate example of acting godly. Truly, "What would Jesus do?" In real life, with genuine love and honest actions.

Conversely, when they killed Osama bin Laden, the conservative Christians led the celebrations and demanded to view the mutilated corpse.

You cannot be pro-war and pro-life, full of hate and full of love.

"Let us not become the evil that we deplore." ~ Congressional Representative Barbara Lee

The Church has had to reinvent itself throughout the ages to keep its power, relevance, and viability. Unfortunately, those took precedence over teaching us how to act and live in love. The messenger became more important than the message. The Church did not do this alone; the followers were lazy. People look to the Church to tell them what to think, how to feel, and whom to exclude instead of searching for ways to find God through acts of selflessness.

Jesus said, *"The Kingdom of God is within you"* (Luke 17:21).
No one can find God when they are looking for the truth outside
of themselves. When we put God in material things, like a book,
building, or artifact, we worship the item, not God. Objects are
material. God is immaterial. God is the all-encompassing, all-powerful
energy of unconditional love—not some old dude in the sky. God is a
verb, not a noun.

During a Sunday morning service when I was a teenager, my
pastor threw the Bible on the ground and put his foot on it. Half of the
congregation gasped; one woman fainted. At a minimum, everyone
was stunned. His intended shock was achieved. He proclaimed the
Bible was just a book of holy stories and sacred words, but just a book.
It had special paper, often edged in gold, and was usually leather
bound, but the book could not get us to Heaven. The book had no
actual power. The power was in the lessons, not the book.

The Church had a growing amount of people who were becoming
fanatical, and the pastor's demonstration completely offended them.
He did not remove his foot from atop the Bible the entire sermon. He
explained the Bible was full of stories of people trying to make God a
material object. It is in our nature.

We have been warned since the days of Moses. Yet, the idolizing
of objects and humans has continued throughout the generations.
We fail when we try to fit "God" into our understanding, beliefs, and
definitions. People get hurt when we act out of instinct instead of
consciousness. *"Trust in the Lord with all your heart and lean not on your
own understanding"* (Proverbs 3:5).

The Church serves many purposes and can be a positive thing.
Fellowship can be a powerful tool that enables our struggles not
to seem so monumental. The Church can be a place of education,
discipline, and growth. But as soon as something is said that is
contradictory to pure love, it is not godly. When something is
said that makes you or your group feel superior, it is not God.
When something is said that encourages you to be more helpful,
understanding, patient, and forgiving, then the message is holy.

So many believers think everything preached within the walls of the Church is divine. When we lack discernment, we spiritually fall asleep and do not use the brains God gave us. And then we forget that Jesus' mission was questioning religious leaders and making them accountable for their hypocrisy, greed, and exclusion. Jesus was unique because, unlike the Torah, Jesus asked us to conquer lands with love, not war.

We walk mindlessly through life, searching for social acceptance rather than emulating God through love. Throughout all my years of church, Christian schools, and Bible studies, I never learned how to love more. I only learned to fear my humanity.

Whenever you hear the truth that ignites your soul because it is based on love, hold on to it, remember and cherish it, and use it to grow. The same is true in reverse. If you hear something that causes you to feel anything other than goodness and love, then reevaluate the source, even if it is from your pastor, priest, rabbi, or imam.

If it makes you feel powerful and separate, it feeds your ego. If it makes you feel humbled and equal, it is invoking love. Our goal should be to grow and become more loving people. Regardless of your religion (or not), everyone can summon love; it is freely given and unconditional.

"The good news is that the moment you decide that what you know is more important than what you have been taught to believe, you will have shifted gears in your quest for abundance. Success comes from within, not from without."
~ Ralph Waldo Emerson.

Section VII: Jesus

"No one else holds, or has held, the place in the heart of the world which Jesus holds. Other gods have been as devoutly worshiped; no other man has been so devoutly loved."
~ John Knox

Chapter 40: The Ultimate Man?

When I was a kid, Jesus was my best friend. He was the most wonderful man I had ever "known." He gave me hope that not all men were monsters out to hurt or abuse me.

Jesus was kind and just. He was humble but a leader. He was firm but loving. Jesus never disappointed me when all the other men had. Whether he was the most remarkable man that ever lived or the ultimate fairy tale, he helped me through many dark days. Even if Jesus was only idyllic, I needed him, and I still do.

I became disillusioned with him when I heard things that tainted my view. It saddened me when he became the purveyor of capitalism and the judge of the poor. I became disenchanted when "love thy neighbor" turned into "except that one, and that one, and those over there...." And my heart broke when "turn the other cheek" was interpreted as "look away," becoming the basis for abandonment instead of forgiveness and love.

Jesus was (allegedly) the ultimate human, someone we are supposed to emulate. He was the greatest role model of them all until the Church said that our greed, ignorance, hatred, and aggression were also his.

Most atheists do not have a problem with Jesus' teachings. Their problem is that (somehow) Jesus is used to hurt others.

And frankly, that is my issue, too.

Chapter 41: Who Was He?

The Church contends Jesus is the only path to God. *"Jesus said to him, 'I am the way, and the truth, and the life. No one comes to the Father except through me."* (John 14:6)

This verse is the foundation of Christian doctrine. And it invalidates every other faith.

Even as a child, I struggled with that. It never stood up as "truth." Truth is valid in all places, times, and for all people. Jesus, being the sole source to God, does not meet those requirements. What about the people who lived before him? Or the Aboriginal people in Australia, the people in China, or the tribes in the Amazon?

I posed these questions to my church leaders. They explained that if someone had not heard about Jesus, they were exempt and would be judged according to their life. The elder explained that is why spreading the word is so important. But that made no sense. The people spared from eternity in Hell were the ones who had not heard about Jesus. But damned if they had. It would make me curse the person who told me about Jesus, not thank them. Religion has so many contradictions, loopholes, contingencies, and requirements for unconditional love.

As part of this journey, I had to find out who the real Jesus was. The good, the bad, and the ugly. The man or the myth. I braced myself to discover all I could about a man who was always my source of hope. After I opened myself up to learn everything they did not teach me, I wondered if I would land in the same place I started. Would my view of Jesus be altered? You never leap without changing positions. That was a scary thought. My entire perception, faith, and source of endless hope were on the line. I steadied myself, reminded myself I was searching for the Truth, and set out to discover what precisely that was.

Foremost, Jesus was not White. He was a brown-skinned Middle Eastern man. I am sure as an effort to enforce Jesus' "whiteness," people in the Middle East and the Horn of Africa, including Somalia and Ethiopia, are considered "Caucasian."

Oh, the irony of racism when viewed through this lens.

They morphed Jesus into a White man with flowing hair, blue eyes, and a thin, elongated face throughout the millennia. This created a "Savior" in the image of the people molding the religion. These are the same people who morphed the image of Satan into looking Jewish—even though Jesus was a Jew.

Scientific studies based on the culture, geography, and era show that Jesus resembled a cave dweller, not an American celebrity. Creating a "Caucasian" Jesus and altering the definition to make him fit is a clear and blatant example of our molding and, therefore, ruining "God."

Creating a White Jesus enabled us to judge and reject people of color. For centuries, our tribal fear and racism overrode our sensibility and enabled us to (conveniently) forget that Jesus was a person of color. We reject the very societies in which Jesus lived, and it is done in his name.

We can determine that Jesus was a real man who lived about 2000 years ago. Jesus tops the historical list for the most books written, songs sung, pictures painted, and thoughts discussed. He is as likely to have existed as Julius Caesar. It is nearly universally accepted that Jesus' baptism and crucifixion are historical facts. What causes all the arguments is whether he rose from the dead and was divine.

The facts are that Jesus was not considered "God" until 431 A.D., and that was only after many debates. Jesus never claimed it, but he also did not necessarily deny it.

Judaism considers Jesus a good man. Islam regards him as a prophet. It should be noted the Qur'an mentions Jesus more times than the Bible.

Chapter 42: Sinner or Saint?

Paul claimed Jesus was without sin (because there is no sin if there are no laws!), but the Gospels say he was innocent, not sinless. Jesus was not a criminal who deserved the death penalty, but based on Jewish law, he was a big ol' sinner.

Jesus violated the Sabbath by picking grain and healing disabled people. He dined with people who did not wash their hands, breaking "the tradition of the elders." Jesus also disregarded the importance of kosher laws. He said what mattered was what came out of your mouth, not what you put in it—dismissing over 1500 years of Jewish nutritional laws.

Jesus turned water into wine, and Leviticus takes issues with that.

> *"You and your sons are not to drink wine or other fermented drink whenever you go into the tent of meeting, or you will die. This is a lasting ordinance for the generations to come." (Leviticus 10:9)*

Or

> *"Wine is a mocker and beer a brawler; whoever is led astray by them is not wise." (Proverbs 20:1)*

Or

> *"They eat the bread of wickedness and drink the wine of*

violence." (Proverbs 4:17)

Jesus even admitted to being drunk.

"The Son of Man came eating and drinking, and you say, 'Here is a glutton and a drunkard, a friend of tax collectors and sinners." (Luke 7:24)

Mark 2:18–20 claims Jesus said fasting was not as necessary as they thought.

He spoke to the Samaritan woman when her nationality (and sex) prohibited it.

When they brought the adulterous woman to Jesus, he refused to stand by Mosaic law and condone her stoning, disregarding the Ten Commandments.

Jesus denounced and disrespected the religious leadership, making him a direct target.

He also touched an "unclean" leper, and cleanliness laws ruled the ancient Jewish world.

He assured "sinners" their sins were forgiven, bypassing temple sacrifices and violating even more religious laws.

Huge sinner!

These laws were the bedrock of Judaism, and Jesus constantly broke them. This fueled Paul's disregard for everything in Judaism.

Jesus flipped tables and made his whips, which he used to clear out the temple from people desecrating it. The religious leaders were silent because of their greed, power, and superiority, and Jesus took control and revealed their apathy. Jesus exposed their hypocrisy, which infuriated them.

What ultimately caused Jesus' death sentence was when the religious leaders thought he claimed to be God.

'Very truly I tell you,' Jesus answered, 'before Abraham was born, I am!' At this, they picked up stones to stone him, but Jesus hid himself, slipping away from the temple grounds." (John 8:58)

The Church leads us to believe that Jesus claimed he was God, the son of God, or God's equal. The Pharisees felt the same way.

However, it can also be a reiteration of, before Abraham, there was God, and professing such a thing meant alignment, not equality.

Claiming equality with God, and therefore their superior, was a massive insult to the Pharisees. To them, he was merely a peasant. Regardless, it was a combative statement and was viewed as such. He was preaching love, not laws, and that was against all religious beliefs—therefore sinful. Jesus was constantly "sinning" and snubbing the religious elite, so he had to die.

How did we go from being sentenced to death for (regularly) breaking religious laws to Jesus being flawless and sinless?

I have found that the only truth about Jesus' "perfection" is that he focused on the two rules that matter: "let go" and "love." If it were any other way, Jesus would be a sinner and a heretic. And, according to religious law, he deserved his death sentence. His rebellion, protests, and being a warrior for social justice made him a hero to billions, but the O.T. justifies his execution.

Chapter 43: His Last Days

In his last days, Jesus struggled with God. His prayers in the Garden of Gethsemane show his agony over relinquishing his will so God's will can be done. The Gospels tell the story of Jesus' first request, hoping God would spare him from being crucified. It reveals his fear by persistently praying to be spared.

During the tough times in my life, "Thy will be done, oh Lord" carried me through. Knowing that I am letting "God" (the Universe, the Flow, Energy alignment, whatever term works for you) guide and direct me through the flow of life gives me a sense of peace. If the fear returns, I repeat it, just like Jesus did when he kept going back to pray.

He went back three times! His first prayer was (paraphrased), "Really? Do we have to do this?"

The second time, "Okay, okay, okay. If we must…"

The third prayer is, "Are you sure? I mean, like, really sure?"

And then he returns, sees his only friends have let him down, and says, "Fine. Let's do this."

Throughout my life, this story gave me strength because there were so many times I could relate.

Living "in the flow" can be terrifying. I equate it to being blindfolded on a roller coaster you have never ridden or seen. You do not know what the experience will be, but you know it will be crazy, scary, thrilling times with unknown curves, loops, and drops. But you also know that when the ride is over, you jump out of the seat, exhilarated and ready for another.

For the record, I am not a huge fan of roller coasters.

It has been my experience that when living in Divine Will, everything always works out. It amazes me, and sometimes I still lose my faith. But the times when I saw I was "going for a ride," Jesus' strength and willingness to let go into the unknown provided me a guide for faith.

Whether Jesus was divine and conquered death has no bearing on the fact that he died for his integrity. He died for his willingness to stand against the hypocrisy, bigotry, greed, and supremacy that was being fostered in God's name. He died because he believed that love was more important than the law. He was martyred because he thought loving was more valuable than being "right."

His level of faith and honoring his beliefs in love should inspire us all. He stood alone when everyone fell asleep or ran in fear. Jesus did not take anyone else down with him. He did not hurt or kill to make his point. He was a servant of the people, giving us the spiritual version of "God." Jesus was unique because he showed us God's unconditional love, not the manufactured beliefs of someone as imperfect as us.

So many of us can relate to Jesus on the cross, *"My God, my God, why have you forsaken me?"* (Psalms 22:1)

In times of despair, I too have cried out, *"Why are you so far from saving me, so far from my cries of anguish?"* But in hindsight, those times were full of fear, not flow.

Sir Isaac Newton concluded the date of Jesus' crucifixion was April 3, 33. A time science determined an eclipse occurred, aligning with the biblical story of the darkened skies during the crucifixion.

It is also widely speculated that the cross was shaped like an "X," not a "T."

Chapter 44: The Resurrection, His Validation

Some scholars assert that when the disciples gave Jesus the sponge on the cross, it was soaked in analgesic, rendering Jesus unconscious, not dead. This is based on Jesus "dying" instantly once they gave it to him.

Immediately, one of them ran and got a sponge. He filled it with wine vinegar, put it on a staff, and offered it to Jesus to drink. The rest said:

> "'Now leave him alone. Let us see if Elijah comes to save him.'
> And when Jesus had cried out again in a loud voice, he gave up his spirit." (Matthew 27: 48-50)

We are told that after they removed Jesus from the cross.

> "And there came also Nicodemus, which at the first came to Jesus by night, and brought a mixture of myrrh and aloes, about a hundred-pound weight." (John 19:38 KJV).

It is believed they noted its weight because it was an extraordinary amount, and the ointments and aloes were reparative, not for embalming. This theory changes resurrection into resuscitation, although there would be no difference in the minds of men 2000 years ago.

We do not know if Jesus rose from the dead. Something so

extraordinary should have references outside of the Bible. But for me, the whole "resurrection" philosophy was always strange. Not for obvious reasons, but because if he isn't dead, why isn't he here? Going to "Heaven," in every other case, is dead.

Paul used Jesus' resurrection to claim that Jesus conquered death because he was sinless since Paul claimed sin caused death. However, that theory is demonstrably false; everything dies. Death is entirely natural and not because we upset some Being.

According to the definition, Jesus is dead. His body is gone. He no longer breathes nor walks the earth. His message, legacy, and love remain, granting him a form of immortality. But we get hung up or overly attached to Jesus' resurrection, diminishing everything he said and did while he was alive.

He beat death! Yay!

Fixating on the resurrection shifts Jesus' priorities from supporter to winner. It makes him a champion over death, not a servant of life and love. Which is a huge reason we are in this mess.

Christianity, using the resurrection as its foundation, means Jesus' message was only validated because he rose from the dead. Think about that. His message of "love" was dismissed until he did the impossible. His life had no meaning unless his death was not real.

Chapter 45: Divine?

Jesus and his disciples never claimed that he was God. He said to focus on God, not him.

> "'Why do you call me good?' Jesus answered. 'No one is good—except God alone'" (Mark 10:18).

Jesus never claimed he had the power. He said it was God's:

> "By myself, I can do nothing" (John 5:30).

> "The Father is greater than I" (John 14:28).

Jesus further distinguishes them.

> "Father, into thy hands I commend my spirit." (Luke 23:46)

The goal was to become one with God, not that Jesus and God were one.

Jesus was not all-knowing.

> "And Jesus grew in wisdom and stature, and in favor with God and man" (Luke 2:52)

> "He turned around in the crowd and asked, 'Who touched my clothes?'" (Mark 5:30).

Jesus only discovered who touched him when the woman

confessed.

That is not "all-knowing."

Mark 13:32 and Matthew 24:36 document how Jesus does not know our "last day," but God does.

> *"But about that day or hour no one knows, not even the angels in Heaven, nor the Son, but only the Father."*

Divinity is not required to understand that God is love.

Jesus' statements are delineations between himself and God. The thing is, Christianity could only differentiate themselves from Judaism if Jesus were God.

The label "Christ" was from the Greek Χριστός/Christós, meaning "anointed one," and was a human title, like "Messiah." In the Torah, the words "Messiah" and "Lord" were used for kings, priests, and prophets. They did not use the term as a sign of divinity; they meant a political leader who was King David's descendant. We are led to believe that the names are unique to Jesus, but the Bible is riddled with them and applied to leaders, teachers, and guides. In this context, Islam also considers Jesus "the Messiah."

We see the term "Son of God" throughout history. I had to compose a spreadsheet to keep them straight and get my head around all of them. Twenty-three different legends mirror and predate the story of Jesus—we see them in mythologies across time and the world. But with Jesus, the Church claims he was using the "son of God" differently than the Greeks, Romans, Egyptians, Persians, Indians, as well as Jews.

Jesus told us we are all children of God.

> *"Jesus said, 'Do not hold on to me, for I have not yet ascended to the Father. Go instead to my brothers and tell them, I am ascending to my Father and your Father, to my God and your God.'" (John 20:17)*

Jesus was not God, but he had a God: The God of Abraham, the God of Judaism, Islam, and (supposedly) Christianity.

Christianity asks us to deny Jesus' words that there was only one God. Instead of seeing Jesus as a fresh path, a teacher of love, a servant of God and man, the Church made him equal to God and told us to worship him instead of learning from him.

> *"Well said, teacher," the man replied. "You are right in saying that God is one and there is no other but him. To love him with all your heart, with all your understanding, and with all your strength, and to love your neighbor as yourself." (Mark 12:32-33)*

There is further proof the disciples did not believe that Jesus was God, even after the resurrection and ascension.

> *"The God of Abraham, Isaac, and Jacob, the God of our fathers, has glorified his servant Jesus." (Acts 3:13)*

> *"When God raised up his servant, he sent him first to you to bless you by turning each of you from your wicked ways." (Acts 3:26)*

Acts was written about 60 years after Jesus' death and details the founding of Christianity. If they believed Jesus was God, they would have said so multiple times.

The Gospel of John calls Jesus "the son of Joseph," not God.

> *"Philip found Nathanael and told him, 'We have found the one Moses wrote about in the Law, and about whom the prophets also wrote—Jesus of Nazareth, the son of Joseph'" (John 1:45)*

> *"They said, 'Is this not Jesus, the son of Joseph, whose father and mother we know? How can he now say, 'I came down from Heaven?'" (John 6:42).*

Later in the chapter, Jesus claims God sent him, but he never claims to be God.

The Church uses two verses to prove Jesus' godship, but other texts contradict them.

> *"All things have been handed over to me by my Father, and no one knows the Son except the Father, and no one knows the Father except the Son and anyone to whom the Son chooses to reveal him." (Matthew 11:27)*

> *"All that belongs to the Father is mine. That is why I said the Spirit will receive from me what he will make known to you." (John 16:15)*

Through the manipulation of texts, wishful thinking, and politics, the monotheistic religion of the God of Abraham became the Trinity of Jesus. Because of continuous changes, Christianity became a contradiction—claiming a monotheistic religion while worshiping more than one entity.

One premise the Church uses to justify Jesus as "God" is that he healed people. So, are all the "healers" throughout time are also "God"?

Every faith has healers.

Another contradiction is that Jesus was God because he forgave sins. But then the Church assumed this power and used it to justify "confession." You cannot have it both ways. Either Jesus was "God" because he could forgive sins and all the priests were also "God," or there was only one "God." Also, of note, Jesus did not say, "I forgive your sins," but, "Your sins are forgiven." His entire ministry was based on our sins being forgiven through unconditional love.

Religion assumed the power of Jesus, claiming it as their own, and used it to advance their agendas. Jesus warned us about this.

The Church also uses John 10:30 to justify Jesus' divinity: "*I and the Father are one,*" but if you continue reading, Jesus said his wish was for everyone to be one with God like he was. *"Holy Father, keep them in your name, which you have given me, that they may be one, even as we are one." (John 17:11, ESV)*

And then again later in the chapter:

> *My prayer is not for them alone. I pray also for those who will believe in me through their message, that all of them may be one, Father, just as you are in me and I am in you. May they also be in us so that the world may believe that you have sent me. I have given them the glory that you gave me, that they may be one as we are one—I in them and you in me—so that they may be brought to complete unity. Then the world will know that you sent me and have loved them even as you have loved me." (John 17:22–26)*

Christianity became a polytheistic faith. It claims that Jesus (Catholics include Mary and the saints) is an intercessor, precursor, or intermediary to God. Putting Jesus, and sometimes a line of people, before God.

Christianity has little to do with Jesus' life. The Beatitudes are footnotes, and Paul's threat of judgment, Hell, and damnation are primary teachings. Faithful followers of Jesus focus on love and only love. Otherwise, we are living like the religious people Jesus tried to correct. They have forgotten that *"Pride goes before destruction, a haughty spirit before a fall"* (Proverbs 16:18)

I am not alone in stating that the Church has completely fallen away from Jesus' teachings. The Church adapted the teachings to their needs, desires, and agendas. And it started with making Jesus divine.

The message of love was always prominent in his speeches. And, while he never claimed that he was God, equal or otherwise, Jesus said he was "love." So, in that context, John 14:6 makes Jesus' statement true: Love is the only way to God.

Jesus' mission was to show the love of God. Before him, God was a vicious, ruthless Being. Jesus gave us God's unconditional love and told us we are all God's children. Jesus said that we obtain the kingdom of Heaven through God's love, not man's laws.

Jesus taught us that we are all special, not just the religious leadership, but all of us. It was a radical concept that the leadership and their egos refused to accept. The Pharisees and Sadducees lived for their power, and Jesus took it away. He freed us.

> *"See what great love the Father has lavished on us, that we should be called children of God! And that is what we are! The reason the world does not know us is that it did not know him. Dear friends, now we are children of God, and what we will be has not yet been made known. But we know that when Christ appears, we shall be like him, for we shall see him as he is. (1 John 3:1)*

And

> *"This is how we know that we love the children of God: by loving God and carrying out his commands." (1 John 5:20)*

For all who saw them, Jesus' miracles solidified his anointing by God, and they are still used to prove his divinity. During his three years of ministry (even that is disputed, with arguments claiming one to three years), he healed two blind men, two who were paralyzed, a leper, a bleeding woman, Peter's mother-in-law, a disabled woman, a man with dropsy, a man's withered hand, and the ear of the Priest's servant after Peter cut it off. Entire towns were healed after Jesus walked through.

Jesus exorcised a mute man, seven demons from Mary Magdalene, and a man at Capernaum's synagogue. He cast a "legion" of demons out of a Gadarenes' man and into a herd of swine, causing them to jump off a mountain. He healed a Gentile woman's daughter, a boy who was foaming at the mouth and gnashing his teeth, and a multitude of people who were brought to him after a Sabbath sunset ceremony.

The N.T. states Jesus raised three people from the dead: Jairus's daughter, a widow's son, and Lazarus. He also turned water into wine and fed 4000-5000 (the Gospels differ) with seven loaves of bread and two fish. On two occasions, he supplied his disciples with nets filled with fish.

Jesus calmed a storm, cursed and killed a fig tree, and paid his and Peter's taxes with coins from a fish's mouth. One of his most famous miracles was walking on water. Which I now think was a metaphor for his need to tip-toe through all the religious and political bullshit.

During Jesus' time, talk of miracles was typical because of the Mesopotamian, Asian, Indian, Greek, Roman, and Egyptian gods. Prophets were already known to have calmed the seas, walked on water, healed the sick, and raised the dead. In their minds, the similarities between these beliefs and what Jesus did verified Jesus' ordination from God. Throughout the centuries, the stories of Jesus' miracles were controversial because people labeled him a copycat, not original or unique.

Elijah, of the O.T., also performed miracles, raised people from the dead, brought fire from the sky, and did not "die" but went to Heaven "alive." Besides the Hebrew Bible, he is mentioned in the Qur'an, the Book of Mormon, and Bahai texts. The last book of the prophets, Malachi, states that Elijah will return on the day of judgment.

Sound familiar?

His miracles are not why I follow Jesus; his reason for those miracles is why. Apart from the Transfiguration, all his miracles were to help the poor and needy in society. He did so with complete humility, instructing several people he healed to tell no one. He was a genuine servant of the people, doing God's work.

Chapter 46: Boys Will Be Boys

The "Infancy Gospel of Thomas" is a non-canonical text that details Jesus's childhood. It is controversial and was deemed heretical long ago, but it was popular in the early centuries. This gospel claims that Jesus was quite the handful.

A one-year-old Jesus cursed a child, causing the child to wither and die. Between the ages of five and twelve, Jesus killed a child who accosted him and one of his teachers. Mary and Joseph reprimanded him for his vicious behavior, so Jesus blinded them. The text claims young Jesus was so arrogant that he continually tried to instruct his teachers. They suspected his supernatural abilities. Their suspicions amused Jesus, and he confirmed their assumptions.

The story claims Jesus had an epiphany (Dare I say, "come to Jesus" moment?) and denounces all his horrific acts. He then does virtuous deeds like resurrecting a friend who fell off a roof and two others who died from various causes. Jesus healed his brother, who was bitten by a snake, and a man who cut off his foot with an ax. Jesus made clay birds and brought them to life (The Qur'an also notes this).

It also documents that Jesus' abilities came in handy. He carried water on a piece of cloth, extended a beam for Joseph that was cut too short, and created an entire feast from a single grain. But, even with new teachers, Jesus still instructed them.

Later in life, stories reflect Jesus became less selfish, more evolved, and more mature.

Chapter 47: The Missing Years

Between the ages of 13 and 29, Jesus' life is a mystery, but there is a lot of speculation.

There is a belief that Jesus joined the traders and traveled to India, Nepal, and Tibet, studying and teaching Hinduism and Buddhism—which were established belief systems, the "pagans." Believers assert Jesus was called Issa, later referred to as Saint Issa. The Unknown Life of Christ (Notovitch N., 1990) details the legend. Jesus was radical, and his teachings vastly differed from Jewish doctrine. This story answered, "Where did Jesus learn his beliefs?" Christians assume he knew all because he was "God," ignoring the scriptures saying he was growing and learning.

Jesus' beliefs portrayed in the N.T. align more closely with Eastern philosophies than Jewish. The problem is that Notovitch wrote it in 1887, and it lacks any supporting evidence. The Unknown Life of Christ was supposedly a translation of ancient scriptures written three years after Jesus' death. But the scrolls that were "translated" were never found. Notovitch mentioned a monastery that denied the document's existence. An overwhelming number of scholars believe the scriptures are a forgery, albeit a good one. (Notovitch, 2018)

Another theory claims Jesus and John the Baptist went to a monastery in Qumran and joined the Essenes—a group resembling today's Christian Monasticism. The Essenes' beliefs were more mystical, messianic, apocalyptic, and monastic than the Pharisees and Sadducees. The Essene monks would have taught Jesus and John. The Dead Sea Scrolls were discovered near Qumran, and archeologists believe the Essenes wrote them. (Feather, 2005)

There is another belief that Jesus went to Japan, became a Buddhist Master, and returned to Judea at 33. This theory also claims that Jesus did not die but escaped and returned to Japan, where he fathered three children and lived until 106. (Lidz, 2005)

The Missing Years of Jesus: The Extraordinary Evidence that Jesus Visited the British Isles. (Price, 2010) claims Jesus visited Cornwall, Stonehenge, and Glastonbury while studying with the Druids.

As with everything, there are dissenters to every theory, and all these theories lack evidence. They are just conjecture, like most religions. But, even if Jesus did not leave the Middle East, somehow, he learned the universal truths of love and letting go. He could have learned from traveling merchants, tribes, or lands. Regardless of where or how he gained this knowledge, in doing so, he changed the world.

Chapter 48: Was He a Blast or Blah?

Throughout the ages, religious leaders dismissed Jesus as having a sense of humor because, somehow, being emotionless relates to godliness. But I cannot believe that someone who was so magnetic and drew so many people to him did so without making them laugh.

I live for laughter. Laughter invokes admiration. Laughter bonds us. Unemotional, monotone individuals are not engaging, and the Bible details how passionate Jesus was. It tells us that people dropped everything and followed him. The Gospel of Luke claims Jesus said our goal is laughter in Heaven. My mom used to say, "No sense of humor, no reason to live!" and I could not agree more. Laughter is the rejoicing of our soul. Again, looking to nature for God's intent: The platypus proves God has a sense of humor.

The O.T. warned against dismissive or scoffing laughter. So, in that aspect, I do not believe Jesus "laughed." But to say that his personality lacked laughter eliminates a pure expression of joy. Laughter is entirely natural and seen across the animal kingdom. To deny that Jesus had this God-given gift is denying his humanity. And Jesus' humanity enables us to relate to him.

Chapter 49: His Humanity

Religions stripped away one vital part of Jesus' humanity: his sexuality. We are sexual beings, and it is often how we are judged. Unlike most animals, we have sex for pleasure and not based on fertilization cycles. We are sexually active for over 75% of our lives.

Our sexuality is often beyond our control, like nocturnal emissions, spontaneous erections, and, frankly, desire. Sex provides connection and intimacy, releases physical and emotional stress, and, of course, creates life. And religion wants to control every aspect.

There is much debate about the marriage of Jesus and Mary Magdalene. However, there is no evidence for this—tons of speculations, conjecture, and searching for missing pieces—but nothing "written in stone." Ironically, more texts are available that detail the possibility of Jesus being gay than there is that he was married.

The first time I heard this theory, I had to catch my breath. It was at my dog's annual visit with the veterinarian—not a place you would expect to have such a revelation. He was my vet for over a dozen years, and we talked about this book on this visit. I told him I was writing about who Jesus really was. He looked at me and said, "Gay, right?"

My first reaction was to laugh at the absurdity. Pfffff! I thought.

He noticed my dismissiveness and said, "No, really. If you don't know about this, you must look into it!"

He dropped everything and left the exam room. Returning with a giant collegiate brochure, he circled all the classes on the topic.

I felt like someone had flipped my world upside down. I was not upset about the possibility of Jesus being gay. I was just perplexed by it. It was definitely a theory I had not heard before and nothing I had ever considered. So, I disregarded it.

But just like the rest of this journey, a few days later, a different conversation with another person resurfaced the topic, forcing me to investigate further. Whenever something presented itself more than once, I researched it. Sometimes, it turned out to be nothing. Other times, it forced me to open my mind and reconsider my previous beliefs.

Religion portrays Jesus as a single man taking on the religious establishment. Throughout his ministry, thousands of people followed him. However, a single man in Jesus' era would have been considered a freak or an outcast. The family unit was central to society, even if that family was the same sex. His lack of a relationship status would have been a source of his invalidation.

The Church likes to claim that he overcame his sexuality, but marriage was a sign of stability and likability. A single person was considered unlovable—a social outcast and pariah. Those societal standards still exist in most of the world.

Marriage was a social platform, and anyone who did not measure up would not have been accepted the way Jesus was. He was flipping tables, telling off the Pharisees, and declaring that love, not laws, would get you into Heaven. Jesus was attacked and eventually killed for this, but if he were single, they would have ignored him, called him a madman, and he would not have been followed.

Scripture states Jesus had a "Beloved Disciple," who we believe was the Apostle John.

"When Jesus saw his mother there, and the disciple whom he loved standing nearby, he said to her, 'Woman, here is your son,' and to the disciple, 'Here is your mother.' From that time on, this disciple took

her into his home." (John 19:26-27)

There are many references to Jesus having a special love for a man. So, for many, it furthers the theory of Jesus' homosexuality. A passage in Mark tells of a young man who was almost captured during Jesus' arrest, but he escaped naked.

> *"Then everyone deserted him and fled. A young man, wearing nothing but a linen garment, was following Jesus. When they seized him, he fled naked, leaving his garment behind." (14:51-52)*

This passage is strange because it has no inherent value to the text. Scholars suggest the author claimed everyone fled when Jesus was arrested, not just his disciples. But that does not address the nudity and why it is in the text.

References about the "Beloved Disciple," are found throughout John, which is considered autobiographical. We see the mentions of this special person in John 13:23: "Now there was leaning on Jesus' bosom one of his disciples, whom Jesus loved." Later translations change this to "was reclining next to him." A major alteration.

"The disciple whom Jesus loved" is repeated in John 20:2 and 21:7.

And reinforcing this love, *"Peter turned and saw that the disciple whom Jesus loved was following them. This was the one who had leaned back against Jesus at the supper."* (John 21:20)

Interestingly, the New International Version references the beloved leaning against Jesus but alters it earlier.

If Mary Magdalene authored John and Acts, one could logically conclude Jesus was married. If she did not, then Jesus may have been gay—neither of which is acceptable to the Church.

A text called "The Secret Gospel of Mark" (Fideler, 1995) added to the theory. A religious scholar, Morton Smith, supposedly discovered the text in 1958. Smith allegedly found notes by Clement of Alexandria in the back of an ancient version of the Gospel of Mark. Clement (150-215 C.E.) was a theologian. In these notes, Clement comments on passages of Mark that do not appear in the canonical text. The notes claim there was a passage about Jesus lying naked with a boy. The following are Clement's notes. He said the text should be placed between Mark 10:34 and 35:

The Secret Gospel brings the following material word for word:

And they come into Bethany. And a certain woman whose brother had died was there. And, coming, she prostrated herself before Jesus and said to him, "Son of David, have mercy on me." But the disciples rebuked her. And Jesus, being angered, went off with her into the garden where the tomb was, and straightway a great cry was heard from the tomb. And going near, Jesus rolled away the stone from the door of the tomb. And straightway, going in where the youth was, he stretched forth his hand and raised him, seizing his hand. But the youth, looking upon him, loved him and began to beseech him that he might be with him. And going out of the tomb, they came into the house of the youth, for he was rich. And after six days, Jesus told him what to do, and in the evening the youth come to him, wearing a linen cloth over his naked body. And he remained with him that night, for Jesus taught him the mystery of the kingdom of God. And thence, arising, he returned to the other side of the Jordan. (Caldwell, 1996)

Clement comments on other entries that he thought were added from the gnostic sect of Carpocratians and not in the original Secret Gospel, like an added phrase, "naked man with naked man." Clement received the Gospel because he noted what was authentic and what he considered altered by the sect.

We do not know if the notations are legitimate; it could be a forgery by Smith, who "discovered" it. If it is legitimate, we do not know if it was a late addition to the book of Mark or if it was in the original text and they later eliminated it.

Some conclude that it is a story of Lazarus, as there are many similarities. We do not know the extent of this "Secret Gospel." But if Clement's notes are authentic, an additional part of the gospel circulated at the end of the third century and erased from history.

I love the way Peter Tatchell, an activist, summarizes the entire theory:

The truth is that we don't know whether Jesus was straight, gay, bisexual, or celibate. There is certainly no evidence for the Church's unspoken presumption that he was heterosexual or devoid of carnal desires. Since nothing in the Bible points to Christ having erotic feelings for women, or relationships with the female sex, the possibility of him being gay cannot be discounted.

In the absence of any evidence, let alone proof, that Jesus was heterosexual, the theological basis of Church homophobia is all the more shaky and indefensible. How can established religion dare denounce homosexuality when the founder of its Faith was himself a man of mysterious, unknown sexuality who could, for all we know, have been homosexual?

The Bible tells us that Jesus was born a man and therefore presumably had male sexual feelings. It would have been more or less impossible, biologically, for him not to have an element of erotic arousal—even if only having the normal male response of waking with an erection. (Tatchell, 1996)

Since Jesus was entirely human—God in human form as the Church prescribes—wouldn't it be heretical to deny any part of his humanity? We know nothing about most of Jesus' life, only fueling speculation. So many unknowns lead to assumptions, and we should focus on his message. However, the absence of information allows the Church to carefully construct "Jesus."

Jesus was probably married, or gay, or some spectrum in between. Through political and personal agendas, Jesus sanitized into something that fits goals, not reality. It is also likely that Jesus smoked hashish, but of course, that would not make the canon either.

But we know, as a human, he went to the bathroom, passed gas, blew his nose, and, yes, had sexual desires.

Chapter 50: My Inspiration

We can speculate and imagine what Jesus' life was like. We can assume and assign theories to our beliefs. But the one thing we should not do is forget his radical message of love.

Why does it matter if Jesus was divine, married, or gay? Would any of that invalidate his message? Would his instructions for love, forgiveness, and peace be any less admirable?

In my lifetime, I have only met a few people who inspired me so much that I wanted to be like them. It is a rare experience to regard someone so highly. And while the meeting of Jesus is only through stories, he is one person I want to emulate.

I want his patience, faith, loyalty, generosity, compassion, and love. He inspires me to serve this planet and everything on it better. He is still the only man who has never hurt me. I will always love his message and mission because Jesus showed us unconditional love. He destroyed the manufactured assumptions of a cruel and vicious "God." Jesus taught that love for our neighbor got us into "Heaven." Not if you washed your hands before a meal, although you really should.

Jesus assured us we are all God's children. That God's love is unconditional and not dependent on who you are. The only request was to give love away to everyone we meet, like he did. Martin Luther

King Jr. said, "Jesus Christ was an extremist for love, truth, and goodness."

Through Jesus, I learn how to be more loving. Jesus is my source of hope because of what he taught and endured and because he never lost his faith or love for humanity.

Jesus is not the path to God for everyone, and that is OK.

God did not create just one of anything, so there cannot be only one way.

If your path is paved in love, you are in the right direction.

Section VIII: God is too Big for One Religion

"The shoe that fits one person pinches another—there is no recipe for living that suits all cases."
~ Carl Jung

Section VIII: God is too Big for One Religion

Chapter 51: Many People, Many Paths

When I was 22 years old, I saw a bumper sticker that read, "God is too big for one religion." It was an earth-shattering statement—a concept I had never even considered. I was always told that Jesus was the only way. But it all came together for the first time in my life; it was a "light bulb moment."

Yes! I thought. *That is the truth!*

There is no rigidity in opinions like that of religion. Can you imagine someone proclaiming the only shoes you can wear are sneakers? It might thrill some, but I know many women who might kill before they gave up their heels. What if we could only eat one type of food? Or if we had only one choice of shampoo?

We have accepted our variations in so many aspects of life, but with our beliefs about "God," we lose all sensibility. We demand adherence from everyone on the planet. We act like spoiled, know-it-all children, trying to claim that "Dad" loves us the most. This way of thinking is selfish and the opposite of what religion is supposed to be.

The only other belief system that can be equally dogmatic is politics. Religion and politics are so intertwined they often become a single ideology, enabling people to proclaim moral authority in governing the masses. Political leaders often use religion to assert "divine appointment," even though their actions and policies are the antithesis of their religious ideals and philosophies. Politics in religion furthers tribal mentalities and deepens divides. But every religion has its breadth because a political leader became a believer.

Most believers' faith is contained in a single book, and most have yet to read it entirely. Scriptures are usually taught line by line from the teacher's perspective (imam, pastor, priest, rabbi, etc.). Most religious leaders never mention the non-canonical texts, what was redacted or altered, or admit that all religious texts have controversial scriptures.

I saw my ex-husband Vince, a few months before he died, and we discussed this book. I gave him section three to review. So, we talked about our "sins." After me, Vince married two more times and was separated from his third wife. He believed that sex before marriage removed all blessings from life and put salvation in jeopardy. He confessed that he primarily married his last wife because of this belief.

He was speechless when I told him how the religious laws changed throughout time. He gasped when I said that adultery was a greater sin than fornication and that marrying his second and third wives was technically adulterous.

I said, "How is making a vow to God during the wedding and then breaking it through a divorce less sinful than just having sex? At least fornication isn't breaking a promise to God—unless you've pledged celibacy."

Vince was dumbfounded and asked, "How do you know all of this stuff?".

I said, "Because I've read more than one book."

However, if I had not been burned by ignorance years prior, I may have never discovered that I, too, was wrong. I also would not have done the research. I would have stood resolute in my faith and proclaimed that my faith was all I needed, as he did. But my life showed me otherwise.

My doubts about the legitimacy of my education snowballed when I was 27 and started working for a tourist publication in the

Tampa Bay area of Florida. The publication's printing company was 2.5 hours north of Tampa in Ocala. We had to go "proof" each issue for errors before they printed it, and it was my first trip.

The proofing room was a large conference room with a 20-foot table with our publication strewn the length of it. Since I was new, I wanted to make a good impression. I promptly got out my markers and started making edits. My boss took the pens when I was done, checked my work, and made his notes.

I looked around the room. Behind me was a giant map and timeline on the wall opposite the table. It reached from floor to ceiling, and the entire wall was longer than the table across from it. Its enormity and information immediately captured my attention. It showed significant details in history, from the beginning of humankind to the present day, the 1990s.

I started walking through this timeline and felt like I entered the Twilight Zone. It dumbfounded me. The map showed that while the Israelites were roaming the Middle East, people lived in China, South Africa, Australia, South America, and (*Oh My God!*) America.

It overwhelmed me with confusion. How could this be? The church taught me other civilizations did not exist until after the Tower of Babel. This timeline detailed cultures for thousands, if not millions, of years before the Bible!

I was assured that everything in history not explained in the Bible was myth, legend, or fable.

My mind raced.

> *How could entire civilizations have existed and not be listed in the Bible?*

I stood there in total awe. I had no idea. Seriously, none. I honestly believed that all of humanity started with Adam and Eve, who were Semites, because the Bible said so.

I wholeheartedly believed the Bible was historically accurate. I was told the Bible was never proven wrong, but on that day, it was. Discovering this was a life-altering moment. It was the first time that I ever doubted what they taught me.

For years, I knew people had flawed interpretations and did

things in the "name of God" that should never be done.

Was the entire foundation of our existence inaccurate?

What about the flood?

What about Adam and Eve?

I realized everything I knew was wrong—at my new job, in front of my new boss and five of the printer's employees. I was experiencing an existential crisis, hours from home, in front of virtual strangers.

I wanted to cry. I trembled and fought the urge to break down. When I thought I would collapse, my boss was done, and we were ready to leave. I steadied myself, grabbed my purse, and made it to the car. We drove back to the office, and I endured a fake smile, keeping my cool. I stared out the window, feeling like my entire life was a lie. I was in complete shock.

I did not know up from down, and if I did "know," was I even correct?

Was there even a God, or was the whole thing a fairy tale?

Was my mom aware of this stuff, or was she misled too?

It shattered me. I was shamed and discarded because of what the Bible said, and I had just discovered the very foundation of it was not even real.

What about my Beloved, Jesus?

I felt like someone kicked me in the gut, and all I could do was act like nothing was wrong. I still had two hours left in the car with my new boss.

After that event, I turned my back on everything religious. The following two years were some of the most difficult of my adult life. My life without faith was desperate and reckless. However, I never abandoned the entire premise of "God." I always believed in something supernatural and part of our existence.

I started looking into other beliefs and exploring what else was out there. It was then that I realized the source of my pain and shame was us, not God. And through the process of studying other faiths, I developed a more well-rounded view of "God."

All religions get some things right and some things very wrong. The truth lies somewhere in the middle.

Theories about "God" originated from us trying to understand and define the world. "God" is based on ancient man's perceptions and observations and how they made sense of everything. These ideas evolved and became corrupted through that evolution—like almost everything humans touch.

Instead of acceptance and love, which unites us, it became about shame and fear for control. They use our insecurities to push their agendas instead of assuring us we are whole and loved. Religion puts conditions on unconditional love.

God and love should always be interchangeable; at one point, they were. Inevitably, egos kicked in, and beliefs became a source of contention, judgment, and hate rather than unity, peace, and love. Throughout history, only one (major) religion has had no war waged in its name (more on that to come).

Generally, the older the religion, the more blood it has spilled. Killing people in the name of God is the ultimate oxymoron. Using a source of love to justify death is moronic and utterly ego-driven.

Killing in the name of God assumes man has the power and wisdom of God. It is replacing divinity with humanity. It is claiming that "God" is so inept at managing his issues that he must use mere mortals to control things he cannot. If killing in the name of God is from "God," then how is he greater, holier, and more righteous than us? If he needs our help, how powerful can he be? Wouldn't a lightning bolt be more effective?

If you created a Venn diagram with all the major religions, they would intersect at "love" and "let go." Everything in religion branches off these two tenets. Each faith has its way of saying these, but they all boil down to being kind and unafraid. But Christianity vilifies other faiths as evil and unjust, primarily because it feeds our egos, making us feel special to claim only we are right. The ego is in complete control when pushing someone down lifts you.

I was only ten when my mom gave me The Kingdom of the Cults by Walter R. Martin. The book views all the other faiths through a biblical lens and a Christian perspective, labeling all other religions as cults. It was complete indoctrination, as well as divisive and damning. My mother thought it was pertinent that Christianity was the only view they exposed me to because she believed that all the others were nonsense or evil.

When I started my studies, I vowed to approach other faiths with an open, curious mind without prejudice. I did not want just to study the doctrine; I wanted to learn why people followed it. What made each religion flourish, and where did it go wrong? I acted like a new convert to each belief system, but a highly skeptical one. I went down every rabbit hole I could find. To find the truth, I had to go beyond the scriptures and research the good and the bad. The complexity of each religion forced me to get outside of my Christian brain and see things from another perspective.

Beliefs are very personal. Most people's religion comes from their parents or culture, but people stay in their faith for many reasons. And there are reasons they leave.

Most assert that their religion makes them a better person. Most people strive to live a good life, believing their faith teaches that. We never live up to our belief systems' standards because we are human. But we focus on other faiths when they do not live up to theirs. Religion is supposed to give us the foundation of love, to build from and highlight a path to righteousness. But historically, it has divided us.

So, where did the ancients get their beliefs?

When did they start?

What was their dogma, and how did it help their believers?

And how did we get to the religions we see worldwide today?

I wondered if, after all my research, I would still be a Christian, or would I prefer another faith? I was treading on the waters of uncertainty, but I wanted to know the truth. So, I was moving forward, regardless of the outcome.

In each religion, I found things I loved, and I understood why they had the followers they do/did. However, they were overtaken by egos and degraded their Supreme Being to mortal tendencies and inadequacies. Abraham, Buddha, Jesus, and Mohammad were all men of faith, trying to lead us to a life of righteousness and away from the stronghold of our ego. They warned of manipulations of their messages, but we either did not listen or dismissed them.

The fact that religions have lost their way does not mean the entirety of their message is wrong. It just means that we must use the minds God gave us to discern the holy from the unholy. We must be able to tell the difference between love and ego—what is from God and what is from humans.

Worldwide, there are approximately 4200 religions, and most of them think theirs is the authentic one—and for them, it probably is. However, if you must proclaim your "God" is better, stronger, grander, etc., you may doubt the topic.

Confidence is not boastful, and security is usually silent. Fanaticism does not equal righteousness and invokes our worst nature, never promoting love and grace. If your "God" hates the same people you do, you need a new god. God is love, and whichever faith helps you realize that and embody that love is the right path for you.

Worldwide, 84% of people are religious. Most believe in one God, but we still fight over who loves him more. The competition is childish, pointless, and lethal. There are approximately 2.4 billion Christians, 1.9 billion Muslims, and 15 million Jews, totaling over 4.4 billion people, or 56% of the world's population, who believe in the God of Abraham. The other top belief systems include 1.1 billion Hindus, 506 million Buddhists, and 26 million Sikhs. (McClendon, 2017)

We have struggled with religious diversity throughout history, but acceptance of it is needed to love your neighbor.

"Truth is one, the sages speak of it by many names."
~ Rigveda, Sacred Hindu Text

"Everyone ought to worship God according to his own inclinations, and not to be constrained by force."
~ Flavius Josephus, Jewish historian, 37–100 C.E.

"Religion is a candle inside a multicolored lantern. Everyone looks through a particular color, but the candle is always there."
~Muhammad Naguib, first Egyptian President; 1901-1984

"We have just enough religion to make us hate, but not enough to make us love one another."
~ Jonathan Swift, writer and Dean of Saint Patrick's Cathedral in Ireland, 1667-1745

"I never told my religion nor scrutinized that of another. I never attempted to make a convert nor wished to change another's creed. I have judged others' religion by their lives, for it is from our lives and not from our words that our religion must be read. By the same test must the world judge me."
~ Thomas Jefferson.

"Half the people in the world think that the metaphors of their religious traditions, for example, are facts. And the other half contends that they are not facts at all. As a result, we have people who consider themselves believers because they accept metaphors as facts, and we have others who classify themselves as atheists because they think religious metaphors are lies."
~ Joseph Campbell

Joseph Campbell was an American mythologist, author, and lecturer who wrote A Hero with a Thousand Faces, The Masks of God, and The Hero's Journey. The books detail how religions all follow the same path. To summarize these books, the journey begins with the calling of the Hero and his rejection of that call. Then, a supernatural being intervenes and offers guidance. The Hero endures trials and tribulations and emerges stronger and wiser. All myths/religions follow this basic premise.

"A myth is a religion in which no one any longer believes."
~ James Feibleman

Campbell noted, "Every religion is true one way or another. It is true when understood metaphorically."

Campbell believed that religion fills four essential societal needs (Valencia College West Campus n.d.):

1. The Metaphysical Function: Awakening us to the wonder of it all.
2. The Cosmological Function: Explaining our universe and nature.
3. The Sociological Function: Instilling social harmony and order.
4. The Psychological Function: Guiding us through the stages of life (coming of age through death and the afterlife).

A relevant Campbell quote:

> Wherever the poetry of myth is interpreted as biography, history, or science, it is killed. The living images become only remote facts of a distant time or sky. Furthermore, it is never difficult to demonstrate that as science and history mythology is absurd. When a civilization begins to reinterpret its mythology in this way, the life goes out of it, temples become museums, and the link between the two perspectives becomes dissolved. Such a blight has certainly descended on the Bible and on a great part of the Christian Cult. (Campbell, 2008)

We miss the point when we take the spirit out of the spiritual or try to define the undefinable. We must remember that religion was supposed to show us the wonder, not confine it. It was meant to enlighten us, not burden our lives. Religion was supposed to give us an image of unconditional love, not place conditions on who receives it.

Joseph Campbell was famous for the saying, "Follow your bliss." So, I cannot mention him without including this quote.

> If you follow your bliss, you put yourself on a kind of track that has been there all the while, waiting for you, and the life that you ought to be living is the one you are living. Wherever you are—if you are following your bliss, you are enjoying that refreshment, that life within you, all the time.

Campbell knew that we must not succumb to daily chaos and routines regardless of our beliefs. We must align with the Divine and discover why we are here. We need to follow where our hearts lead us, where our passion lives, and what adds meaning to our lives.

Getting into that flow aligns us with our purpose. Campbell said,

One has only to know and trust, and the ageless guardians will appear. Having responded to his own call, and continuing to follow courageously as the consequences unfold, the Hero finds all the forces of the unconscious at his side. Mother Nature herself supports the mighty task.

That sentiment is the epitome of writing this book.

The journey of the Hero is in us all. I feel like I have undergone my own. But historically, only the Hero's story is told, not the Heroine's. Everyone has a journey and travels it at their own pace. We should honor that and try to live righteously by accepting that with love. You cannot force someone into a belief. You can only be an example and a servant for them to grow.

Throughout history, we have questioned which religion is correct. Is it Ahura Mazda, El, Jehovah, Zeus, Jah, Ra, Krishna, Baal, Molek, Thor, or other gods in myths and religions? Posing that question assumes any of them were entirely correct. Since humans have carried the message, the doctrine tends to be as flawed as we are.

Our entire existence is a rainbow with a magnificent spectrum. In between all the colors are vast distances and no singularities. There are many truths in every faith. The only goal should be how to love more, and we should disregard anything contradictory.

Breathe in the good shit, breathe out the bullshit. However, discerning between the two requires an open mind, sound judgment, and knowledge.

Chapter 52: The God Before God

Occasionally, archeologists find something that forces us to rethink our beliefs. The Ugaritic texts were discovered in 1929 in modern-day Syria, and they confirmed a lot of suspicions. Originating from 1450 to 1180 B.C.E., as far as discoveries go, they were a significant find. (Spar, 2009)

The Ugaritic texts share similarities with the Torah/O.T. and fill in some blanks from the Bible. They confirmed the Israelites worshiped many gods until the destruction of the Temple in Jerusalem in 586 B.C.E.

The Ten Commandments state that "there should be no gods before Me" because there were many. The Bible says the "One True God" had many names. The first was given to Abraham in Genesis 17:1: "El Shaddai." God repeated it in Genesis 35:11 when he renamed Jacob "Israel."

"El" means god or judge and dates to 3000 B.C.E. (900 years before Abraham and 1500 years before Moses). El and 'l-h-m is Ugaritic and describe the temple and the Canaanite gods. Combined into "Elohim," it meant the followers of El. At one point, "El" covered the Canaanite's Trinity of gods, but in Hebrew, it became a singular masculine deity.

The term "El" was first used in Babylon (present-day Iraq), where the ancient Akkadians lived and worshiped a Trinity. It was El (father god), Ea (Lord of the Earth and creator of man), and Enlil (lord of the air). Elohim is mentioned over 2500 times in the Bible. The Israelites adopted El and gave it their distinction: "El Shaddai." (Robinson, 2010)

When God introduced himself to Moses in Exodus 6:3, the name changed.

> "I appeared to Abraham, to Isaac, and to Jacob as El Shaddai– 'God Almighty'–but I did not reveal my name, YHWH, to them." (N.L.T.)

Some scholars take issue with this change, claiming God deceived Abraham, Isaac, and Jacob by not giving them his real name.

It is difficult to find modern Bibles that use "El Shaddai" and "YHWH." Most of the translations use "Lord," which causes a misreading of the text. "God" told Abraham, Isaac, and Jacob his name was "El Shaddai," then it changed to "YHWH."

The Israelites were trying to separate themselves and their "God" from the "pagans." Pagan is defined as: "a person holding religious beliefs other than those of the major world religions." (Oxford English Dictionary, 2023) So, everyone else believes in pagan gods, but we believe in the correct one!

The prophet's names also began to change. They went from an "el" ending, like Ezekiel, Israel, Daniel, Samuel, and Ishmael, to ending in "ah" like Elijah, Uzziah, Hezekiah, Josiah, etc.

The Israelites took the pagan gods, made them their own, and tried to erase all evidence of their preexistence.

Chapter 53: The Sun Before the Son

Another Canaanite god was Baal, and according to the Bible, he was YHWH's archenemy. The Ugaritic texts show that by the early 14th century B.C.E., Baal was the "Ruler of the Universe" and was the primary religion. Known as El's son, Baal was the Sun and Storm god. He brought fertility and heralded his arrival with thunder. As the Sun, Baal brought life, and his rains brought prosperity through bountiful crops and healthy livestock. They believed as he giveth, so he taketh, and if Baal was not happy, it would show through floods, droughts, or famine.

He was often depicted as a bull and called "Adon," which the Israelites later claimed and changed to "Adonai." Baal was widely accepted within the ancient tribes of Israel and followed by the religious leaders of ten Jewish tribes.

The original Hebrew texts show that YHWH was also called a bull. The "bull" was changed in future translations to distance themselves from any association with Baal. The KJV uses "unicorn" in Numbers 24:8.

Most current translations use a ram instead of a unicorn. Young's Literal Translation (YLT) uses Reem. Darby's Translation has buffalo, and Douay-Rheims 1899 American Edition (DRA) uses rhinoceros. The "Common English Bible" (CEB), New Life Version (NLV),

Orthodox Jewish Bible (OJB), and The Voice all still use the term "bull."

The full name of Baal was Baal-Zebul, which means Prince Baal. In the Bible, Baal's name was morphed into Beelzebul and then Beelzebub and was labeled the "lord of the flies" and the "prince of evil." In John Milton's Paradise Lost, Beelzebub was Satan's chief lieutenant. The Pharisees accused Jesus of being possessed by Baal in Matthew 12:24.

The Bible considers Baal evil (after all, he was "God's" archenemy!), but for hundreds of years, he was worshiped, revered, and considered vital to life.

The Bible justified the Canaanite's destruction because of their rituals involving child sacrifice. Many Christians gasped in horror, lowering their heads and whispering, "No wonder God asked them to be destroyed."

However, outside of the Bible, there is no evidence the Canaanites performed child sacrifice. It does not appear in ancient Canaanite, Ugaritic, or Phoenician texts. Claiming child sacrifice "as directed by God" was limited to pagan religions is utterly hypocritical. Abraham, the founder of Judaism, Christianity, and Islam, believed in child sacrifice. We see proof in his attempt to sacrifice Isaac. Some ancient texts, like the Jewish Midrash, claim neither an angel nor a ram appeared, and Abraham killed Isaac.

Jesus was the ultimate child sacrifice. If we believe Jesus was the son of God, "God" sacrificed his child. Back then, it was the thing to do! The Bible is riddled with stories of people regularly killing kids; it was standard practice. We see it with Abraham and Isaac, Moses as a child, the "Passover," and Herod in Jesus' time. But the Canaanites get blamed—it was all Baal's fault!

The Egyptians worshiped Baal, too. Baal and the Egyptian god, Set, are interchangeable. In art, Baal was often displayed wearing the crown of Lower Egypt. When the Canaanites became the Phoenicians and started sailing up and down the coast, their religion spread and influenced the Greek and Roman mythologies. The Bible states their breadth of influence:

"Again, the Israelites did evil in the eyes of the Lord. They served the Baals and the Ashtoreths, and the gods of Aram, the gods of Sidon, the gods of Moab, the gods of the Ammonites and the gods of the Philistines...." (Judges 10:6)

"The children of Israel dwelt among the Canaanites, Hittites, and Amorites, and Perizzites, and Hivites, and Jebusites: and they took their daughters to be their wives, and gave their daughters to their sons, and served their gods." (Judges 3:5-6)

Monotheism was not relevant or widespread until the seventh and sixth centuries B.C.E., nearly 1000 years after Moses.

Some theorize the Egyptian Pharaoh Akhenaten emboldened the monotheist movement. After his death, the next Pharaoh erased Akhenaten and his monotheism from Egyptian history. Moses was born about 50 years after Akhenaten's death.

Chapter 54: God's Wife

A pleasant but shocking discovery was that for over 3000 years, God had a wife. The Goddess' name varied by region and dialect. Assyrians and Babylonians knew her as Ishtar. The Sumerians called her Inanna and Attar by the Aramaic tribes. The Greeks called her Aphrodite. The Canaanites called her Asherah, Ashtoreth (or Ashtaroth), Anat, Astarte, or Elat.

Most of the history of the ancient Canaanite religions and gods was clouded or erased to hide any assimilation. There are many debates on whether these were different names for the same feminine deity, separate deities, or a combination of both—various goddesses called other names according to the era and region.

Asherah is mentioned over 40 times in the Hebrew Bible, all negatively. For over a millennium, her identity was lost because we believed "Asherah" was a name for poles, trees, or groves. The Ugaritic texts revealed the concealment of the Goddess.

She was the consort of El, Baal, and YHWH. The book of Jeremiah, written approximately 628 B.C.E., called her the "Queen of Heaven." Jeremiah 7:17-18 mentions the cakes made for her as an offering. Asherah poles—shrines to the Goddess—were placed at the entrance to Solomon's Temple by King Manasseh and removed by King Hezekiah, which means they stood at the temple gates for over two-thirds of its existence for over 300 years.

Jeremiah 44:15-18 says they tried YHWH, and they preferred the Goddess.

> *Then all the men who knew that their wives were burning incense to other gods, along with all the women who were present—a large assembly—and all the people living in Lower and Upper Egypt, said to Jeremiah, "We will not listen to the message you have spoken to us in the name of the Lord! We will certainly do everything we said we would: We will burn incense to the Queen of Heaven and will pour out drink offerings to her just as we and our fathers, our kings and our officials did in the towns of Judah and in the streets of Jerusalem. At that time, we had plenty of food and were well off and suffered no harm. But ever since we stopped burning incense to the Queen of Heaven and pouring out drink offerings to her, we have had nothing and have been perishing by sword and famine.*

King Solomon became a worshiper of Asherah (1 Kings 11:1-6). Of course, like Jeremiah, their "transgressions" were blamed on the women. Religion depicts women as the root of evil. It was never the man's fault; it was always those annoying women!

In 1 Kings 18, the followers of Baal and Asherah completely outnumbered Elijah. In verse 22, he states he's the only prophet of God remaining. As a believer, I looked at this story as one of strength, perseverance, and God's power. I never looked at it in terms of history and the possibility monotheistic beliefs were the minority, not the majority.

King Josiah demolished all the temples and shrines to Baal and Asherah (2 Kings 23:4-14).

> *The King ordered Hilkiah the high priest, the priests next in rank and the doorkeepers to remove from the temple of the Lord all the articles made for Baal and Asherah and all the starry hosts. He burned them outside Jerusalem in the fields of the Kidron Valley and took the ashes to Bethel. He did away with the idolatrous priests appointed by the kings of Judah to burn incense on the high places of the towns of Judah and on those around Jerusalem—those who burned incense to Baal, to*

the Sun and moon, to the constellations and to all the starry hosts. He took the Asherah pole from the temple of the Lord to the Kidron Valley outside Jerusalem and burned it there. He ground it to powder and scattered the dust over the graves of the common people. He also tore down the quarters of the male shrine prostitutes that were in the temple of the Lord, the quarters where women did weaving for Asherah...

... He pulled down the altars the kings of Judah had erected on the roof near the upper room of Ahaz and the altars Manasseh had built in the two courts of the temple of the Lord. He removed them from there, smashed them to pieces, and threw the rubble into the Kidron Valley. The King also desecrated the high places that were east of Jerusalem on the south of the Hill of Corruption—the ones Solomon King of Israel had built for Ashtoreth the vile Goddess of the Sidonians, for Chemosh the vile god of Moab, and for Molek, the detestable god of the people of Ammon. Josiah smashed the sacred stones and cut down the Asherah poles and covered the sites with human bones.

Recent archeological discoveries confirmed it was a regular practice to convert "pagan" shrines into latrines—the ultimate desecration (and a literal shitting on) of competing gods.

"My God is bigger and better than your God" has killed millions and destroyed historical relics for over 5000 years.

The Goddess was often depicted naked with horns or a crescent moon (which, when rotated horizontally, resembles her horns). Her sacred symbols were the dove, lion, and horse. The Sphinx and Venus were also representations of her. She was known for fertility and walking on water. She was the Tree of Life. They revered her as "our mother," as she was mighty and nurturing. Some scholars link her with Eve because she was called the mother of all creation. Discovering the Goddess added an entirely unfamiliar perspective to Genesis 1:26, which was altered in modern translations: "Then God said, 'Let us make mankind in our image, in our likeness."

I always found it strange that "God" designed women as the birth givers, but we are told there are just two guys up there: a father and son. Had no one else ever wondered what happened to Mom?

My question was always dismissed. Or they claimed God was so powerful he was not created, and since Jesus was technically part of God, neither was he. So, "God" is an exception to his own rules, and in this single instance, women were unnecessary?

It is just another example of Western Religion's dismissal and degradation of women. They erased feminine deities from history, all to bolster the ridiculous claim that only a man was significant and worthy of praise.

So, along with Baal, Asherah (in all her depictions and names) was removed from history.

> "...When he makes all the altar stones to be like limestone crushed to pieces, no Asherah poles or incense altars will be left standing." (Isaiah 27:9:)

Their goals:

> "In that day, people will look to their Maker and turn their eyes to the Holy One of Israel. They will not look to the altars, the work of their hands, and they will have no regard for the Asherah poles and the incense altars their fingers have made." (Isaiah 17:7-8)

When anyone destroys ancient temples or churches, we roar with condemnation. But in the Bible, they justified it. For 2400 years (3000 B.C.E. to 600 B.C.E.), these religions were the fundamental beliefs of the ancient world. From modern-day Iran to Morocco and Spain to Turkey, hundreds of generations lived according to their theology, worshiping their gods, fearing the wrath of upsetting them, and building temples and erecting monuments in their honor. But according to the Bible, they were all to be destroyed.

> "I will uproot from among you your Asherah poles when I demolish your cities." (Micah 5:14)

It was genocide, glorified by a "holy" book.

By 1 Samuel, we are told the Israelites finally "saw their error" and were converting to monotheism.

The Canaanite religion predated Christianity by at least three thousand years and lasted longer than Christianity has existed. It was still relevant after Jesus because Paul mentioned Baal in Romans 11:4.

Sadly, the Bible, known as the "Word of God," details their death, destruction, ethnic cleansing, rapes, and slavery, claiming it was "God's" will. If these stories were in any other book or from another "God," we would decry their theology as heretical and label it a terrorist cult.

The Bible illustrates what happens when the ego is in complete control and how our need to win causes terrorism and genocide. We should view the biblical stories as a warning of what happens when people use "God" to justify immoral or deadly behavior. This ego-maniacal, self-centered, insecure mentality caused millions of people to be slaughtered, all in the name of "love?"

How does that even make sense? We have turned "God" into the ultimate abusive relationship.

For centuries, the Church admonished meditation and yoga because of tribal rivalry with the "pagans." Meditation silences the ego, and yoga is muscle strengthening and breathing, which should be encouraged, not demonized.

And seriously, what was their problem with incense?

Chapter 55: Which Was One First?

The Bible encompasses the view of Middle Eastern cultures and political climates. However, each region was developing its spiritual belief systems throughout the world. Wars and migrations forced assimilation and eventually formed the top five religions. All religions have pieces of each other, just like the strands and building blocks of our DNA.

Archeologists have found sacred iconography worldwide, dating back tens of thousands of years. The Native Americans, Polynesians, and Aboriginal Australians have belief systems that predate anything that is widely practiced today. Almost all theologies have three things in common: a prominent god, the spirit/soul in life, and some form of afterlife.

I went back 6000 years and studied the origins and history of the most prominent religions still around today—any deeper and this book would be a million pages.

Along with fighting over which god is more powerful, there's debate over which is the oldest or original belief system. Judaism claims Adam and Eve as the first inhabitants and the flood, where only the Israelites survived, so they assert they are the original. Because of my upbringing and education, I had as much confidence in this assertion as my next breath, but it is untrue.

The Chinese Book of Changes, written around 2800 B.C.E., is the most ancient divination text and details the I Ching. However, while it claims divine intervention, it is not a religion but a philosophy. Confucianism was based on the I Ching.

Hinduism is the oldest theology that is still practiced today. However, Dravidianism predates Hinduism by 1200–2200 years. Dravidianism was founded in the Indus Valley and was a pre-Vedic religion. It established "The Four Paths of Yoga" and the "Six-fold Desires"—these tenets are still the foundation of Hinduism. Hindus were among the "pagans" of the Bible.

There is some debate about whether Dravidianism established these practices. Still, there is little in any religion to which everyone agrees. Hinduism, like Judaism, claims to be original and something that predates our time. However, based on my research, Dravidianism wins as the founder of Yoga and the Six Desires, as well as "original" theology.

These treasured philosophies are:

The Four Paths of Yoga
1. Karma Yoga—Yoga of Action
2. Bhakti Yoga—Path of Devotion or Divine Love
3. Raja Yoga—Science of Physical and Mental Control
4. Jnana Yoga—Yoga of Knowledge and Wisdom

The Six-Fold Desires:
1. Tranquility / Right
2. Training / Wisdom
3. Withdrawal / Might
4. Forbearance / Harvest
5. Faith / Peace
6. Focus / Love

Followers of Dravidianism believed in a God that was a guardian of all, and they also had a Mother Goddess. She was known by many names, such as Parvati, Amman, or Mariamman (Mother Mari). She was the Goddess of strength, power, fertility, love, and devotion.

She was born to a virgin and was the mother of all of humanity. Archeologists in India discovered drawings and figurines of the Goddess that were carbon-dated to around 20,000 B.C.E.

Dravidianism spawned the Vedas, the oldest known religious texts written between 1500 and 1000 B.C.E. The Vedas added rituals, priests, temples, and rules to the previously only verbal belief system. The Vedas are the holy texts that led to Hinduism, Buddhism, Jainism, Taoism, and Sikhism. Hinduism purports the Vedas are divine wisdom heard by humans but not made by humans. Buddhists and Jains do not believe in the divinity of the Vedas but view them as more of a guide map.

Dharma is the core philosophy of the Eastern religions. Dharma does not easily translate into Western faiths. My summation would be that it is a set of religious, cosmic, and moral laws instructing how to transcend the ego and reach enlightenment. The meaning and context of dharma evolved over the millennia and varied slightly across the Indian religions. It is the Vedic path to righteousness.

Dharma means "practice, customary observance or prescribed conduct, duty, virtue, morality, religion, religious merit, good works, according to right or rule, rightly, justly, according to the nature of anything." (William, 2013)

The Vedas teach and expand on dharma, showing the correct way of living. The opposite of dharma is adharma, which means unnatural, immoral, or unlawful.

One of the Vedas, the Katha Upanishad, says,

> *"The goal, which all Vedas declare, which all austerities aim at, and which humans desire when they live a life of continence, I will tell you briefly it's Aum." (Sastri, 1928)*

"Aum" or "Om" is a declaration of the divine, a cosmic sound or mystical syllable said to be the essence of breath, life, and everything that exists. The Vedas teach that to reach Om, one must live a life of self-restraint, temperance, and moderation.

I first experienced "Om" when I was 27 and went to a yoga class with a girlfriend. She and the rest of the group were middle-aged, but I had heard good things about yoga and wanted to try it. I was always flexible, so the stretches and poses did not faze me.

But as the older participants pushed through their poses, things happened. The grunts turned into farts, and deep breaths turned into snores. I lay there with tears flowing down my cheeks. I was turning purple, nearly breaking a rib, holding in belly-busting laughter, and the only way I could express it was through tears. I bit my lip so I did not crack a smile. Noxious gases started flowing my way. I stuck my face inside my t-shirt to hinder the smells. Under the circumstances, the struggle to stay silent for an hour prevented any focus or relaxation.

We gathered around the instructor in a semi-circle when the session was over. She clicked her fingers, which had cymbals at the ends, and the sound brought everything into focus. Although, for me, it was more like a school bell, jolting me into the present and out of the daze of sweat, noxious fumes, and the sounds of bodily functions.

The instructor asked us to stay silent or join her in reciting the "Om." We sat with our legs crossed, and I put my thumb and index finger together like the rest of the group. I closed my eyes, and the "Om" started. On the second "Om," the man beside me, guilty of gas and snoring, let out a giant burp.

That was it! I burst out laughing. I had held that laughter in for an hour; that was the icing on the cake!

When I realized there was no way I could stop laughing, I wiped the tears from my face, gathered my towel and belongings, apologized to the group, and promptly exited the room. I stood outside, laughing, smoking a cigarette, but fearing my friend's judgment.

About five minutes later, she came out and gave me a smile that tried to hide her embarrassment and control her overwhelming desire to scold me. When I saw her, I again erupted in laughter and apologized profusely. I thanked her for the invite and agreed that yoga was not my thing. I figured that even if I found a younger group who did not have all the ailments of aging, I could not remain silent for an hour. No jokes or sarcastic remarks? For me, it was something I tried but did not enjoy.

Learning that "Om" is trying to mimic the sacred sound of the Universe or God changed everything for me. My Christian upbringing taught me it was cultish or demonic. But the peace that surrounded the people reciting it contradicted that. It was no longer a funny sound that mimicked all the other bodily noises I heard that day. It was divine.

Without religious prejudice or fear of the unknown, I took a deep breath, exhaled with a hum, and felt peace. The beauty of the syllable enveloped me like a warm blanket. It felt ancient but new, universal, and timeless. It made me feel connected when so much made me feel isolated. Understanding the meaning of the mantra and experiencing the breathing technique invoked deep emotions and a genuine connection.

The first time I was part of a large group, and we did the Om in chorus, it overcame me with peace and love. Tears uncontrollably flowed down my cheeks. Strangely, I was not crying; it was like a joyful soul cleansing. People were coming together peacefully, breathing and releasing positive energy in unison. It was the definition of a sacred moment. For me and the billions of followers of the Eastern philosophies, Om is an instant connection to the present and God.

Twenty years after my first yoga disaster, my daily practice is a source of my sanity and physical strength. Right before quitting my last sales job, I went to a yoga session out of desperation. I was so stressed that I feared if I did not exert some energy and be quiet for an hour, I might explode—and there was no good coming from that.

As I stretched and kept my balance, my mind was forced into the present and away from mentally recycling my work grievances and frustrations. To avoid falling, one must concentrate. And I was not about to add embarrassment to the list of stresses that day. The instructor approached me after the class and asked me what I thought of the session and how I felt. I told her she saved a life—mine or my boss's.

Speaking of not killing people…Karma is fundamental to Eastern philosophies. Karma is the law of action. It aligns with Sir Isaac Newton's third law, "For every action, there is an equal and opposite reaction." Karma is about morals, not physics, but both are based on the laws of nature and address the results of energy. Hindus believe that if you are righteous in this life, your next life will be better. If you cause harm and do evil, in the next life, you will be born into a life deserving of those actions.

The Vedic texts state this about Karma: "Happiness comes due to good actions, suffering results from evil actions, by actions, all things are obtained, by inaction, nothing whatsoever is enjoyed. If one's action bore no fruit, then everything would be of no avail, if the world worked from fate alone, it would be neutralized." (Mahabharata)

"As a man himself sows, so he himself reaps; no man inherits the good or evil act of another man. The fruits of the same quality as the action." ~ Mahabharata, xii.291.22

One issue with Hinduism is the Caste system is intertwined with Karma. This system imposes harsh judgments based on our understanding of reincarnation. It does not allow for expansion beyond one's (perceived) fate of birth or plight. Caste systems are now being viewed as old-fashioned and are slowly being phased out, but as humans, we are always looking for ways to prove that God loves us the most. The ego creeps in and permeates our societies and religions, even when the doctrine vehemently warns against it.

Hindus do not believe there is a singular path to God because God surpasses all understanding. They do not view other religions as greater or lesser, right or wrong, simply different. Their belief system is complex and diverse, but it can be called henotheistic (worshiping one god without denying the existence of other gods). However, that is an oversimplification of such an encompassing and intricate religion.

Hinduism embraces all belief systems, and its followers encompass all the theories, such as monotheists, polytheists, agnostics, Gnostics, pantheists, and even atheists. Most Hindus believe everyone has an Atman, the eternal spirit or soul—the authentic "self." They aim to grow into oneness with our Atman and realize that we are one with God. How you get there is personal and not up for judgment.

Durga is the Hindu Goddess, and they believe she created humanity—everything exists because of her. Equality is fundamental to Hinduism, so Shiva, Vishnu, and Krishna are also prominent and considered manifestations of each other: different forms bring unique gifts, undivided and equal.

I love that they leave the path open to the individual. Hinduism is beautiful because it is accommodating and diplomatic, which ensures harmony. Emphasis is not on the beliefs but on the believer's actions. Their lack of commitment to dogma and no feelings of superiority influences the entire faith. They rest in the fact that "no one really knows."

The "Nasadiya Sukta," the Hymn of Creation in the Rg Veda:

> *But, after all, who knows, and who can say*
> *Whence it all came, and how creation happened?*
> *The Devas (minor gods) themselves are later than creation,*
> *so who knows truly whence it has arisen?*
> *Whence all creation had its origin,*
> *he, whether he fashioned it or whether he did not,*
> *he, who surveys it all from highest Heaven,*
> *he knows-or maybe even he does not know. (Vedas, 2018)*

From a Christian mentality, Hinduism was hard to grasp. If you Google "How many gods are in Hinduism?" The answer is "330 million." The results made me laugh aloud, and I realized why I was chasing my tail. I was thinking as a Christian and looking for a single and prominent deity. Each time I thought I found the "top god," it said, "but there's also…who is considered an equal."

Within their philosophy of the god or gods, there is no competition. It is such a beautiful thing, albeit from a Christian mindset; it was mind-boggling initially. The goal is enlightenment, so whichever "God" gets you there is accepted and revered. Whether it is one god or 330 million, Hindus believe in the oneness of them all. Schisms occur over the importance of deities and dogma and how to implement those in your life.

"According as one acts, so does he become. One becomes virtuous by virtuous action, bad by bad action"
~ (Brihadaranyaka Upanishad 4.4.5)

Like the Abrahamic religions, the bull is divine and associated with the Hindu gods. They believe cows are a representation of motherhood and Mother Earth. They consider them benevolent because they give more than they take. Hindus consider cows to be a manifestation of all 330 million gods. Because they are holy, everything that comes from a cow is holy. Vedics use the dung in sacred fires and fertilizers. They use the urine as a disinfectant for humans (treating illnesses, removing hard minerals, and as a spermicide) and household cleaning.

Cleaning with urine is a little much for me.

The Hindus are responsible for some of the most significant architectural wonders of the ancient world. Over the millennia and throughout the East, they built thousands of temples that dot the world's landscape. Angkor Wat is the most extensive temple complex in the world, covering over 390 square miles or over 1000 square kilometers. The second largest are the temples at Karnak, Egypt, which are less than half the size of Angkor. It is also the biggest pre-industrial complex in the world, supporting more than a million people before being abandoned around the 13th century and eventually transitioning to a Buddhist site.

Islam reached the Indus Valley (now, Pakistan to northeast Afghanistan to northwestern India) through trade routes in the seventh century but did not gain prominence until the Muslim conquests in the 12th century. From the 12th to the 15th centuries, Hindus were tortured and forced to convert to Islam. Because of the religious persecution, Buddhism in the area also dramatically declined during the same period.

Not to be upstaged in the realm of religious torture, in the 15th century, the (Christian) Inquisitions started. The Goa Inquisition was truly brutal and lasted for almost 300 years. Christian Historian Dr. T.

R. de Souza described the atrocities that occurred from the 15th to the 18th century:

> A particularly grave abuse was practiced in Goa in the form of 'mass baptism' and what went before it. The Jesuits staged an annual mass baptism on the Feast of the Conversion of St. Paul (January 25), and in order to secure as many neophytes as possible, a few days before the ceremony the Jesuits would go through the streets of the Hindu quarter in pairs, accompanied by their Negro slaves, whom they would urge to seize the Hindus. When the Blacks caught a fugitive, they would smear his lips with a piece of beef, making him an 'untouchable' among his people. Conversion to Christianity was then his only option. (DeSouza, 1975)

Catholic Priest Diogo de Boarda and his advisor, Vicar General Miguel Vaz, devised a 41-point plan for torturing Hindus. Dr. De Souza further elaborated on the barbarity of the Inquisition:

> The screams of agony of the victims (men, women, and children) could be heard in the streets, in the stillness of the night, as they were brutally interrogated, flogged, and slowly dismembered in front of their relatives. Eyelids were sliced off, and extremities were amputated carefully, a person could remain conscious even though the only thing that remained was his torso and head.
>
> They forced anyone over the age of fifteen to convert to Christianity, or they would incur the same treatment. Women were raped, tortured, and burned alive; children were kidnapped and indoctrinated. They outlawed Hindu marriage customs and destroyed over 300 Hindu temples. (DeSouza, 1975)

The archbishop at the time and the one responsible for overseeing the area said, "The post of Inquiry Commission in Goa is regarded as holy."

The Hindu's use of idols and iconography fueled the Catholic's justification for holy war. As a Protestant, I find that especially ironic.

Krishna has similarities with Jesus, such as immaculate conception, a father "God," healing, and exorcism powers. Both were called Savior and are the second seat in a Holy Trinity. A king tried to kill both when they were infants. They viewed themselves as servants, and they both washed people's feet. They focused on love above the mortal law and showed us the unconditional love of God.

All the belief systems, including mythologies, have things that set their holy men apart from the rest of society: a miraculous birth, righteousness in the face of adversity, and an attitude of servitude. They defy the "norm," rebuke unbridled power and injustice, and do it all in the name of a Higher Power. These are the reasons their message resonates and why they accumulate followers. They are "special" people who inspire us to be more contemplative. These "Lords" come in forms familiar to us and speak to each of us in a way we understand.

Anyone claiming that one person, in one language, culture, and era, could suit all of humanity, satisfying all spiritual needs and questions, denies the diversity in which we were created. It is limited and egotistical thinking, and exactly why so many people are murdered.

The goal of Hinduism is the complete awareness and acceptance of oneness with God and all of existence. This knowledge brings detachment from material things, eliminating expectations, and the recognition of the self through releasing selfishness. Their religious practices and icons are to help people find divinity and, therefore, bliss in their everyday lives.

I saw nothing "evil" about the tenets of this ancient sacred philosophy. On the contrary, the Upanishads are an excellent source of wisdom and direction when we strive to become better people. Another path with the same sentiments leads us all to a life of less ego and more love.

"From untruth lead us to Truth. From darkness lead us to Light. From death lead us to immortality. Om Peace, Peace, Peace."
Brihadaranyaka Upanishad (1.3.28)

Chapter 56: Judaism's Prequel

All major religions have their roots in ancient tribal ideologies. The first monotheistic, organized religion was Zoroastrianism. In a world of polytheism, Zoroaster (aka Zarathustra) detailed one supreme God: Ahura Mazda, "The Wise Lord." Ahura Mazda was the ultimate source of wisdom and benevolence and aided all the righteous. But he was not omnipotent.

Before Zoroaster, Ahura Mazda was known as a spirit. Zoroastrianism spread throughout the ancient world and formalized Ahura Mazda as the Supreme Being. There is no agreement on when Zoroaster lived. Theories range from 6300 to 522 B.C.E., But Zoroastrianism entered the written historical record in the sixth century B.C.E. It was the official religion of the ancient Persian king and queen. It lost its prominence during the Muslim conquests in the seventh century C.E. In 2003, UNESCO declared and celebrated 3000 years of the Zoroastrian culture.

Zoroaster was 30 years old and taking Haoma (a plant used for spiritual connection, possibly ephedra, aka Soma) for a sacred ritual. He saw a radiant Being at the river who revealed the truth of Ahura Mazda and Angra Mainyu. The message altered his life, and he vowed to spread the word.

The Zoroastrian tenets are:

Good thoughts, good words, good deeds.

There is only one path, and that is the path of Truth.

Do the right thing because it is the right thing to do, and then all beneficial rewards will come to you. (Ghosn, 2018)

It was the first religion to believe in dualism: good vs. evil, Heaven and Hell. Ahura Mazda was good, and his antithesis and nemesis was Angra Mainyu—or as we now call them, God and Satan. Ahura Mazda was the creator, and Angra Mainyu was the destroyer. Zoroastrianism taught that Ahura Mazda was superior and would ultimately win the spiritual battle.

Zoroastrianism gave us monotheism, free will, Heaven and Hell, and messianic and apocalyptic prophecies. Zoroaster taught a Savior would return for the soul's last judgment—living and dead. The dead would rise out of their graves and be judged accordingly. Souls and bodies reunited to serve eternity according to their judgment.

Zoroaster and his followers were known as magicians, astrologers, and wizards. They were known as magi or wise men for over a thousand years. They were physicians and healers and were widely respected for putting the needs of others ahead of themselves. The three Wise Men detailed in the story of Jesus' birth were Zoroastrians. They predicted the birth and followed the star to find him (Matthew 2). Two Zoroastrians are mentioned in chapters 8 and 13 of Acts: Simon Magus (the singular of Magi) and Bar Jesus.

Zoroastrianism, in many ways, mirrors Christianity, so it was easy to understand, accept, and appreciate their doctrine. The differences between the two endeared me to the faith. First was their love of dogs. They saw dogs as sacred and stood against any mistreatment, as well as condemning the pervasive ritual of animal sacrifice. Second, they were considered the first ecological religion, teaching that our obligation was to protect the planet. Zoroaster emphasized we must make the world a better place through good words and deeds. Not in isolation, like a monastery.

As of 2011, they believe in priestly leadership roles for women unless they are menstruating, which they consider an "impure" time. Consequently, most women do not become full priests until after menopause, but at least there is a chance. No religion is perfect. They all have their inconsistencies and flaws; they are, after all, managed by humans.

Zoroaster emphasized personal responsibility, teaching that our free will gives us the choice of right or wrong. The doctrine states that it is up to us to accept the Divine Will or live in ignorance and chaos. The more "good thoughts, good words, and good actions" one does, the closer one becomes to the divine creator. They believed it was our choice, not a demand. But if we sought a partnership with Ahura Mazda, the world would be better, and the afterlife would reflect our goodness.

Zoroaster started the ten percent tithe, wore sacred undergarments like the Mormons, and believed everyone's head should be covered: men, women, and children. Ahura Mazda was the leader of a triad; Mithra and Anahita joined him. Mithra was the judge and protector of Truth. Anahita was the Goddess of fertility and health. The triad or trinity is documented throughout religious history and is not unique to Christianity.

Chapter 57: Jainism

Jainism is the only religion with no wars fought in its name. The Jain's core beliefs center on non-violence and non-absolutism— nothing is black and white. They are only absolute about their regard for all of life. With only four million followers, they are no longer a major religion. But I wanted to highlight them because of their dogma of non-violence, and Jainism was the foundation of Buddhism.

Jains believe one reaches salvation through the Five Great Vows:

1. Ahimsā (Non-violence)
2. Satya (Truth)
3. Asteya (Non-stealing)
4. Brahmacharya (Chastity)
5. Aparigraha (Non-possession)

Jainism can be traced to the ninth century B.C.E., but most claim it started in the sixth century B.C.E. It is a non-theistic belief system, believing the Universe is eternal. We are part of a complex system managed by Karma and reincarnation.

Jains believe each of us has a perfect soul, and our souls and everything in the Universe have always existed. They believe everything exists and functions through the laws of nature, Karma, and reincarnation, not because of a deity.

Jains believe their religion is eternal, and their first spiritual teacher lived 85,000 years ago. They assert he was Krishna's cousin—albeit thousands of years apart. They do not pray or worship gods, but their religious leaders, Tirthankaras, are their role models. That is who they strive to emulate. The three tenets of Jainism are the right knowledge, the right vision, and the right conduct.

Their commitment to non-violence endeared me to this religion. Jains believed in microorganisms long before science discovered them. To ensure they do no harm, even to invisible creatures, they filter their water and sweep the ground before them as they walk, not to step on or kill anything.

Their regard and respect for all life forms changed my life. Before studying Jainism, I killed any bugs that came near, especially ants, spiders, and bees. Now, I understand that even those creatures (that irritate or scare me) are also just trying to get through their day. They're looking for food, a safe place to sleep, or a mate, and just because our paths crossed, it should not mean they must die.

Bees always terrified me because I am allergic, but now I understand their value and significance to our existence. Without their pollination, one-third of our food supply would be gone within six months. The Jain philosophy also helped me to realize that these insects are not looking to kill me, so I should not be concerned with killing them. I now look at these creatures with a new respect and gratitude as I watch them live their lives and fulfill their purpose.

Like other Indian religions, Jainism practices yoga and believes in Karma. But unlike Hinduism, Jains believe actions, deeds, thoughts, and emotions affect Karma. They assert we must conquer anger with forgiveness, pride with humility, deceit with honesty, and greed with contentment. If the mind is not controlled and hostile emotions tamed, the consequences can lead to violence, which must be avoided at all costs. Meditation is fundamental to Jainism and is their path to purity.

Jainism believes that every soul has the potential for divinity, infinite knowledge, power, perception, and bliss. Understanding this leads to empathy and kindness toward all living creatures. This path of non-judgment acknowledges that every soul is the architect of their life and on their karmic path, both now and in the hereafter.

Because the goal is peace, understanding and accepting that others have different beliefs and convictions leads to tolerance, elimination of prejudices, and compromise. The Jain doctrine, Syādvāda, teaches that everything is based on our perception and how we view it. To make sure they remain open-minded, they look at every proposition from these seven standpoints:

1. In some ways, it is.
2. In some ways, it is not.
3. In some ways, it is, and it is not.
4. In some ways, it is, and it is indescribable.
5. In some ways, it is not, and it is indescribable.
6. In some ways, it is, it is not, and it is indescribable.
7. In some ways, it is indescribable.

They often use the tree as an example because some may see it as stationary, but from the perspective of space, it is moving with the planet. Perspective is everything, and Jains realized that thousands of years ago. Seeing a faith that tries to make the world more peaceful is beautiful.

Jains do not pray to a Higher Power but use mediation to maintain their system of peace and openness. During meditation, Jains focus on the Four Virtues:

1. Peace, love, and friendship to all.
2. Appreciation, respect, and delight for the achievements of others.
3. Compassion to souls who are suffering.
4. Equanimity and tolerance in dealing with other's thoughts, words, and actions.

Like all Faiths, Jainism is not perfect. Their texts are full of misogyny. They believe menstrual blood kills microorganisms, making female bodies "more violent" than men's. Hence, they think women have not evolved to the highest form like men. However, one of their Tirthankaras was a woman—one out of 24.

All the Eastern ideologies share philosophies. Buddhist texts state that the Jains were the first Buddhists, and Buddha encouraged them to keep their Jain traditions. The influence between the two is apparent.

One of the holiest symbols throughout the Eastern philosophies was the swastika. Before its high jacking by the Nazi party in the 1930s, the swastika was a symbol of good luck and well-being. Archeologists found swastikas all over the world, dating back to 10,000 B.C.E.

The word "swastika" originates from the Sanskrit word "swasti" and is used often in the Vedas. Its Vedic meaning is: "well, good, auspicious, luck, success, prosperity." It is associated with the dharma wheel and symbolizes the eternal cycle. In Hinduism, when written clockwise, it represents the Sun; when written counterclockwise, it means the night. In Buddhism, it is the footprints of Buddha. And in Jainism, it is their seventh Tirthankara. In ancient Greece, it was a symbol linking heaven and earth. To the Romans, it meant "life of life."

But today, it is a symbol of hate, racism, and genocide. The evolution of the swastika from good luck to hate is a perfect example of what we do to God. We take something beautiful and use it to control and manipulate the masses to achieve greater power. We take holy symbols and use them to justify atrocities, turning peace into war, good luck into tragedy, and fortune into fatalities.

Chapter 58: Buddhism

Many Buddhists argue Buddhism is a philosophy, not a religion. Still, I could not discuss the top belief systems without including it. Buddhism was founded around 563 B.C.E. by Siddhartha Gautama or the Buddha. Because of communist regimes and the fear of reprisal, it is challenging to get an accurate number, but the total varies between 230 million and nearly 1.7 billion followers. (Pew Research Center, 2012) People often practice Buddhism alongside other faiths and philosophies, as only a lack of knowledge about the ideology would cause one to view it as an infringement or competition with different belief systems.

Buddhism's faith is in the Three Gems:

Buddha (the teacher)
Dharma (the teachings)
Sangha (the community)

Someone who "takes refuge in the triple gems" commits to a clear mind, open heart, and a life of integrity, respect, and compassion. The term "refuge" means "safe place." Buddhists find security in the wisdom of Buddha's teachings, the path of an awakened life, and the interconnectedness of all of us.

Buddhism does not have any set of religious texts or dogma, but it offers guidelines for navigating the philosophy. This set of instructions is in the Four Noble Truths and Noble Eightfold Path.

The Four Noble Truths:

1. Life is Suffering: pain, frustration, agitation, jealousy
2. The Origin of Suffering is ignorance, selfishness, craving
3. The Cessation of Suffering, or perfect peace, can be achieved through the elimination of ignorance, selfishness and craving
4. The Path to extinguish ignorance, selfishness and craving is the Eightfold Path

The Noble Eightfold Path

1. **Right Views**-to keep ourselves free from prejudice, superstition, and delusion and to see the true nature of life.
2. **Right Thoughts**-to turn away from the evils of this world and to direct our minds towards righteousness.
3. **Right Speech**-to refrain from pointless and harmful talk, to speak kindly and courteously to all.
4. **Right Conduct**-to see that our deeds are peaceful, benevolent, compassionate, and pure; to live the Teaching of the Buddha daily.
5. **Right Livelihood**-to earn our living in such a way as to entail no evil consequences.
6. **Right Effort**-to direct our efforts incessantly to the overcoming of ignorance and selfish desires.
7. **Right Mindfulness**-to cherish good and pure thoughts for all that we say and do arise from our thoughts.
8. **Right Meditation**-to concentrate our will on the Buddha, His Life, and His Teaching. (Cirlea, 2021)

Meditation is the root of Eastern Religions. Some practices include clearing your mind, citing mantras, or focusing on positive things. The "Four Immeasurables" is a mantra central to Buddhist meditation.

1. May all beings enjoy happiness and the root of happiness.
2. May we be free from suffering and the root of suffering.
3. May we never be separated from the great happiness devoid of suffering.
4. May we dwell in the great equanimity, free from passion, aggression, and prejudice. (Chodron, 2017)

Buddhists do not believe in an Eternal Soul, or, as the Eastern Religions call it, the "Self." Buddhism teaches that attachment to anything causes suffering. Buddha was asked about the soul and would not answer. His disciple asked why he would not respond. Buddha explained that any answer he gave would cause suffering, so it was better to say nothing.

Buddhists believe the concept of the soul is an attachment to our immortality and the afterlife. We hope to see our loved ones again, to see our God, and to be proven good or bad. Those attachments are ego-based and will ultimately cause us suffering.

Buddhism asserts that everything in the universe lives and dies and changes forms, so they do not accept the concept of an eternal soul that does not change. However, if you think otherwise, in classic Eastern religious tradition, that is OK.

This theory gave me pause. My soul was always the focus of everything.

Was it clean and worthy, or was it dirty and undeserving?

Would it burn for eternity in Hell or sit with God in Heaven?

Each Sunday, it was like the pastor was issuing report cards on how healthy our souls were that week. As Buddha said, it was genuinely consumptive.

If we no longer believed in an "eternal soul," how different would our lives be? My mother would not have disowned me. The LGBTQ+ community would not be told they are going to Hell. And dying might not be so scary.

Without belief in a soul, one might assume there would be immorality and everyone running amok, hurting others. It is a premise the Church has always claimed. But that's where karma offers balance. There are always consequences. And most people do not enjoy causing harm.

Buddhism tries to bring its practitioners to the ultimate present moment. Do not focus on tomorrow or especially the next life. Do not look back at yesterday, particularly if it causes shame and regret. Focus on right now, right this minute, and breathe.

The Bible mentions meditation often, and Christian leaders warn against Eastern meditation. They claim opening your mind could let evil spirits in, and doing any of their "chants" could summon demons. That assertion is ignorant. Not understanding the mantras and assigning fear to them is even more ignorant. Concentrating on peace, love, and material detachment will never be wrong. A lack of knowledge breeds fear. Instilling the notion of evil is to keep Christians scared and blinded to the beauty of other traditions, faiths, and philosophies.

It is the ego exemplified when we claim we know everything and dismiss anything we do not understand. It is entirely egotistical to think our way is the best, and there is no need to learn anything else. Most people do not do this with any other aspect of their lives. Most people strive to learn new things, experience new cultures, and learn new ways of doing things. But with religions, we are told to close our eyes, ears, hearts, and minds to any other faiths, their followers, and their knowledge. This mentality keeps people loyal to their religions but divided as people and at war as a society.

There are a lot of similarities between the Buddhist traditions and the Catholic Church. Buddhism has mala beads; Catholicism has the rosary. They both ring bells at the beginning and end of their rituals. They use iconography and holy water. The Christian tradition of praying with your palms together is Buddhism's greeting and symbol of prayer. The Catholic and Buddhist hierarchical system within the clergy and their monasticism mimic each other down to the way they dress. Siddhartha Gautama was conceived after his mother, Maya, received a message from a supernatural spirit, like Christian's Mary, receiving the news of her pregnancy from the angel Gabriel. But Buddhism is over 800 years older than Catholicism.

All religions of notoriety gained prominence because someone in authority and power became a follower. Buddhism is no different, and since political power helped spread the philosophy, it was influential and intertwined with the government. When politics and religions collide, wars and destruction ensue.

And, also like the Catholic Church, Buddhism has had its share of sex scandals. The power and the sexual repression that comes with some religions are a recipe for disaster. This combination has made monsters out of men and turned children into the sacrificial lambs of doctrine and indecency.

To claim that God requires celibacy is like being given a gift, the best gift of all, and then being told you are evil if you play with it. Doctrine demands you give up innate pleasure to prove your faith and use it to measure your righteousness.

Now, keep in mind, everything in moderation, or you will break it! But instead of giving up our instincts of companionship and love, we should learn to give up our hate and fear. Our righteousness should not be measured in what we have forsaken but in how much hope, kindness, and love we have given.

> We can reject everything else: religion, ideology, all received wisdom. But we cannot escape the necessity of love and compassion. This, then, is my true religion, my simple faith. In this sense, there is no need for Temple or Church, for Mosque or Synagogue, no need for complicated philosophy, doctrine, or dogma. Our own heart, our own mind, is the Temple.
> The doctrine is compassion. Love for others and respect for their rights and dignity, no matter who or what they are: ultimately these are all we need. So long as we practice these in our daily lives, then no matter if we are learned or unlearned, whether we believe in Buddha or God, or follow some other religion or none,

if we have compassion for others and conduct ourselves with restraint out of a sense of responsibility, there is no doubt we will be happy. ~ Dalai Lama XIV.

Chapter 59: Islam

Next on the historical timeline is Christianity, but since that is covered in all the earlier sections, let's move on to Islam. This is such a sensitive topic. There is so much focus on the radical sects of Islam and so little information about why it has 1.8 billion followers.

Muhammad Ali said,

> The word 'Islam' means 'peace.' The word 'Muslim' means 'one who surrenders to God.' But the press makes us seem like haters. I can assure you, if Muslims were as frightening and destructive as the media leads us to believe, then I could not address this topic.

Enver Masud, the founder of The Wisdom Fund and the recipient of the 2002 Gold Award from the South African Human Rights Foundation, describes the essence of Islam and its core beliefs and edicts. His description is the perfect summation of why Islam has so many devotees.

The Truth About Islam:

> Islam means "submission to the Will of God." In its ethical sense, Islam signifies "striving after the ideal." A Muslim is one who submits to the will of God. "Islam" and "Muslim" derive from the same word as the Arabic for "peace." The traditional

Muslim greeting is "Peace be unto you."

Islam offers hope for salvation to the righteous and God-fearing of all religions. Muslims believe in the divine Revelations of many prophets including Abraham, Moses, Jesus, Muhammad, but do not believe that God assumed human form. The Qur'an, Muslims believe, is God's word and Final Revelation to The Prophet Muhammad. Revealed over a period of 23 years, the Qur'an was compiled and distributed to distant lands within 25 years of The Prophet's death in 632 C.E. This is the only Qur'an recognized by Muslims.

Comprising laws, moral precepts, and narratives, the Quran's timeless text remains an inspiration and guide for over one-fifth of humanity. Together with the Qur'an, the epitome of classical Arabic, Muslims' lives are guided by the examples and sayings of The Prophet. Thousands of sayings have been attributed to The Prophet. Some are accepted as authentic; some traced to The Prophet's companions; some are the subject of debate. Some examples:

"The first thing created by God was the Intellect."

"The most excellent Jihad is that for the conquest of self."

"The ink of the scholar is more holy than the blood of the martyr."

"One learned man is harder on the Devil than a thousand ignorant worshipers,"

"Riches are not from an abundance of worldly goods, but from a contented mind."

"Reflect upon God's creation but not upon His nature or else you will perish."

"He who wishes to enter Paradise at the best door must please his mother and father."

"No man is a true believer unless he desires for his brother that which he desires for himself."

"When the bier of anyone passes by you, whether Jew, Christian, or Muslim, rise to your feet."

"The thing which is lawful, but disliked by God, is divorce."

"Modesty and chastity are parts of the Faith."

"Heaven lies at the feet of mothers."

"Women are the twin-halves of men."

"Actions will be judged according to intentions."

"That which is lawful is clear, and that which is unlawful likewise, but there are certain doubtful things between the two from which it's well to abstain."

"The proof of a Muslim's sincerity is that he pays no attention to that which is not his business."

"That person is nearest to God, who pardons... him who would have injured him."

"... yield obedience to my successor, although he may be an Abyssinian slave."

"Assist any person oppressed, whether Muslim or non-Muslim."

"The creation is like God's family... the most beloved unto God is the person who does good to God's family."

Islamic law is based upon the Qur'an, examples, and sayings of The Prophet, consensus among the learned, analogical deduction, and individual reasoning. Islamic society comes closer than any other society to the ideal democracy. All persons are equal before God; goodness is the only criterion of worth. There is no priesthood in Islam; even a child, with greater knowledge of the Qur'an than his elders, may lead them in prayer. To become a Muslim, one need only profess, "There is no god but God; Muhammad is the Messenger of God." (Masud, 1995)

Most people would find minor faults in Masud's summation. Not so scary, right? Our tribal brains turn ignorance into fear. The words are different, but the message is like that of the other religions. Understanding invokes empathy; empathy invokes oneness. When we realize we are all searching for the same thing, it turns aggression into collaboration, and knowledge replaces fear. The Qur'an mentions Jesus 25 times. Muhammad is only named five times. "Allah" is "God" in Arabic. Judaism, Christianity, and Islam all worship the same God—the God of Abraham.

Islam follows the Six Articles of Faith:

1. Belief in Allah, The Only God
2. Belief in the Angels
3. Belief in Holy Books (Qur'an)
4. Belief in the Prophets
5. Belief in the Day of Judgment
6. Belief in God's predestination

We get hung up on our differences and scream "heretic" instead of allowing variations. Jews and Muslims acknowledge Jesus as a prophet but deny that he is the son of God. Remember, Jesus never claimed divinity. This makes the divide between these religions about who takes Jesus' words more seriously. Crazy, right?

Muslims assert that the worship of the Holy Trinity is polytheistic, and the God of Abraham is monotheistic. So, while they revere Jesus in Islam, they did not believe that he was divine. They do not worship Muhammad either; they view him as the last of the messengers.

The differences between the two largest sects of Islam, the Shia and the Sunni, are like the differences between Catholics and Protestants. An example is Sunnis, like Protestants, who do not believe in iconography, and Shias love their symbolism like the Catholics.

Muslims believe everything is predetermined, so whatever happens, both good and bad, God controls it. Whatever happens is because God allowed it.

This offered a new perspective on how radical Islamics could warp this belief into terrorism. A twisted ideology would assert that if the bomb did not go off, God prohibited it; if it did, it was God's will. By turning the philosophy of "let go" into destruction and killing in the name of God, Islam is now feared around the world. The self-proclaimed "Religion of Peace" is viewed as the fanatical faith of death.

Steve Slocum, author of *Why Do They Hate Us: Making Peace with the Islamic World*, documents an essential edict in Islam that is ignored by the terrorists and unknown to the West:

> What set the Muslims apart from the Hebrews and the Christians was the strict prohibition against initiating conflict and the requirement to cease fighting the moment the enemy surrendered. Whereas Israel was commanded to take the land from its inhabitants and 'not leave alive anything that breathes.' And the Christians conquered most of the Middle East and large swaths of Europe and North Africa. (Slocum, 2018)

Another common misconception is that the women's head covering is oppressive. Mostly, the Hijab (head covering) and the Niqab (covering the head and face) are worn with a sense of pride by Muslim women. The Burka is the entire face and body covering. It is usually a sign of oppressive rulers. Still, those are a minority—although the media would lead us to believe differently. Most Muslim women only wear a head covering, and they do so for modesty, not submission.

What the West views as restrictive, Muslim women see as freedom—freedom from societal concepts of beauty, makeup, and fashion expectations, the leers of men, and freedom from being objectified. Many times, I wished I could throw on a niqab and hide from the world. But in today's climate, it would have the opposite effect, drawing more attention, judgment, and ridicule.

Most would find it surprising and ironic that Muhammad could be considered the world's first feminist. His treatment of women was far more progressive than his era. His edicts dramatically improved the status of women in the seventh century.

Islam prizes knowledge and made significant contributions to science and education. Al-Zaytunah in Tunis and Al-Azhar in Cairo are the oldest universities in the modern world, dating back over a thousand years. The graduation cap and gown originated at Al-Azhar University. Muslims introduced algebra and trigonometry, which could be good or bad depending on who you are.

We can also credit Islam with founding the first hospitals. A Muslim invented the first bone saw, the syringe, a surgical hook and needle for closing incisions, and the scalpel. These are just some ways Islam improved our lives. Islam contributed many important things, but today, only the negative views are presented.

For this chapter, I took 40 pages of notes, single-spaced, 11-point-font of almost 29,000 words. I researched the good and the bad. At times, I "got it." I understood why this faith resonates with so many. And sometimes, I became enraged, and I felt like my head would explode. I said aloud, "How can anyone follow this? How could anyone believe this is a peaceful religion? How does this faith invoke more love?"

I saw the faults and why things are the way they are. It is easy to see where terrorists get their justification. There are significant issues regarding the treatment of women in Islam.

And then it occurred to me: While I was then focused on Islam, I wrote over 65,000 words on how, why, and when Christianity did the same things. I wrote an entire book about it!

I was enraged over Islamic views on slavery, using the "sword" to solve issues, and frankly, never evolving past its inception. But most of the commands and edicts are also biblical. The biblical laws about women, slavery, and conquering other tribes are just as grotesque in the Qur'an. The messengers are only different. Only focusing on the messengers creates an us-v-them mentality. We fight over who is right when they say the same things.

At one point, I was so confused and distraught over what I found I phoned a friend. I needed to speak to a Muslim woman and see why she was a believer. I got straight to the point and asked her why she loved her religion. Her answer was, "It's peaceful. The prayers bring me peace and make me feel love and warmth in my soul."

She talked about how she loved the charity aspect of Islam and told me stories about giving to the poor and homeless. "Alms" is a tax demanded by the Qur'an, but unlike tithing in churches, they give it directly to the poor. It is calculated according to income status but is usually around 2.5%. My friend told me about her family feeding people before and after Ramadan and how it filled her with love and hope. She spoke about how the faith and holidays brought her family together and were some of her fondest childhood memories.

I asked her how she reconciled being a woman (a progressive woman at that!) and a Muslim. She was confused and told me the Qur'an held women in the highest of regards, and men were told to treat their wives well, even going as far as instructing husbands to kiss their wife's feet.

Then, I read her the verse:

> Men are in charge of women by [right of] what Allah has given one
> over the other and what they spend [for maintenance] from their
> wealth. So righteous women are devoutly obedient, guarding in [the
> husband's] absence what Allah would have them guard. But those
> [wives] from whom you fear arrogance-[first] advise them; [then if they
> persist], forsake them in bed; and [finally], strike them. But if they obey
> you [once more], seek no means against them. Indeed, Allah is ever
> Exalted and Grand. (4:34)

My girlfriend was as shocked as I was when I found the same sentiments throughout the Bible. She was adamant that something like that would never be part of her faith! She wondered if it was just something on the internet or if I had a fake Qur'an because she could not believe it would be there. My response was: "It's OK. Most Christians don't know that the Bible tells us to kill our children."

Just like most Christians, most Muslims are unaware of the texts saying anything other than peace, love, acceptance, and charity.

The significant difference between Judaism, Christianity, and Islam is that most of the hateful instructions for war and genocide found in the Bible are now widely disregarded. Broadly speaking, Judaism and Christianity have evolved beyond those proclamations, and their followers no longer recognize them. And, as of the publication of this book, historically, the amount of death and devastation committed by Jews and Christians far exceeds that of Muslims.

The critical problem is that one of the central tenets of Islam is that the texts are eternal and are never to be altered or abolished. It leaves the religion stuck in the seventh century, and while it was progressive then, it is now archaic. Like Christianity, there are progressive sects who use love as their guide to the Qur'an and common sense about ancient laws. And, like Christianity, these modern views have not taken hold in most of the leadership. Patience, perseverance, and love-centered doctrine will get us all where we should be, regardless of our religion.

Our tribal mentalities, which are sourced by our ego, always want us to pick sides. The ego says, Oh, My God! How/Why does that religion do that? I would never believe/do any of that!

Our ego wants us to find an enemy so we can look down on them and feel better about ourselves. These "enemies" vary. It could be your neighbor, co-worker, an organization, or religion. Whatever we focus on grows exponentially. Focusing on fears and how bad they are makes us more afraid and insecure. It results in irrational generalizations that lead to racism, xenophobia, and even death. The truth is, we are not better than "them." God does not love you, or "them," more. Unconditional love is unconditional love, regardless of the stipulations we add. Everyone is on their own journey and doing their best with what they have. We are all looking for the same thing: love.

I have met no one who claims their religion makes them want to do terrible things. People look for faith because they want something greater than themselves: to be a better person or just be able to sleep at night. It is our ego that turns good into evil.

Terrorism is subjective. Some people consider the United States a terrorist country. ISIS felt righteous in their quest. The Crusades and Inquisitions were supposedly doing Jesus' bidding. The attempted genocide of the Canaanites was "directed by God." The perpetrator believes every terrorist act to be a righteous cause. However, the recipients view it as a version of Hell. Ironically, if you ask extremists why they follow their religion, they will say that it brings them closer to "God" and teaches peace and love.

Except for the Jains, every faith is guilty of terrorism; it just was not called terrorism. Thousands of years of "holy wars" have terrorized billions of people. What was supposed to teach us how to be more loving killed millions in the name of a "loving God." It is insane.

There are many truths to be found in every religion. The ancient faiths taught me a history hidden from so many and brought me the divine Goddess. Hinduism taught me the diplomacy of beliefs and how the ancient directives are truly divine. Jainism taught me respect for all life, even those annoying and sometimes scary insects. Buddhism taught me meditation, being present, and detachment. As the foundation of my faith, Christianity showed me the love of God. And Islam taught me that freedom is subjective and true monotheism means only one "God."

Instead of focusing on our religious differences, we should only be held accountable for the person it helps us become. Whichever faith or philosophy makes you more loving is the right path for you. But the right way for you does not mean it is appropriate for everyone. We must accept that everyone is on their own path. We must respect and honor their commitment to love and peace—not use their journey as a source of division, hate, and war. We are all in this together, and the sooner we realize that the sooner we will live in love and peace.

Section IX: Science vs. God

"Science without religion is lame. Religion without science is blind."
~ Thomas Edison

Chapter 60: Can We Believe in Both?

The biggest misconception about science and God is they contradict each other and are mutually exclusive. Science and spirituality speak different languages—science attempts to understand the "natural" and religion, the "supernatural." I could quickly summarize this chapter in one word: ego.

As the earlier sections detailed, our ego divides us and, in doing so, ceases collaboration, expansion of knowledge, and, therefore, the advancement of humanity. Science and religion cease to understand each other when myth and logic meet.

Our universe is algorithmic, so we should assume that "God" is logical. However, religion prefers constructing a magician rather than an expert in logic and physics, whose design is shown across the universe.

Most of my childhood education in science was based solely on creationism. My science book only had four paragraphs with opposing theories; the Big Bang theory was one of them. I do not remember the other three, but they were listed as absurd hypotheses. Our science fairs were full of basic science tricks, like cleaning water through rocks or sucking an egg through a bottle. Some kids built models of the solar system, or in my case, hatched chickens—for which I won an award. At best, it was rudimentary.

One night, when I was 23, I could not sleep, so I was flipping through the TV channels. I came across a documentary on the Big Bang theory hosted by Tom Selleck. I watched because, if nothing else, he was easy on the eyes and had a soothing voice to put me to sleep.

Instead, I was on the edge of my seat, fascinated by what I was hearing. I learned that the Big Bang was a legitimate theory, not some insane hypothesis, and it made sense!

I realized that Christianity and science were essentially saying the same thing, albeit in different terms and for different reasons. But I could not understand how each side dismissed the other as useless babble while claiming a spontaneous start of our universe. It was as if they spoke different languages but were saying the same thing—one spiritually and one rationally.

The following day, I tried talking to my fiancé, Glenn, about it, but he looked at me like I was an idiot. It amazed him that I was not aware of the theories of evolution, and since he was a narcissist, he shamed me and called me stupid. But I was not. I was ignorant about science because creationists educated me. They taught me that aliens could not exist because God would not send his son to die more than once. One son + one planet with life = one crucifixion and resurrection. All these made sense to me, the 12-year-old, but not at 23.

For almost 1500 years, the Church believed we were the center of the Universe. In the second century, Claudius Ptolemy, a mathematician, astronomer, geographer, and astrologer, asserted that everything in our Universe revolved around the Earth. Western religious leaders liked the geocentric theory because they already believed in our ultimate supremacy. To them, the Ptolemaic system confirmed that God planned our existence, ensuring everything revolved around us. The ego is always self-centered.

In 1543, Nicolaus Copernicus developed a Heliocentric model, claiming our Solar System revolved around the Sun. It contradicted what the Church purported, so it did not gain traction. In 1611, the Roman Inquisition ruled that the Copernican theory was "foolish and absurd in philosophy, and formally heretical since it explicitly contradicts in many places the sense of Holy Scripture." (Graney, 2018)

In 1632, Galileo championed the Copernican theory in his book *The Dialogue*. The Pope took it personally, resulting in Galileo facing the Inquisition and being declared a heretic. He spent the rest of his life under house arrest. For over two hundred years, *The Dialogue* was forbidden. Instead of knowing better and doing better, historically, the church just forbids the information

No scriptures support the geocentric hypothesis. Stubbornly holding onto this belief was pure ego. No one would tell the Church that the Universe did not revolve around us! No one would ever change the "fact" that we are the center of everything! The smugness of the Church, the unwillingness to relinquish the ego, and the denial of progress laid down the gauntlet between Christianity and science.

"I do not feel obliged to believe that the same God who has endowed us with sense, reason, and intellect has intended us to forgo their use." ~ Galileo Galilei

Your religion and denomination within that religion generally dictate whether you believe in the validity of science. Pew Research (2020) claims The Assemblies of God, Baptists, Evangelicals, and Mormons have the most considerable disdain for science. Hindus, Buddhists, and Jews are the most accepting. The middle has Catholics, Lutherans, Methodists, and Muslims. Nearly 60% of people polled agree that there's a conflict between religion and science, but only 30% claim it is their religion—everyone else has a problem, not me.

In 2012, the United Methodist Church issued the following statement on their views of science:

> We recognize science as a legitimate interpretation of God's natural world. We affirm the validity of the claims of science in describing the natural world and in determining what is scientific. We preclude science from making authoritative claims about theological issues and theology from making authoritative

claims about scientific issues. We find that science's descriptions of cosmological, geological, and biological evolution are not in conflict with theology.

We recognize medical, technical, and scientific technologies as legitimate uses of God's natural world when such use enhances human life and enables all of God's children to develop their God-given creative potential without violating our ethical convictions about the relationship of humanity to the natural world. We reexamine our ethical convictions as our understanding of the natural world increases. We find that as science expands human understanding of the natural world, our understanding of the mysteries of God's creation and word are enhanced.

In acknowledging the important roles of Science and Technology, however, we also believe that theological understandings of human experience are crucial to a full understanding of the place of humanity in the Universe. Science and theology are complementary rather than mutually incompatible. We, therefore, encourage dialogue between the scientific and theological communities and seek the kind of participation that will enable humanity to sustain life on Earth and, by God's grace, increase the quality of our common lives together. (2016)

That says it all.

Chapter 61: Our Genesis

The main contention between religion and science is the origin of the Universe. Where you fall on the spectrum of believing in science coincides with what you think was our own genesis *(pun intended)*. More than any other religious sect, Protestants believe the Bible is the literal truth of our inception. A sizable portion of them home-school and are against higher education because they fear it causes people to leave religion. That fear is not baseless.

If the truth is hidden, ignored, or dismissed, when it becomes known, everything else is questioned, doubted, and then disregarded. I know. I have been there. But that is just a section of Protestants; many people of faith accept evolution and are open to the discoveries of science.

Theodosius Dobzhansky, a geneticist and evolutionary biologist, stated there could be a synthesis between religion and science:

> I am a creationist and an evolutionist. Evolution is God's, or Nature's, method of creation. Creation is not an event that happened in 4004 B.C.E.; it is a process that began some 10 billion years ago and is still under way...Does the evolutionary doctrine clash with religious faith? It does not. It is a blunder to mistake the Holy Scriptures for elementary textbooks of astronomy, geology, biology, and anthropology. Only if symbols

are construed to mean what they are not intended to mean can there arise imaginary, insoluble conflicts...the blunder leads to blasphemy: the Creator is accused of systematic deceitfulness. (Dobzhansky, 1973)

"The Bible tells us how to find abundant life, not the details of how life became abundant." ~ Thomas J. Oord

Creationists developed an "Intelligent Design" theory and a "Fine-Tuning" concept to address the Big Bang theory. However, thousands of church leaders criticize both arguments and state that Christianity is compatible with evolution.

Richard Dawkins, a renowned biologist and atheist, said the "Fine-Tuning" argument is the best theory religion has offered but claims it still doesn't provide a complete explanation—like, who did the fine-tuning? Another problem with the Fine-Tuning argument is the Church asserts that only the Christian God could have designed it, excluding and isolating all other religious beliefs. All sides (religions and science) are trying to prove they are right and everyone else is wrong. All of this is proof that the ego knows no religious affiliation.

After Glenn and I split up, I returned to California for a few months to stay with my mom. Since my "sinful relationship" was over, she could get my soul saved again. She and I once discussed the origins of the Universe. My mom grew frustrated because I argued against the biblical creation story and the age of our Universe. I told her there was no way the biblical account was correct. There was too much missing, like the dinosaurs. I was 25 and only had the Tom Selleck documentary. I was actively trying to reconcile my faith with what I was learning.

Since our planet is billions of years old, I explained how the six days of creation had to be allegorical. I told her I had been thinking and was starting to believe that the "days" mentioned in the Bible were not measured like we now view time. I suggested that the "days of creation" could be millions or billions of years. She became agitated and dismissed me by saying, "We don't know all the ways of the

Lord!"

I pressed on, asking, "How do we know the dinosaurs weren't just lizards that lived thousands of years, growing to their massive size? The Bible says humans lived a thousand years, so what about the animals?"

She laughed and said I was being absurd. I responded, "Not as absurd as thinking the Earth is only 6,000 years old or that people lived hundreds of years!"

We headed to different rooms at that point so the discussion did not turn into a war.

A few weeks later, she burst into my room at 7 am, jolting me out of a deep sleep. Throughout my life, she never woke me up gently. It was always with an intrusive and demanding shout, "GET UP!!! GET UP!!"

This morning was no different, but she was not angry and storming this time. She was enthusiastic and wanted me to run downstairs to watch an episode of 700-Club, which was the last thing I wanted to do.

She would not leave and told me she had just watched a "Jewish scientist" explain the same thing that I was saying about Genesis. Full of enthusiasm (probably because she no longer feared for my soul), she ripped the covers off me, demanding I get up and watch this episode. I angrily (she woke me up for this?) grabbed the blankets, rolled over, and said, "I told you so."

Because she had heard the information on a religious program, she concluded it was factual. If it was from the "godly realm," she accepted it; it was entirely dismissed outside of it. She said psychics were demon-possessed until one came to her church as a "Christian psychic" and was accepted with open arms.

The "Jewish scientist" on the 700 Club was Dr. Gerald Lawrence Schroeder, an Orthodox Jewish physicist. Dr. Schroeder claims he synchronized Creationism and evolution. Schroeder used Einstein's theory of relativity and calculations based on the space-time continuum to formulate his theory. He then converted the biblical "days" to a mathematical equation.

Based on space's expansion, Schroeder decided that before the

Universe formed, a trillion days was equivalent to what we now consider one day. He took the age of the Universe (13.8 to 15 billion years), applied Einstein's theory of relativity equations, and aligned the scriptures to evolutionary theories. His calculations resulted in the start of time on the "sixth day," when humans finally arrived to see and judge time based on day and night.

Schroeder said this about the beginning of time:

> The further philosophical problem of there having been a beginning arises with the idea that the beginning of our Universe marks the beginning of time, space, and matter. Before our Universe came into being, there is every scientific indication that time did not exist. Whatever brought the Universe into existence must, of course, predate the Universe, which in turn means that whatever brought the Universe into existence must predate time. That which predates time is not bound by time. Not inside of time. In other words, it is eternal. If the laws of physics, or at least some aspect of the laws of physics, did the job of creation, those laws by necessity are eternal. (Schroeder, 2001)

Quantum theorists assert that reality is shaped by how we observe it. Schroeder applies that theory to time and the beginning of existence. Time had no inherent value until "humans" arrived to see day and night.

Many people praise Schroeder's work, but he has critics. He made a believer out of philosopher Antony Flew, an atheist, before reading Schroeder's theories. Flew's atheist views changed to a deist perspective, and he was seen as a traitor by the atheistic science community. He denounced his critics, noting that "none of them have read a word that I have ever written."

Schroeder used the term "metaphysical," which made most of his fellow scientists' heads explode. To figure out, "Why is there an 'is'?" And "Why is there something rather than nothing?" Science and religion must turn to the metaphysical.

The rigidity of scientists can be as dogmatic as religion.

The fact is that we do not know what instigated the Big Bang. But we know that if it varied in even the most minuscule of ways, life as we know it would not exist. Astrophysicist Michael Turner states that the likelihood of our existence equates to throwing a dart across the Universe and hitting a one-millimeter bull's eye on the other side.

Roger Penrose, Professor of Mathematics, calculated the precision of the Universe:

> An accuracy of one part out of ten, to the power of ten, to the power of 123. This is an extraordinary figure. One could not possibly even write the number down in full, in our ordinary denary (power of ten) notation: it would be one followed by ten to the power of 123 successive zeros! (That is a million billion billion billion billion billion billion billion billion billion billion billion billion billion zeros.) (Penrose, 2006)

The precision needed for our existence is incomprehensible. If science and religion worked together, they could be unstoppable, and in doing so, one day, we could have the answers to currently elusive questions.

Chapter 62: Collaboration Instead of Condemnation

In 1950, the Catholic Church tried to end the war with science, but it left most scientists feeling like it was a little too little and definitely too late. Pope Pius XII and then Pope John Paul II confirmed in 1996 that there is no contradiction between evolution and Catholicism. Pope Francis tried to bridge the divide and was bolder than any other member of the papacy.

In 2014, Francis addressed the Pontifical Academy of Sciences.

> When we read the account of Creation in Genesis we risk imagining that God was a magician, complete with an all powerful magic wand. But that was not so. He created beings and he let them develop according to the internal laws with which He endowed each one, that they might develop, and reach their fullness. He gave autonomy to the beings of the universe at the same time in which He assured them of his continual presence, giving life to every reality. And thus Creation has been progressing for centuries and centuries, millennia and millennia, until becoming as we know it today, precisely because God is not a demiurge or a magician, but the Creator who gives life to all beings. The beginning of the world was not a work of chaos that owes its origin to another, but

derives directly from a supreme Principle who creates out of love. The Big Bang theory, which is proposed today as the origin of the world, does not contradict the intervention of a divine creator but depends on it. Evolution in nature does not conflict with the notion of Creation, because evolution presupposes the creation of beings who evolve. (Francis, 2014)

Pope Francis said that while God gave us freedom and autonomy over everything, we must be stewards of the planet, not rulers. Unlike the "Christian Right," which dismissed global warming, the Pope stood with the climate scientists. In the U.S., this deepened the divide between Evangelicals and Catholics.

The lack of support for climate science has dominated the political spectrum and affected funding for research and prevention. With science, the Religious Right took a stand of predestination.

Instead of being responsible, loving caretakers of this fantastic planet, we have left a wake of devastation. We have caused Mother Earth to look like a victim of abuse, with scars of devastation on the forests and lands, poisoned waterways and dead oceans, and massive holes bored into the ground because of greed and consumerism.

Can you imagine the funding for research that would be available if the Church and science worked together? The Vatican is the wealthiest "country" on Earth. In the interest of humanity, it requires science to be the adult in the room and work with open-minded believers.

Unfortunately, both claim superiority: religion by divine right and science through scrutiny. Religion tries to justify their faith through ancient texts and feelings. Science establishes physical laws by what can be seen, repeated, and documented.

But some of the most incredible things in life cannot be duplicated yet.

Instead of trying to understand "God" through examination and science, religion holds on to ancient beliefs and the humanization of God. We envision "God" as a Being, which limits "him" to our human capabilities, thoughts, and imaginations. Religion holds these beliefs so tightly that anything other than a God in human form is heretical.

Because of this stubbornness and closed-mindedness, religion stayed in the Middle Ages, and science made fools of them.

Not only are science and religion not mutually exclusive, but they need each other. The Jains knew about microorganisms over 2000 years before modern science. People who believe in a loving God tend to be healthier and happier than non-believers or those who believe in a mean, judgmental "God." Our brain is wired for belief, and instead of being open to the possibility of the supernatural, science considers it delusional.

However, the scientific community is more open to competing theories than religion is. Carl Sagan, a scientist and American legend, said:

> In science, it often happens that scientists say, "You know that's a really good argument; my position is mistaken," and then they would actually change their minds, and you never hear that old view from them again. They really do it. It does not happen as often as it should because scientists are human, and change is sometimes painful. But it happens every day. I cannot recall the last time something like that happened in politics or religion. (Segan, 1987)

As the divide and hostility between religion and science deepens, we delay, if not lose, answers to our questions. Even if science can figure out "how" we got here, we will still want to know "why."

For some people, it gives them peace, believing that we do not matter in the grand scheme of things--we will decay in the ground and become worm food. For others, the afterlife makes this life worth living. The thought of our insignificance is overwhelming and terrifying. But for most, accepting that we do not know for sure is unacceptable—the ego cannot handle that. We must know everything.

Throughout civilization, our perceptions dictated our beliefs and fears. The way they explained things a millennium ago is not how we now view things—both in science and (most) religions. We do not condemn 5-year-olds for not knowing and understanding physics. So, we must not blame our ancestors for their (lack of) comprehension of their world.

But we should not hold on to their ignorance either. If 5-year-olds refuse to learn as they grow, they stay ignorant, stifled, and possibly become a detriment to society. The same goes for everyone; our scientific, religious, and political beliefs should continuously evolve and make us better people.

Chapter 63: The Flood

The Bible is not the only set of ancient texts that tried to define our surroundings. Before the Bible, there were at least three other "flood" stories. The Sumerians told their story in 3000 B.C.E., the Babylonians in 1640 B.C.E., and the Mesopotamians with the "Epic of Gilgamesh" in 1100 B.C.E. The Hebrew's story of the flood appeared in their texts between 1000 and 500 B.C.E.

Geologist Cesare Emiliani, the father of paleoclimatology and paleoceanography, Professor James P. Kennett, a marine geologist and member of the National Academy of Sciences, and Nicholas John Shackleton, also a geologist and paleoclimatologist, studied core samples taken in the Gulf of Mexico. They found that a universal flood caused a sudden and significant drop in salinity approximately 11,000 years ago. They found whale bones 500 feet above sea level in Vermont and 600 feet above sea level in Quebec. Archeologists and geologists worldwide uncovered evidence that shows a massive, sudden flood—although the timelines vary.

Geologists William Ryan and Walter C. Pitman suggested that the melting at the end of the last ice age, around 7000 B.C.E., was responsible for the flood stories. Others assert that since most of the population lived near the water's edge, an unusual and catastrophic flood became legendary among the tribes.

For most examining the biblical legend, animals on the Ark are the breaking point. What about their food, sex drive, and waste? As a child learning this story, it never occurred to me, but it makes me laugh now. Most religious leaders claim the animals were vegetarian at the time (Really?) or all the creatures hibernated during the rains.

Some studies claim Noah saved 35,000 species, and 70,000 could have fit on the Ark (per biblical dimensions). But it is beyond reasonable to believe it happened. If there was a flood, studies show animals sense pending dangers and flee to higher ground or safe areas—the most logical conclusion. But that is not miraculous like believers want it to be.

I grew to view Noah's story as heinous. It is one of massive and utter destruction. It is a story where only one family and "two of each animal" survive; everything else is dead. And not a peaceful death; they were banging on the side of the Ark pleading for their and their loved ones' lives before drowning. It is a story that should horrify everyone.

But in religion, it is glorified. Christians made it into children's songs.

When my son was growing up, and I was feeling obnoxious and wanted him to get out of bed, I would wake him up singing the old children's song about the flood:

…. Rise and shine

And give God the glory, glory…

The animals, they came in; they came in by twosie, twosies

Elephants and [Big clap!] kangaroosie, roosies

Children of the Lord…

[Soooooooooooo] Rise AND shine… (Rise And Shine (Arky Arky), 2023) (2022)

At that point, Joey would scream, "Mom! Stop!" or throw a pillow at me, but those moments always brought me so much joy. When he became an adult, it did not stop me from waking him up like that or hindering my joy.

The story activates our ego and makes us want to be part of Noah's lucky and "righteous" family. We condemn those killed as wretched sinners and claim they deserved their punishment. Since this story is in religious text, our response is one of judgment and disdain, or at best, indifference. Outside of scripture, it is a horror story.

This flood supposedly destroyed the entire planet, and in 2016, a Christian man built a theme park in its honor. Attendance in its first year was less than expected. So, the park's creator, Ken Ham, blamed atheists and bad press for the lack of participation. Not that this theme park was a tribute to mass destruction. It was the non-believer's fault.

The people who celebrate the flood story are the same people who wish for Armageddon when billions of people will supposedly die.

It is the ultimate "win" and utterly egotistical. It is a "win" where you hope you are the only one left and everyone else dies. It is a death wish for most of the planet—one of utter destruction and hoping most will burn in Hell for eternity. That is not godly, nor righteous, and definitely not moral.

Chapter 64: God's Wrath or Natural Phenomena?

Science has explained the ten plagues. The first plague, when the water turned to "blood," and all the fish died, was probably a red algae bloom that happens in Florida annually.

The frogs falling from the sky in Plague Two could be a phenomenon called "raining frogs," which they have documented worldwide, usually because of weather patterns.

There were no longer frogs to eat the lice, so lice overtook the village, fulfilling the third plague.

The fourth plague was not about wild animals but a swarm of flies caused by plagues one and two.

The fifth plague mirrors a well-known and existing plague called rinderpest. This disease has an 80% mortality rate and killed over 200 million livestock in the 18th and 19th centuries.

The lice from Plague Two could have caused the boils of Plague Six, or it could have been smallpox.

The fiery hail of the seventh plague could be linked to the eruption of Santorini, which consequently would have provided an ideal environment for the locusts in the eighth plague.

Santorini's explosion also would have caused the ninth plague: darkness.

The Tenth Plague can be attributed to the First Plague, the algae bloom. The algae could have contaminated the grain, passing on deadly mycotoxins to the firstborn who ate first. (Marr JS, 1996)

We often take the wonders and mysteries of the Universe and label it "God." Ancient humans took the things we did not understand and attached God's judgment to them. Christian leaders are still doing it! After science deciphered weather patterns and gained knowledge about our world, they turned to religion and asked, "Now what?"

A lot of us have been asking the same thing.

Religion has held on to the belief that God is a magician. Like the Wizard of Oz, the illusion is revealed when the curtain is pulled back, leaving religion scrambling and making excuses.

Religion fears becoming obsolete and invalidated, so it holds on to archaic thinking instead of trying to understand, grow, and see the wonder of it all.

Chapter 65: Our Brains: Contained or Connected?

The brain is still a phenomenon, and its complexity still inspires and bewilders scientists, but they learn more daily. The cerebral cortex is the mass of wrinkled gray matter that envelopes the halves of our brain and sits right below the skull. It is believed to manage our language, memory, attention, awareness, and consciousness. Our senses and perceptions all flow through the cerebral cortex. Scientists have determined the thickness of the cortex can indicate personality traits, intelligence, and disease.

A research team worked together for a UCLA study to understand if the cortex's and intelligence's thickness correlate. They concluded the thicker the frontal cortex and temporal brain regions, the greater the chance for higher levels of intelligence. These are the same areas of Einstein's brain found to be "extraordinarily" large. (Katherine L Narr, 2007)

Scientists have found that the temporal lobe section of our cerebral cortex dictates whether we are believers. In the mid-twentieth century, Wilder Penfield, a Canadian neurosurgeon, mapped the human brain. He discovered that stimulating the temporal lobe caused his patients to have out-of-body experiences, hear voices, and hallucinate. He hypothesized he had found the location in the brain that invoked religious events. (Coles, 2008)

Another set of researchers from the New York State Psychiatric Institute and Columbia University, led by Dr. Lisa Miller, says the thickness of one's cortex corresponds to the importance of spirituality or religion. The study also showed that a person's view of God could dramatically decrease instances of predisposed depression.

They found that if you view God as kind, compassionate, and loving, you were 90% less likely to develop hereditary depression than the non-spiritual participants. Miller asserted, "A thicker cortex associated with a high importance of religion or spirituality may confer resilience to the development of depressive illness in individuals at high familial risk for major depression...." (Miller L, 2014)

Conversely, Miller found that if you believe in a "God," that is a judgmental disciplinarian who could abandon you, your chances of depression significantly increase. People believing in such a god have shown signs of significant and profound depression, which directly affects their overall health and life expectancy. Dr. Miller concluded that meditation and other affirmative practices could increase the thickness of the cortex, decreasing symptoms of anxiety and depression.

Neuroscientist Dr. Andrew Newberg suggests meditation and repetitive prayer (like mantras or memorized prayers) to activate the frontal lobes responsible for our emotions. He asserts that strengthening these parts of the brain results in "more calm, less reactionary, better able to deal with stressors." (Rettner, 2015)

Harold G. Koenig, director of the Center for Spirituality, Theology, and Health at Duke University Medical Center, agreed with these studies. "People who are more involved in religious practices and who are more religiously committed, seem to cope better with stress." (Koenig, 2012)

Koenig added, "One of the reasons is because [religion] gives people a sense of purpose and meaning in life, and that helps them to make sense of negative things that happen to them."

Koenig also notes that religious communities can provide support and encouragement, which improves people's overall well-being.

I have experienced all levels of these studies. I experienced a deep depression because of the shame and fear of "God." And I felt the depression ease as I realized that "unconditional love" meant unconditional. I felt the unity of the church community and the isolation because of cliques or my "sinner" status. I saw the chaos of my control turn into the bliss of letting go.

Wayne Dyer said, "Change your thoughts. Change your life." (Dyer, 2009) Perspective is everything. Our brains and our thoughts control our lives.

Some scientists regard these brain discoveries as proof that "God" is just in our heads. They attribute the religious revelations throughout history to frontal lobe epilepsy. But others view this discovery as perfection in design and uncovering our source to the divine.

Education, influences, and choices drive our beliefs and perceptions about science and God, but so does our anatomy. Our brains are diverse. People think, see, and hear differently. Some view our brains as iPods, contained. And others, as a cellular tower, connected.

The assumption that there is a universal religious or scientific philosophy is naive. No matter how much evidence is provided, someone will always disagree. We see this in all aspects of life, but especially in religion, science, and politics.

Chapter 66: Drugs: A Gateway to God?

Drugs are another way to activate our brain receptors and enable us to "talk to God." For thousands of years, religions used plants as intoxicants to reach various aspects of the spiritual realm. The Native Americans used tobacco smoke to send their prayers to Heaven. They also ground down the tobacco and sniffed it for health benefits, clarity, and serenity. They believed tobacco was a holy plant and a gift from God before the White man corrupted it.

A shaman once told me the White man's use of tobacco altered it from a sacred experience to a selfish one. She claimed that cannabis kept its spiritual connections because of its intoxicating qualities. Her example was the way people hold "joints." The thumb and index finger are together, and the palm faces outward, showing an open, communal experience.

Conversely, we hold cigarettes between our index and middle fingers and palms facing inward. It creates a boundary instead of openness. Each cigarette is intended for one person, while groups can share a single joint.

Ironically, I started smoking cigarettes to be part of the group. Now I sit outside by myself in the "shame spot," aka the smoking section.

Some scholars believe they used cannabis in ancient Hebrew

anointing oil. The Hebrew Bible mentions "Kaneh-bosm" several times. Prophets, priests, and kings used the oil but forbade it for anyone else.

The Rastafarians use cannabis (ganja) to discuss and be with God (Jah). The Rastas cite Proverbs 15:17 to justify their use,

> "Better is a dinner of herbs where love is than a fattened ox and hatred with it" (ESV).

For over 4,000 years, the Hindus used "bhang," which is made from cannabis. They used bhang in religious rituals to connect with Shiva. They also used it medicinally to cleanse their sins and avoid the misery of Hell. However, they considered recreational use morally wrong.

The Vedas detail a ritual of drinking "Soma," a plant derivative, but there are many theories about which plant. The Vedas state Soma induces immortality, causes the blind to see, disabled people to walk, the sick to be well, what is lost will be found, and those who seek will find the truth.

Hallucinogens have been used in South America for over 10,000 years for spiritual connection, growth, and healing. Peyote and Ayahuasca are used in religious rituals in the quest for higher spiritual knowledge and connection to God. Benny Shanon, a psychology professor at the Hebrew University of Jerusalem, asserts Moses was under the influence of Ayahuasca when he had his interactions with "God." Shanon was not accusing Moses of being high but finding a means of communication with the Divine.

Ayahuasca is a tea made from vines and leaves that are found in different areas of the forest. Shamans call it "Mother Aya" and claim the Divine gave them the recipe. There are similarities between Aya and the Goddess Asherah—both are Goddesses characterized as trees (literally, in Aya's case) that offer protection, healing, and love. Whether from the Goddess or God, they used plants as medicine to silence the mind, open other senses, and reach ultimate oneness with the Divine.

Ayahuasca's popularity is growing across the world because of its therapeutic benefits. It has made tremendous advancements with anxiety, depression, PTSD, and childhood trauma. The latter is why I tried it.

Some say an Ayahuasca ceremony is ten years of therapy in four hours. In my mind, this was an excellent way to knock out all my pain, shame, and heartbreak in just a few hours—boot camp style. Unbeknownst to me, that meant that I would have to process ten years of intense therapy in just four hours. It was overwhelming, and that is an understatement.

However, no therapist, doctor, family member, or friend could have healed me as Aya did. No amount of therapy or prescriptions could have eased my shame or given me the gifts each ceremony offered. Each session with Aya enabled me to see and, therefore, heal my pain, which helped me become a whole person.

It was no party. It was heartbreaking, gut-wrenching, horrific, and utterly confusing. It was also pure beauty, love, clarity, understanding, and acceptance. And through it all, there was healing. It may not be for everyone, but if every adult participated in a ceremony, there would be world peace.

Ayahuasca is a gift from the Divine, giving us what we need to heal, be whole, and be more loving. Science is still researching Aya, but for the past 5,000 years, tribal spiritual leaders have been aware of its healing potential.

Scientists have used hallucinatory drugs to simulate Near-Death Experiences (NDEs), communicate with "God," and ease the emotional stress and sadness of terminal patients. They used ketamine, a dissociative anesthetic used by veterinarians, to replicate an NDE.

For some scientists, this confirmed that spirituality was solely cerebral and had no basis in, or requirement for, any outside influence. However, unlike those who had natural NDEs, Ketamine produced no lasting changes. Most individuals who survived an actual NDE report fundamental changes in their lives. I will address NDEs in the next chapter.

Because of drug laws instituted in the 1960s and 70s, research on the medical benefits of hallucinogens was stagnant. However, recently, a study at the Johns Hopkins University School of Medicine used 51 cancer patients with "life-threatening diagnoses and symptoms of depression and/or anxiety" as test subjects for his Psilocybin experiment. The results were remarkable.

> Psilocybin produced significant decreases in clinician and self-rated measures of depressed mood and anxiety, along with increases in quality of life, life meaning, and optimism, and decreases in death anxiety. At 6-month follow-up, these changes were sustained, with about 80% of participants continuing to show clinically significant decreases in depressed mood and anxiety. Participants attributed improvements in attitudes about life/self, mood, relationships, and spirituality to the high-dose experience, with [more than] 80% endorsing moderately or greater increased well-being/life satisfaction. (Griffiths RR, 2016)

Psilocybin has been used for over 10,000 years to access higher intelligence and invoke religious experiences. Archeologists found artwork depicting the mushroom in Africa and the Mayan ruins.

Religion and drugs trigger the same areas of the brain. Both activate the dopamine and serotonin neurotransmitters, our pleasure and reward centers. When those parts are stimulated, we always want more. Whether that be more love and communion with others or more food, cigarettes, alcohol, or heroin, it all depends on the individual. These parts of the brain are our feel-good receptors; when they are activated, we are happy. Catnip has a similar effect on cats. "God" also gave cats a way to elevate their serotonin levels.

For thousands of years, spiritual leaders from all religions used their local plants and fungi to form more profound levels of communication with the Divine. A deep spiritual awareness can occur when we use nature's gifts in religious experiences—the natural to reach the supernatural—no wonder these events generated stories that have lasted generations.

Chapter 67: God Would Not Break His Rules

The laws of nature dictate our existence and are cosmically all-encompassing. One of those laws is that everything in our universe consists of matter and energy. Matter is everything in our physical world. It is all the surrounding stuff: the ground we walk on to whatever you use to read this book.

Except for some subatomic particles, all matter decays and decomposes. Everything we can see or touch will one day "die." All of us, the trees, flowers, stars, and even our sun, will someday cease to exist in its current form.

But energy neither dies nor decays; it can only be maintained or transformed. "Energy cannot be created or destroyed, but only changed from one form into another or transferred from one object to another." (Law of Conservation of Energy, 2022)

The laws of nature are the highest form of truth because they consistently apply to everything since the Big Bang.

If there is a God, suggesting that he would break his laws is unreasonable. Religion created a God who is a Being, made of mass and matter, breaking a fundamental rule of nature: matter decays.

Energy causes things to change form. The Big Bang was a burst of pure, extraordinary energy. Energy is not an object or a thing. But it is a part of everything and characterizes what the object is, what it does, and how it relates to other things.

Federico Faggin, a physicist and inventor of microprocessors, is now devoting his time to bridging the gap between science and spirituality. He states:

> For a scientist, generally, God is the unnecessary hypothesis.
> Well, to me, God is that undivided energy, that undivided
> wholeness of which everything is made—that's God.
> What else can it be? Since everything is made of that. And
> that's all that you have to say about it. Obviously, God
> is not anthropomorphic. It's something way beyond our
> comprehension. But we can connect with that energy because
> we are made of it. Everything is made of it. (Faggin, 2013)

I discovered the Truth about "God" through studying science. "God" is not matter or mass; "he" is energy. God is the energy of love. I do not mean "God is love" as some cliche, but in the most literal sense. Love is what ancient people were trying to describe when he labeled God. Science cannot prove love but can document its effects. We cannot put love in a beaker and evaluate its properties, but we can see changes in our brain, body chemistry, and behavior.

Thinking of God as an energy instead of matter puts the onus on us. No longer is someone else responsible for all the good and evil in the world. No longer is it someone else's fault. The number one question posed by atheists is, "If God is benevolent, then why do babies die?" Religion's answer is always: "We do not know the ways of God."

God as a Being cannot offer support for dying children, so the atheist's argument stands. But God, as the energy of love, means it is up to us to provide comfort and care. Either we tap into the power of love, or we ignore it. Either we invoke the love of God, or we do not. Our actions dictate our lives and the lives of others. Not some old guy in the sky who we blame for everything we have ever done.

No religion in its entirety stands up as Truth. But love does. It applies to all times, cultures, and people. From ancient people to modern people, the North to the South Poles, we are looking for love from the day we are born till the day we die. Our lives have meaning because of love.

Love creates, expands, and alters everyone it graces. Love is the muse for all beauty, like art, literature, and music. Love gives us hope, encourages us to offer help, and comforts all in need. I could go on, but trillions of things have been said about love. It is the motivator for us all.

However, some scientists say love is just an illusion, a trick of our brains, like belief in "God." Love is an emotion that cannot be measured and has the same chemical reactions in the brain as someone having a spiritual experience or is on drugs. Some scientists claim it is just a mental mirage.

Science cannot prove love, but that has no bearing on our confidence in its existence. There was no one to see the Big Bang, but we are assured of its accuracy. There may always be things that science does not fully understand or cannot explain, which is OK.

The things beyond the physical world are for spiritual perspectives, imagination, and wonder. And in the same fashion, religion must stop looking to ancient minds for scientific knowledge. If religion focused more on the love of God rather than a book of laws, they would see Divine Law in action.

Albert Einstein said for scientists, "Religious feeling takes the form of a rapturous amazement at the harmony of natural law, which reveals an intelligence of such superiority that, compared with it, all the systematic thinking and acting of human beings is an utterly insignificant reflection."

Both perspectives of religion and science show us the extraordinary nature of our existence. We all have spiritual experiences. Attaching a Supreme Being to it is an individual's prerogative. There's genuine awe and amazement when looking at DNA, celestial bodies, the brain, or the wonders of our planet. It does not require belief in a Supreme Being to see our universe's miraculous and exceptional aspects. The labels and descriptions we assign to such bewilderment divide the logically minded from the spiritually motivated.

We will realize the magnificence of it all when we work together and harness collective energy and knowledge.

Section X: Death

"No one wants to die. Even people who want to go to Heaven don't want to die to get there. And yet death is the destination we all share. No one has ever escaped it. And that is as it should be, because Death is very likely the single best invention of Life. It's Life's change agent. It clears out the old to make way for the new."
~ Steve Jobs

Chapter 68: Consciousness

For those of us left behind, death is a wound that never truly heals. We learn to cope and move on with life, but it is a loss we will always feel. Mostly, if we take measures for renewal, everything else in life that causes us pain will eventually heal. We can seek treatment from a doctor for physical ailments or therapy for emotional pain. But the death of a loved one is a pain only soothed with time and never truly abates. As a friend said, "When you love someone, you will always miss them; that shows your love, and death doesn't change that."

Every other section of this book was cathartic. While often difficult, it provided healing. But this one shoved in my face the enormous loss of my mother and Vince. It also highlighted that I had no feeling of loss with my father. And it forced me to face my mortality. Death sucks, but nothing gets out of here alive.

Death would not be so sweet or horrifying without religion. *"For the wages of sin is death"* (Romans 6:23) is the most psychologically destructive doctrine ever issued. Those seven words took the natural life cycle and turned it into a punishment. Consequently, for many religious people, death and, therefore, judgment are their greatest fears.

A month before my mother passed away, she was in bed,

and suddenly, she was terrified. As she faced her mortality, she questioned everything she lived for. Panicked, she grabbed my arm and asked, "What if I got it all wrong, Sheri? What if I picked the wrong God?" The fear on her face saddened me so much. She was an amazingly strong woman; I had never seen her so terrified. I could feel her fear; she was squeezing my arm.

I offered her comfort. While stroking her hair, I said, "Mom, if anyone is going to Heaven, it's you. God loves you and will accept you, if only because you tried so hard to get it right. You did everything asked of you. Don't be afraid. I'm sure you're going to Heaven."

The only good thing about cancer is that it gives you time to say and do everything you can before death. Cancer affords us a chance to minimize the regrets that death causes. Throughout my mother's struggle with terminal cancer, I swore to myself there would be nothing left unsaid, no unanswered questions, no should've, would've, or could've. In those last days, I would lie awake every night, trying to think of every question, apology, and way to say "I love you" before she left me.

At the time, I was 32. By then, I no longer had faith in the Christian doctrine, especially believing that the Bible was the only answer to every question. I saw viable arguments for each religion's perspective on death.

A few days after her existential crisis, I had another long, sleepless night, staring at the ceiling, thinking about my mom's imminent death. My thoughts raced, but I came up with the perfect question. I hoped it would ease my grief in the days/weeks/months ahead when I was missing her.

Aha! I thought, *this will tell me so much!*

I could not wait to talk to her the next day and take a small step in making this horrible situation a little easier. She was frail, but she could always find a reason to laugh.

I was acutely aware that I had to approach this question with extreme sensitivity and choose my words carefully. I found the right moment, one of levity and clarity, and asked, "Mom, if you get to

Heaven and God says, 'Job well done, my child. What would you like to do next?' What would you say?"

She looked at me as if I had lost my mind and dismissively said, "I've never considered such a thing!"

I smiled and said, "What if? Come on, Mom, I'm just asking! Play along for a moment…"

While she was pondering my question, I tried to plead my case and ease her confusion and concern that I had gone off the deep end. Excitedly, I proclaimed, "I would like to be a marine animal! Like a dolphin! Wouldn't that be cool?"

I desperately tried to find something to hold on to that would comfort me somehow. Something that would reassure me that my mom was still with me, even after her body was gone. Something I could see as my life went on without her. It would make me smile instead of focusing on the immense loss.

She looked at me with a mischievous grin and said, "My dog!"

I laughed at the ridiculous statement and asked, "Not my dog?" Playfully but adamantly, she replied, "No. You don't groom yours often enough." We laughed, and I did not press any further.

Her dog? Really? What was I supposed to do with that? How could she have a dog after she was gone? I walked away, disappointed and frustrated.

She obviously had not taken my question seriously. It went against everything she stood for and the core of her identity. The night before, I imagined she would say a butterfly, a robin, maybe an elephant, but she said her dog. I was deflated and felt like there would be nothing to keep her memory alive. I hoped I had found the perfect way of maintaining my mother's presence. Instead, she answered the question as ridiculously as the amount of weight I put into asking it.

The word "reincarnation" stems from the Latin word "renascentia," which means rebirth. Key figures in ancient Greek cultures, like Pythagoras, Socrates, and Plato, believed in the transfiguration of the Eternal Soul. Today, over 50% of the planet believes in the afterlife. (2011)

That statistic shocked me, so I wanted to see what the people I knew thought about the afterlife. In my super-non-scientific Facebook poll, most friends felt that our essence or soul transforms into another form of life. About 15% believed we just become worm food, and another 15% thought we would be in Heaven with our loved ones for eternity.

How one feels about death directly correlates to how one views life. If one believes in a soul or some form of consciousness, then they (likely) believe in some form of afterlife. If one thinks there is only the here and now—the science community calls it "materialism"—they probably believe our bodies just become worm food.

Science is based on the observable and the soul is literally beyond that realm. So, most scientists dismiss it. Today, we cannot scientifically prove consciousness beyond electrochemical activity in the brain. So, most scientific views are monism. Monism is "a theory or doctrine that denies the existence of a distinction or duality in some sphere, such as that between matter and mind, or God and the world." (Oxford University Press, 2023)

But just like with everything else, not everyone agrees.

Sir John Eccles, a neurophysiologist, philosopher, and winner of the 1963 Nobel Prize, and René Descartes, a 17th-century French philosopher, mathematician, and scientist, often referred to as the father of modern Western philosophy, asserts a dualist theory. Dualism contends that consciousness, the soul, is separate from the physical mind and that our mind includes more than just our brain. It has a non-material, conscious, spiritual aspect to it. Descartes' famous quote is, "I think, therefore, I am."

Federico Faggin founded the Federico and Elvia Faggin Foundation to support "A Framework for the Union of Science and Spirituality." Faggin states, "The Foundation is interested in the scientific investigation of consciousness under the assumption that it's an irreducible property of nature." (Faggin, 2011)

He notes computers are a hundred million times more advanced than 40 years ago, but "we're not even one iota closer to having the first microwatt lamp of consciousness lighting up inside a computer."

Regardless of how advanced machines become or how they can

mimic and exceed our brains, consciousness cannot be replicated, yet.

Faggin notes:

> Believe it or not, Quantum Physics and General Relativity let
> the genie out of the bottle when they discovered the intimate
> connection between the observer and the observed.
> The observer affects what is observed, and there is no
> totally objective world out there that is independent from
> its observation. [In other words, your thoughts create your
> reality and what you put your attention on is affected by that
> observation].
> These new findings can no longer be wished away, and
> their implications about the nature of reality must be deeply
> explored, despite being difficult to accept...
> ...I believe that physics cannot afford to ignore the study of
> consciousness because it might just be the missing link. By
> refusing to accept that consciousness may be fundamental or
> perhaps the fundamental property of nature, physics may not be
> able to unify its two most successful theories.

Faggin proposes our bodies are holding us back from realizing the
depth and magnitude of our consciousness:

> ...death may be necessary also to dissolve the identification
> of consciousness with the body, thus freeing consciousness
> to recognize its own true nature. This happens because
> death destroys the only source of information the embodied
> consciousness has relied upon, and therefore, only after the
> destruction of the body would consciousness realize that it is
> still alive. Without the disappearance of the body, it would
> be impossible to convince consciousness that its existence is
> independent from the body's existence. (Faggin, 2014)

Faggin uses Virtual Reality (VR) as an example. In a VR
experience, the participant often becomes so engrossed in the
experience they forget about the outside world. Faggin believes this
happens to us as we grow and age. When we die and shed the body,
we return to the reality of the soul, our consciousness.

Neurosurgeon Eben Alexander had an NDE after contracting meningitis. He affirms that science's reductive materialism blinds us to our natural state as spiritual beings. Alexander contended, "Consciousness is at the core to unfolding all of reality."

> The old paradigm of birth to death represents an outdated concept that is woefully inadequate in defining the unfolding reality of expanded awareness. Materialist science is at the end of its days, as most scientists are changing their views. The old concepts are soon to be relegated to the same dustbin as "the Earth is flat" as we develop a more mature understanding and transcend old beliefs. (The Brain Does NOT Create Consciousness, 2014)

While some scientists continue to try to make robots feel emotions and claim that we are technically just walking zombies, advancements are slowly bringing life into the living. Two hundred years ago, we would not have even considered animals to be conscious, but now we know many species have exhibited consciousness. Technically, science is just catching up to Islam and the Eastern Religions, which have long believed animals were sentient.

Science estimates that 95% of our universe is dark matter and energy. What if "dark matter" is some level of consciousness? What if the energy science is trying to define, is what people like Faggin and Eben (et al.) report as our conscious energy or universal soul?

Buddhism has described this for over 2000 years and asserted there is nothing more—nothing less, but nothing more than a universal consciousness. Consciousness gives life meaning, connects us, and makes death impermanent. Our soul is our connection to the afterlife.

Consciousness makes death a disbursement of energy, not just a disintegration of matter.

Chapter 69: Reincarnation

Hindu scripture declares, "As, after casting away worn-out garments, a man later takes new ones. So, after casting away worn-out bodies, the embodied Self encounters other new ones." (B.G.)

Eastern Religions believe our afterlife and rebirth depend on our karmic debt. Karmic reincarnation answers a lot of life's questions, like why some are born into poverty and others into riches, some into freedom and some into slavery, some are healthy, and some are sick.

Eastern Religions assert humans are the highest life forms and, therefore, returning as anything else is a punishment. I do not believe in the supremacy of people, so it was easy for me to want to try something different—another species, a different kind of life. I see balance, magic, and magnificence in all the life on our planet. As noted in the "Animals" section, in many ways they are superior. Only our ego would say otherwise.

Eastern philosophies (and early Christianity) believe men are the highest form of rebirth. Women have at least one more incarnation because they are women and, therefore, are not fully evolved like men. Women, the givers of life, are diminished to a "second-class" soul.

Reincarnation is prominent in the apocryphal texts, and because of its widespread acceptance, it also appears in the Bible. It was a part of Christian doctrine until 553 C.E. and is another example of Jesus' full story being glossed over or ignored.

The Torah prophesied Elijah would return to pave the way for the Son of God. Jesus said that his cousin, John the Baptist, was Elijah reincarnated, fulfilling the prophecy.

> And the disciples asked him, saying, 'Why then do the scribes say that Elijah must come first?' But he answered them and said, 'Elijah indeed is to come and will restore all things. But I say to you that Elijah has come already, and they did not know him, but did to him whatever they wished. So also shall the Son of Man suffer at their hand.' Then the disciples understood he had spoken of John the Baptist. (Matthew 17:10-13)

Jesus named John as the reincarnated Elijah, proving Jesus as the Messiah.

> "See, I will send the prophet Elijah to you before that great and dreadful day of the Lord comes" (Malachi 4:5).

Naming John as Elijah was a clear sign to the disciples that Jesus was the one who was predicted, fulfilling the prophecy.

The Bible asserts Elijah's return showed the Messiah's presence— not someone like him, but Elijah himself. Jesus' affirmation that John was Elijah confirms the cultural beliefs in reincarnation. Without it, Elijah did not return as John, and Jesus was not the Messiah.

One fascinating parallel between John and Elijah leads some to conclude that the beheading of John was the karmic consequence of Elijah decapitating the Baal priests.

So, what happened to the belief in reincarnation? Paul. He did not believe in reincarnation but thought the soul remained with the body until Judgment Day. I saw it called "The Night of the Living Dead theory," where bodies come crawling out of graves and walking among us on the day of judgment. Think of Michael Jackson's "Thriller" video. This belief concludes there are billions of properly dressed skeletons just below the Earth's surface, ready to crawl out and start dancing for Jesus.

Reincarnation directly opposed Paul's Hellenistic beliefs. The elimination of the philosophy in Christianity was from Paul's history, not Jesus'. It was through Paul that reincarnation became resurrection. Resurrection originated in Zoroastrianism.

And so, it became the new doctrine of the Church. However, without reincarnation, Jesus is not the Christ but is a false prophet. He promised his disciples would see his second coming.

> *"Truly I tell you, some who are standing here will not taste death before they see the Son of Man coming in his kingdom" (Matthew 16:28).*

The disciples are all dead, so how does that work? Paul claimed they're all still in the ground waiting for their "Thriller" dance to begin. Paul is a glaring example of the winner changing and pushing his-story.

Not all Christians believe in the dead's resurrection. Growing up, I was not led in any direction. My mom used to say it was an unending debate. What beliefs one holds depend on one's Christian denomination. The Evangelicals and the Latter-Day Saints have the highest percentage of believers in bodily resurrection—between 60% and 80%. Less than 50% of believers from other Christian denominations believe in bodily resurrection. The remaining percentages believe we either reach Heaven or Hell immediately or reincarnate (24% of Christians). Western Religions think our souls depend on our bodies for the eternal destination. Belief in reincarnation assumes the soul is an energy that changes and is reborn into a different physical nature. (Pew Research Center, 2013)

I hope we are given a chance to experience all of life, not just this one. Human life is hard and full of suffering. I want to surf the waves with a few dozen others in my dolphin family. Or swing from the trees and scream like chimps. Humanity is overrated.

From dust to dust. May our souls live on.

Chapter 70: Our Attachment to Our Bodies

For almost 2000 years, and like the Egyptians, Christians have had a fascination with the body and believe it is required for the next life. Not until 1963 did the Church lift its ban on cremation, but most doctrine states that we should bury the ashes.

Generally, the Abrahamic faiths believe the body will be resurrected, which is another attempt at making the soul, which is intangible, into something tangible. It is also wholly ego-driven. Ironically, because of the ego, most people would gladly trade their current bodies for a new and revised version. Our bodies bend and break before eventually decaying, but Christianity places our worth in its form.

Adopting Egyptian mysticism with the body afforded the early Christian founders a clear delineation against Eastern beliefs in cremation. It was safe to copy the Egyptian burial rites because the civilization was extinct. In doing so, their beliefs differed vastly from the other philosophies—those "evil pagans."

Catholic doctrine states that cremation hinders the grieving process because the living cannot confront death without seeing the body. I saw my mom's body before cremation.

Ram Dass, formerly Richard Alpert, was a Harvard psychologist, professor, and a self-proclaimed "philosophical materialist." As

Richard Alpert, he gained notoriety while hanging out with Timothy Leary and Ralph Metzner, who were also psychologists, authors, and researchers. They all participated in the psychedelics research at Harvard University in the 1960s. In 1967, Alpert went to India and had a spiritual transformation. He was renamed "Ram Dass," meaning "servant of God." He was a spiritual teacher and author. Ram focused on comforting the dying and teaching how to "die consciously."

Ram Dass wrote a piece titled "Dying is Absolutely Safe – Awareness Beyond Death." It reads there is "a tombstone in Ashby, Massachusetts that reads, 'Remember friend, as you pass by, as you are now, so once was I. As I am now, so you must be. Prepare yourself to follow me."

Dass asserts that because we conflated our dying process with religion and fear, it lurks in the shadows as something to be avoided:

> It's [only] now becoming acceptable in our culture for people to die. For many decades, death was kept behind closed doors. But now we are allowing it to come out into the open. Having grown up in this culture, the first few months I spent in India in the 1960s were quite an experience. There, when someone dies, the body is placed on a pallet, wrapped in a sheet, and carried through the streets to the burning grounds while a mantra is chanted. Death is out in the open for everyone to see. The body is right there. It is not in a box. It is not hidden. And because India is a culture of extended families, most people are dying at home. So, most people, as they grow up [in India], have been in the presence of someone dying. They have not walked away from it and hidden from it as we have in the West.

On the ego:

> Prior to my first experience with psychedelics, I had identified with that which dies—the ego. The ego is who I think I am. Now, I identify much more with who I really am—the soul. As long as you identify with that which dies, there is always fear of death. What our ego fears is the cessation of its own existence. Although I didn't know what form it would take after death—I

realized that the essence of my Being—and the essence of my awareness—is beyond death.

He goes on:

> People ask, "Do you believe that there is continuity after death?" And I said, "I don't believe it. It just is." That offends my scientific friends to no end. But belief is something you hold on to with your intellect. My faith in the continuity of life has gone way beyond the intellect. Belief is a problem because it's rooted in the mind, and in the process of death, the mind crumbles. Faith, consciousness, and awareness all exist beyond the thinking mind. (Dass, 2013)

This is where it gets weird, but the philosophy is intriguing.

> In the Theravadan Buddhist traditions, they send monks out to spend the night in the cemetery, where the bodies are uncovered and discarded for the birds to eat. So, the monks sit with the bloated, fly-infested corpses, and the skeletons, and they get an opportunity to be fully aware of all the processes of nature. They watch their disgust and loathing, and their fear. They have a chance to see the horrible Truth of what 'as I am now so you must be' really means. Seeing the way the body decays and meditating on the decay opens you to the awareness that there is a place in you that has nothing to do with the body—or the decay.

I understand the need for closure when someone dies. When Vince passed, I was out of the country and could not return for the funeral. A part of me still does not, or cannot, believe he is gone. My mom wanted to be cremated. I still have her ashes. She did not want to be spread anywhere. And since I move around a lot, a cemetery plot made little sense. She and I would joke that after she died, her ashes and I would watch her favorite movies together.

A ceremony of respect, remembrance, and the ability to say "goodbye" is what we need. Not the worship of our physical form.

When my grandfather died, they held the funeral according to his beliefs and customs. Since immigrating to the U.S., he was a founding member of the Russian Molokan Church in San Francisco. The Molokans (meaning milk drinkers) are a Christian sect with pieces of other denominations and faiths intertwined. In the 17th century, Russia ostracized them for being too passive.

The Molokan's funerary practices are unlike what we see in the West. First, everyone wears white, not black. Second, the funerals last several days. Unlike in America, the "viewing" of the body lasts a minimum of eight hours and a maximum of thirty-six. It is not a passive display. You must sit quietly in front of the open casket for eight hours. Women may not cross their legs, and everyone's hands must be folded in front of them.

I was fourteen when he passed, and when my mother informed me how the funeral would be, it horrified me. But a unique healing process occurred. After a few hours, you are kind of cried out. This practice helped me realize my grandfather was no longer in that body. What was lying in front of me was nothing but a shell.

During this ritual, there was healing, and we were no longer consumed and overwhelmed by grief. Our focus shifted from the death before us to the surrounding life. After about five hours, I started to notice things. Who were the other mourners? Why did my mom and her siblings buy pants that were too short for my grandfather?

The women elders continually scolded my mom and me for crossing our legs. So, we saw how long it took them to catch us. Feistiness is in our DNA; we got it from him.

They opened the doors at the end of the viewing, and church members flowed in and filled the grand hall. There was an enormous feast, and the congregation joined to commune and celebrate his life. Tears dried; smiles appeared. There were stories of his life, and everyone laughed and cheered his existence. Throughout the experience, there was beauty, peace, and letting go of my grandfather's shell. It was a healing process and something I am thankful I could experience.

Chapter 70: Our Attachment to Our Bodies

I imagine it is a similar reckoning the Buddhist Monks undergo when sitting among all those corpses. It is harder saying goodbye to a loved one than a stranger, but being able to see death in its harsh reality can be a spiritual encounter.

Regardless of the religion, they all have an event of closure, which forces you to realize the body is just a shell where the soul no longer lives.

Chapter 71: The Soul Moves On

Both the ancient Egyptian and Tibetan cultures had funerary texts. The Egyptian books, now called the *Book of the Dead*, were originally the *Book of Coming Forth by Day*. The Egyptian obituary texts date back to the 26th century B.C.E. They drafted unique books for each royal funeral but often used the same "spells."

Initially, for Egyptian royalty, around 2000 B.C.E., the books became coffin texts. This ritual change opened the afterlife to the rich, not just the powerful. According to Egyptian culture, this released a flood of souls to eternity.

There are 192 known spells, but "Spell 125" puts our life's actions into perspective. It changed my thoughts from "you're never good enough" to "you can always do better." Spell 125 is the weighing of the heart against a feather of truth. If the heart is lighter than the feather, that soul could continue into the afterlife. If the heart is heavier than the feather, then Ammit, the Egyptian version of Satan, devoured the soul. For thousands of years, many cultures detailed the afterlife as a heinous eternal tragedy for the sinner, which kept us controlled by fear.

The Tibetan Book of the Dead (or the *Bardo Thodol* or *The Great Liberation upon Hearing in the Intermediate State*) was supposedly written in the eighth century but not discovered until the fourteenth.

Buddhists believe the texts were revealed when the world was ready to receive them.

Buddhists believe the soul lingers in Bardo for 49 days after death. During that time, the soul undergoes various stages of judgment. The funerary texts help the deceased cross over to the next life. The book notes that most people do not want to move on at the end of life. So, the scriptures offer comfort and guidance for the troubled soul trying to remain in the body.

> O nobly born, that which is called death hath now come. Thou art departing from this world, but thou art not the only one; [death] cometh to all. Do not cling, in fondness and weakness, to this life. Even though thou clingest out of weakness, thou hast not the power to remain here. Thou wilt gain nothing more than wandering in this Sangsāra. Be not attached [to this world]; be not weak. Remember the Precious Trinity. (Karma-glin-pa, 1992)

I found it interesting that some verses resemble NDE reports. The text guides the dying "into the clear light," where the Holy Trinity greets them and helps them move through the various stages of Bardo. These prayers align with the reports of those resuscitated, but the Buddhists wrote them 1200 years ago.

Some unsettling texts were instructions for the dying person who lingers instead of moving through the death process. The llama recites the above passage and compresses the major arteries in the neck to speed up the dying process.

> If the expiration is about to cease, turn the dying one over on the right side, which posture is called the "Lying Posture of a Lion." The throbbing of the arteries (on the right and left side of the throat) is to be pressed. If the person dying be disposed to sleep, or if the sleeping state advances, that should be arrested, and the arteries pressed gently but firmly. Thereby the vital-force will not be able to return from the median-nerve and will be sure to pass out through the Brahmanic aperture.

Having witnessed my mother's death, it was time for her to go.

The suffering became too great. But there was no way I could have hastened it. I wanted her for every second I could have her. Every one of her breaths was precious to me. I can mentally understand that Buddhism's goal is complete non-attachment, but detaching from the love and bond with my mother is not something I could do.

When a loved one dies, we cry because of our own selfish needs. All we can think and feel is our pain, loss, and the unquenchable longing to see and speak to them again. Mostly, when someone passes, it is an end to their suffering. But the loss, pain, and hole in our hearts consume us because they are gone and will never be back.

I still do not know how I made it home from hospice the morning my mom died. One of her mix-C.D.'s was in my car stereo, and I sobbed as it played. There was a deep, aching pain in my chest from a loss like no other. For the people left behind, death is so horrendous; the only comfort we often have is the hope of an afterlife and reuniting with them.

Before my mom died, I asked if she could "write in the sand." To send me a sign, a message, to let me know she was still here with me—somehow, someway. She promised me she would if she could.

After she died, I planned two funerals: one in Atlanta, her last home, and one in California, her first. The memorial in Atlanta was beautiful, and the support I received was an unexpected blessing. My friends, dozens of coworkers, and a few people from her church came to pay their respects and offer support. Most of them had never met my mom. I had no family, so their support was something I will always cherish.

It also gave me a valuable lesson: When you truly need someone, someone will always be there—maybe not when you want them to be, but when times arise, when you really need someone, life gives you that friend. Dozens of people blessed me with their support during my greatest heartbreak.

Instead of flowers, I requested donations in my mother's name to the charity she selected. A few special people did both, so my mom would have flowers at her service. Typical of flowers for funerals, they came in the shape of a cross and a wreath. Two days after the Atlanta funeral, Joey and I stopped at the Chattahoochee River before heading to the airport to go to California. I did not want to come home to dead funeral arrangements. So, I thought it would be a healing experience for us to release them down the river.

Joey grabbed the cross, and I grabbed the wreath. It was October, and the Chattahoochee was a rushing river with white caps. He and I leaned over the bank and gently placed the flowers in the rapids. The arrangements were immediately caught in an eddy. So, instead of rushing down the river, they circled back to the shore. Joey and I held hands as they slowly spun in front of us. Tears streamed down my cheeks.

After circling for a few seconds, they locked into each other and became one. They moved to the center of the eddy and stopped spinning. They stayed below our feet instead of going down the river as expected.

I was perplexed, assuming they were stuck. I had a million things on my mind. We were rushing to the airport, so it was difficult to absorb the moment, and I was still consumed with grief. I was not looking forward to another funeral, and letting go of those flowers was just one more thing I needed to release but did not want to. I was stressed and focused on the next task: getting to California.

Even though the cross and wreath were still floating before us, I looked at Joey and said, "C'mon. We have to go!"

I looked down again, mentally said another goodbye, and walked away. Joey lingered and said, "Mom, what do 'X' and 'O' mean again?"

The cross and wreath had moved into the perfect position of X and O. I was not paying attention, so I got in the car and ordered him to do the same. We had a flight to catch!

That night, after an exhaustive day traveling across the country, I was lying in bed and finally heard what Joey said. I burst into tears, sobbing, heaving tears. That was my sign! She could send me one! And I almost missed it.

Looking back, I wish I were not so preoccupied. It was such a special moment, and I almost missed it entirely, even though it was right before my eyes. I could not have made that happen if I tried. In the rushing waters of the Chattahoochee, two three-foot objects joined and stood still. The thought is even absurd. But she did it! She sent me a message, letting me know she was still with me.

The other time was six weeks after she passed. I was standing in the breezeway of my apartment, taking in the Georgia Fall. The building backed up to a small forest full of fall colors. I stood there, wishing my mom had seen it. In her last days, I brought her a single red leaf so she could see a little piece of the South's change of seasons.

Standing there, taking in the beauty, I was sad but smiling, missing her but knowing she was no longer in pain. A fall breeze blew my hair, and suddenly, I was enveloped by the smell of her perfume. I freaked out and turned around, thinking Joey was playing a cruel joke. I looked to my left and right, down and up. I was alone. I leaned over the rail, looking at my neighbor's windows. I assumed an open window was responsible for the aroma, but they were closed.

Later, I discovered I was the only one home in the building. If I had doubted the cross and wreath message, there was no doubting this one; it was overwhelming. She was sending me the signs she promised. My head denies it, but my heart absorbs the supernatural love sent just for me.

The Church claims we are only supposed to feel Jesus' spirit— only his soul is transmittable. Yet through these experiences, through my mother's love, I felt closer to "God"—to an afterlife and the spiritual realm. The Church teaches she was in Heaven, purgatory, or waiting to resurrect on the day of judgment. But I felt her presence and spirit there with me on those days.

If we are souls and energies, then these events are entirely possible. Only our narcissism binds death and tries to understand "God's" goals. I do not know how, but I know it happened. I believe it because I saw, felt, smelled, and experienced it.

However, only someone open to the wonder of our universe will ever catch these events. My closed, preoccupied mind would have missed it if it had not been for Joey. Now, when I attend funerals, I urge the mourning to be open to seeing or feeling their loved one's presence. Some thank me; others think I am nuts.

Chapter 72: The Other Side

Because of medical advancements, the number of people being resuscitated has skyrocketed. Sometimes, these resuscitations come with vivid stories of what they experienced after they "died."

Raymond Moody, a philosopher, psychologist, physician, and author, coined the term "Near-Death Experience." He started doing NDE research in 1975 and penned several books. There are thousands of books on the subject—Amazon lists over 5000 [2]. In his first book, Life after Life, Moody documented over 200 cases of people clinically dead but had vivid experiences.

They estimate that over the past 50 years, twenty-five million people have experienced an NDE. Religion has no impact on these visions, as atheists also report these experiences. The circumstances vary, but they have three things in common: feelings of a force, they are overwhelming, and it is authentic to the person experiencing it.

Most people report a light, warm, non-judgmental love. Unlike drug-induced NDEs, actual near-death experiences cause significant and profound changes. Most NDEs are positive. However, for some, they are terrifying. Regardless of the experience, the lasting changes in the person's life are positive.

After my mother passed away, a dear friend sent me the

2 As of Oct 2023

book *Embraced by The Light* by Betty J. Eadie. I have since bought several copies for friends and family and still highly recommend it to anyone who has lost someone. The book tells the story of Betty, who was clinically dead but was resuscitated and lived to tell her story of Heaven. Her stories confirmed my beliefs that our lives are a journey of learning and knowledge. It also made sense of things that confused me during my mother's death.

The last week of her life, she was inundated with drugs, trying to breathe, and saying the craziest things. I would sit up with her all night, watching her rest, taking care of her, and writing everything she said. The next day, when she was more lucid, we would laugh at her overnight antics.

One evening, after being silent for over an hour, she sat up, turned, looked at me, and asked, "Do you still want to move back to Florida?" I said, "Of course!"

She shook her head, chuckled, relaxed her composure, and said, "Oh Sheri… always chasing those pink elephants under the sea!"

Pink elephants under the sea? Huh? I was laughing so hard that I had to leave the room.

Most nights, it appeared she was talking in her sleep. At one point, she thought her girlfriend was there, and my mom told her she needed to wear more makeup. She matter-of-factly proclaimed, "Even a barn needs paint every once in a while!"

Each night, I hoped the following day would give us time to laugh about what she said.

The night before she died, she continually talked to the empty chair in her room. She was focused. It differed from the ramblings of earlier days. She was conversational. She saw a parade of people coming to see her. She continuously looked towards the chair and asked, "What are you doing here? I have not seen you in 30 years!" or "Oh My God! Hi! I thought you were dead?"

Her confusion at seeing these people was evident. But she was elated, and I was fortunate to see her innermost thoughts and experiences. I asked her who was there, and she looked at me like I was crazy. Agitated, she would say, "Sue!" or "Mary!" and turn back towards "them" like I was interrupting their chat. She was never lucid again, so I never got to ask her about those "visitors."

According to *Embraced by the Light,* Betty Eadie called those who visited my mom "The Monks." Betty described people dressed as monks who came to escort her to the afterlife. When I read about these guardians, it made sense out of what I had only considered delusions. I instantly understood what my mom experienced on that last night.

She died less than 24 hours later. I believe her loved ones came to help her pass, and I was fortunate enough to see them welcome her. Some say we die alone, but based on what I saw and read in Betty's book and the reports of millions of NDEs, we all have someone to hold our hand on that journey, too.

Science dismisses NDEs as nothing more than cerebral hallucinations from a lack of oxygen to the brain. This is another belief attached to how you generally view your life. However, many NDE stories have been corroborated by outside sources.

Like the woman who was technically dead but overheard (floating above them) her family's conversation in the cafeteria on the other side of the hospital. Or another who, while drifting out of her body and above the hospital, noticed a shoe on the roof. After hearing the report, the hospital staff checked, and a shoe was there. There was no way anyone, unless from the perspective above the hospital, could have seen the shoe.

"AWARE—Awareness during Resuscitation" was a four-year international study on NDEs at the University of Southampton. Researchers interviewed 140 survivors of cardiac arrest (CA) to learn more about their near-death experiences.

This study revealed:

> 46% had memories with seven major cognitive themes: fear;
> animals/plants; bright light; violence/persecution; Déjà vu;
> family; recalling events post-CA and 9% had NDEs, while 2%
> described awareness with explicit recall of 'seeing' and 'hearing'

actual events related to their resuscitation. One had a verifiable period of conscious awareness during which cerebral function was not expected. (Parnia S, 2014)

The survivors spoke of increased senses, bright lights, being pulled through the water, or having an out-of-body experience (OBE). Sam Parnia led the study, which concluded:

> While it was not possible to absolutely prove the reality or meaning of patients' experiences and claims of awareness, (due to the very low incidence of 2% of explicit recall of visual awareness or so-called OBE's), it was impossible to disclaim them either and more work is needed in this area. Clearly, the recalled experience surrounding death now merits further genuine investigation without prejudice." (Parnia S, 2014)

Only with open minds will we find the truth of our existence. We will achieve greater understanding only when we learn to discover, without preconceived notions—which only dismiss and divide.

When we acknowledge the measured and the mystical, we will uncover the true magnificence of our reality—the here and now and the afterward.

Chapter 73: Heaven and Hell

Eastern Religions view our afterlife as a rebirth into another life. Western Religions believe our afterlife consists of Heaven or Hell, except in Judaism, Western Religion's foundation. Genesis 3:19 generalizes Judaism's ancient beliefs, which have varied significantly over time and sects: "By the sweat of your brow you will eat your food until you return to the ground, since from it you were taken; for dust you are and to dust you will return."

Like the belief in the resurrection of the dead, the concept of Heaven or Hell originated with Zoroastrianism, not Judaism.

I was raised under the "Hellfire and Brimstone" doctrine. The pastors passionately screamed, "Release your evil ways or burn in Hell for eternity!" The threat of burning in Hell terrified the 8-year-old me. Every time I would accidentally burn myself, my mom would say, "Imagine what Hell is like!" It caused nightmares, irrational fears, shame, and a mentality of always expecting punishment.

The first time I heard of an NDE was when my mom told me the story of George Ritchie. He died and claimed to have gone to Hell. George encountered different rooms in Hell. The rooms were full of damned souls trying to continue their "sinful" lives of smoking cigarettes, drinking, and sex but were prevented from doing so. It left them burning in Hell and longing for the things that got them there.

The mental images terrified me; I was just a child.

Episcopalian Bishop John Shelby (Jack) Spong said:

> I happen to believe in life after death, but I don't think it's got a thing to do with reward and punishment. Religion is always in the control business. And that's something people don't really understand. It's in the guilt-producing control business. And if you have Heaven as a place where you are rewarded for your goodness, and Hell as a place where you are punished for your evil, then you sort of have control of the population. And so, they create this fiery place which is quite literally scared quite the Hell out of a lot of people throughout Christian history. And it's part of a control tactic. But I think there is a sense in most religious life of reward and punishment in some form. (Spong, 2006)

This philosophy of shame caused me to live in fear. I always looked for problems because I was definitely due some pain and punishment from God. The ranges of my "sin" varied so greatly that if Hell existed, I was doomed for eternity. I would be condemned for being a single mother, lying to my boss about why I was late to work (which was usually because of) partying on the weekends, (which resulted in) fornication, and, of course, not attending Church regularly (Who can get up on a Sunday after drinking all night?). The Church said I was a full-fledged sinner, and I was casting my eternal fate.

Because of my upbringing, I assumed everyone had the same fears about judgment and eternal penance in Hell. I included the question, "Are you afraid to die?" in my Facebook poll, and it was reassuring that most did not fear judgment. They were more afraid of the pain of the death. A few respondents said life can be Hell, so there was no need to look further.

"Religion is for people who're afraid of going to Hell. Spirituality is for those who've already been there." ~ Vine Deloria Jr.

Each culture has its version of Hell, but only Christianity and Islam believe it is an eternal destination of fire and brimstone. The third-century text, "The Apocalypse of Paul," states there are rivers of fire and ice in Hell. The philosophy of the lake of fire originated with the Egyptians. It was where Ammit devoured the condemned souls—the gnashing of teeth in a lake of fire.

Judaism believes when someone dies, they go to Hades or Sheol, which is more of a waiting room for the afterlife. The Torah does not mention it until the Book of Daniel, which allegedly took place in the sixth century B.C.E. but was written in the second century B.C.E., during the Hellenistic period.

Judaism teaches that "Hell" is not a place but a state of being—separated from God. It is not a future destination to be feared but the present moment. The Torah teaches that suffering occurs when one is out of alignment with God's will, and that is the ultimate punishment. However, they believe through repentance, one can always return to God's love.

Jainism and Buddhism's "Hell" is Naraka. It has hot and cold places and is temporary until one has fulfilled their karmic debt—which could be billions of years. Hinduism also has a Naraka, which they believe has 28 different hells, where one's sins dictate the punishment. For example, it blinds someone who was deceptive or adulterous. Or someone who commits heresy is sent to a forest of palm trees with leaves made of swords that whip them as they move through.

I was shocked to find philosophies that believed in reincarnation also believed in a version of Hell. I assumed all the "sins" of one's lifetime were addressed in the next incarnation. But even the Eastern philosophies believe in some penance besides the karmic rebirth—sometimes a double-whammy.

The Christian vision of Hell was influenced by poets, philosophers, pastors, popes, and pagans, but not the Bible. The word "Hell" was not in the scriptures until the Latin Vulgate in 400 C.E., and not again until 1611, with the King James version. "Hell" was a mistranslation of Gehenna, Sheol, Tartarus, and Hades. Sheol and Hades translate as "grave." Tartarus originated in Greek Mythology.

Jesus mentions Gehenna eleven times in the Hebrew Bible. In ancient times, Gehenna was in the Valley of Hinnom, located south of Jerusalem. In the O.T., they referenced it as the place for pagan child sacrifice, so it was known as dark and evil. Legend states after King Josiah desecrated it (1 Kings 23:10), they turned it into a trash heap. Along with trash, they burned pagan statues and altars and the corpses of criminals, derelicts, beggars, and prisoners of war.

The fire never went out because the heap was continually refilled. The toxic smell would burn an onlooker's eyes and nose. To be associated with Gehenna meant you were trash. To have your body left there meant no one loved you enough to bury you. A person's remains discarded in the trash heap indicated a social pariah. So, when Jesus referenced Gehenna as a hellish place, it was. But it was not about eternal implications because the Jews did not believe in Hell. It was about being such a horrible person who would be tossed away as trash.

Augustine (354—430) turned God back into the unforgiving, relentless Judge who sends us to burn for eternity. Based on Plato's belief in an eternal soul, Augustine postulated we would be in Heaven or Hell for eternity. Dante's (1265–1321) Divine Comedy and John Milton's (1608–1674) Paradise Lost gave us the poetic, dramatized, and terrorizing depictions of Hell, which the Church appropriated as doctrine. All our current beliefs about the Christian and Islamic Hell are not based on the Bible but the dogmatic adaptations driven by imagination and creativity.

The more frightening the depictions of Hell, the bigger the tool of control. Ask a parent about the power of fear. Hell became the ultimate threat. There is no redemption, just eternal suffering.

The concepts of Hell and the unconditional love of God are mutually exclusive—both cannot be true.

"There is no fear in love. But perfect love drives out fear because fear has to do with punishment. The one who fears is not made perfect in love." (1 John 4:18)

The Church labeled death as the ultimate penalty for sin. The concept of Hell also leaves us wondering about the fate of our loved one's soul. Because of religious doctrine, we speculate if the death was a curse, terrifying the imagination of the indoctrinated. Belief in a torturous eternal destination only adds to our pain when a loss occurs.

There are many stories of churches refusing to perform funerals for people they consider "sinners." This bigotry was prominent during the AIDS crisis, where hundreds of churches closed their hearts and doors to the people who died of AIDS. Today, we see it in funerals for LGBTQ+ or those from different beliefs.

Religion holds death hostage and uses it as the absolute and eternal weapon—we are so easily controlled in such vulnerable and sad times.

Manipulating our emotions is cruel.

Chapter 74: God is Pro-Death

Let me be truly clear: God is pro-death. The proof is in the entirety of our existence. Every bit of matter in the known universe dies: stars, planets, galaxies, plants, animals, and people. Not one thing gets out of it alive.

If this is God's creation, then how could he be pro-life?

It does not make sense. It is not logical. If everything dies, then death is part of our journey. Death is not something to be feared (or rushed!); it is just a completion of one life and off to another.

What if death was not a terrible thing? I fully understand that the loss we feel when a loved one dies is not something that ever goes away. But, if we eliminate our beliefs of the ultimate judgment and examine our world logically, we can only surmise that death is simply part of all life.

Not before our time, but the ones who are no longer in human form are free from the confines of a flawed body and the hostage of their ego. They have learned their lessons, completed their tasks, are done with their part of this world, and are no longer suffering. They are returning to the ultimate source of love.

If we viewed death as more of a completion of our job, would we still blame "God" for all the terrible things that happen? Would a child's death or a natural disaster still be the act of an "evil God?" Or an act of mercy that ends all the suffering of life?

If Heaven is so grand, why is it so dreaded?

Many cultures mourn but then celebrate one's passing with parties, parades, and dancing. But Western Religions view death as the ultimate punishment because they believe God is pro-life. We see the signs waved at protests, abortion clinics, Washington, DC, and many times on the news.

I cringe every time someone says, "God will save my life!" Vince stopped doing his chemo treatments because he thought God would save him. I argued with him and yelled that if God wanted things to live, everything would not die! We do not know why, but nothing lasts forever.

What we know is death causes action. Death forces us to live. Our pending demise tells us to act today, not tomorrow. Death ceases procrastination because we know our time is limited.

But for the living mourning the dead, everything stops in its tracks. When someone you care for dies, you are no longer too busy, preoccupied, or angry. It is an unfamiliar perspective when those things no longer matter because that person is gone. The rush of life stops and forces you to see what is important. Unfortunately, most of us realize this too late.

Again, we should look to nature to understand our existence and death. Look at the trees and the changing seasons. They die in the winter and are reborn in the spring, more vibrant, robust, and with fresh growth. We see the beauty in their death with the colorful falling leaves, knowing one day those leaves will return. A caterpillar is reborn as a butterfly. Some stars' demise starts the birth of new celestial bodies.

Yet, Western Religions do not consider this possibility in us, the "greatest creation of all?"

There is nothing we will not confine to our understanding.

Chapter 74: God is Pro-Death

Chapter 75: It's All about the Lessons

We are here to learn and grow as spiritual beings, having a human experience. The trials and tribulations of our lives strengthen us or make us wiser, which is why those lessons are repeated when we do not learn. Happiness would not be so sweet if it were not for sadness.

A year before my mom passed, she had a revelation—a massive "aha" moment. She was reading a book that revealed the errors in her role as a mom. She called me, crying hysterically. As a child, I only saw her cry twice. On that day, she called me sobbing. I could barely understand her.

Through her tears, she profusely apologized. She explained she did not know any better. She told me how she was unloved and unaccepted as a child, so she did not learn how to love or nurture me. She admitted to trying to control me for her own goals and used God as an excuse. There were long pauses as she wept.

She expressed her regrets about disowning me and not being able to teach me the things she wanted to as my mom. I had never heard my mom so vulnerable, apologetic, or human. This call was something I dreamed of but never thought would happen. I was not only caught off-guard; it floored me.

Two weeks later, she was diagnosed with breast cancer and given three to six months to live. I believe she learned her lessons, and therefore her journey was complete. She fought for an entire year, but when the day came that she gave up, she was gone in less than a week. I miss her so much.

In seeing my mother pass, in telling her I loved her as she took her last breath, I saw the shell emptying. "She" was no longer there. When I was 28, a friend of mine was killed. When he died, his body also seemed empty. I never experienced such a thing, but there was no dismissing it. A framework was all that remained, like a vacant home.

After seeing their deaths, there was little that I was sure of, but I knew they were no longer in their bodies.

I will not pretend to know what happens to our soul and energy after we leave this body, but I struggle to believe there is nothingness. Or that we sit in Heaven for eternity. As Joey used to say, "How boring!" Or that a source of unconditional love would consider or condone eternal, endless suffering.

It is also hard to believe that out of all the life on our amazing planet, this human experience is our only one. I really hope I have done a respectable job here so I can try many new things the next time.

"What a caterpillar calls the end, the rest of the world calls a butterfly." ~ Lao Tzu

On the day I die, when I am being carried toward the grave, do not weep.
Do not say, He is gone! He is gone.
Death has nothing to do with going away.
The Sun sets, and the moon sets, but they are not gone.
Death is a coming together.
The tomb looks like a prison, but it is really release into union.
The human seed goes down in the ground like a bucket into the well.

Chapter 75: It's All about the Lessons

It grows and comes up full of some unimagined beauty.
Your mouth closes here and immediately opens with a shout
of joy there.~ "On the Day I Die" by Jamal ad-Din Muhammad
Rūmī (Rumi)

Section XI: What I Now Know

"I no longer think that any principle or opinion is worth anything if it makes you unkind or intolerant."
~ Karen Armstrong

Chapter 76: When You Jump, You Never Land in the Same Place

At the age of 28, I decided that after Joey grew up and moved out, I would sell everything I owned. I would buy a 45-foot boat and run a scuba diving charter in Bimini, Bahamas. I wanted to spend the rest of my life breathing underwater, swimming with dolphins, and dying in 30 years of skin cancer or something like that.

I had a plan and took steps towards this goal. I had no dreams of authoring a book, although everyone who has ever known me said I should. Fast forward 20 years, and I could not imagine my life without this book. It has thoroughly changed me. The charter was a cool idea, but there was no way I could live on a boat.

I did not understand that I was embarking on a pilgrimage that would forever change my life.

The book was initially an emotional idea brought on by rage, but it became a mission of truth and love. The lessons I have learned, the pain I faced, and the faith I had have forever altered who I am. This book aligned my priorities in life, shifting my focus from what was lacking to one of giving. I became a student of life, a sponge of learning and knowledge. And through it, I grew spiritually and emotionally; in both cases, I am stronger.

Religion tells us we are inadequate and uses our insecurities to control us. It causes us to beg for love and worthiness. One of the greatest lessons I learned is that I am not lacking, unworthy, or insufficient. I am complete—humanly flawed but whole. Perhaps not everything I want, but I have everything I need. I am not a vessel that needs to be filled; I am a boat that can carry others.

We are not broken souls, damaged merely because we were born. And some magician in the sky need not rescue us. We need to focus more on love than man's law—more on our pure wholeness and less on judgment—as Jesus said.

Religion often fuels a superiority complex, claiming ultimate knowledge, sacred lineage, and divine appointment. Our feeling of inequality is all in our heads. The ego must be tamed, controlled, and used for good—not for division, status, power, and greed.

"The ego constantly competes with the spirit for control over your inner voice." (Johnson., 2023)

Our goal is to have our ego thrive on the laughter or kindness we give others. A productive ego shines in someone's joy; an unhealthy ego delights in another's misery.

"It's love alone that leads to right action. What brings order to the world is love, and let love do what it will."
~ Jiddu Krishnamurti

My outgoing and assertive demeanor perfectly covered a shattered and insecure soul. I was weak, weary, and always looking over my shoulder. I constantly waited to receive my penance and suffering.

But my energy shifted when I no longer focused on what could or had happened. If we only realized how powerful our thoughts and words are and the energy they produce, we would control our negative thoughts and never repeat another dooming word.

I now understand that the energy we emit, we must also endure. Our lives are mirrors. Words have power. They carry our intentions and reveal our hearts. If we are afraid, life will give us an overabundance of things to fear. If we are angry, most of our interactions will be tense. One of my favorite sayings sums up this philosophy: "Attitudes are contagious; is yours worth catching?" Even though I always had a smile, my energy communicated more than my appearance.

I am not saying the ride of life has been smooth—it is still a roller coaster. But instead of living in a terrifying free-fall, I can now raise my arms and scream, "Wheeeeeeeee!" I now know that once the terrifying or exhilarating ride is over, I will be better prepared and eager to go again.

I use this analogy because the drops still scare me, but the twists, turns, and loops elate me and make me laugh. Sometimes, I am scared, but now my fear is a blip, not a brick wall. The steps I had to take for this book were some of the scariest I have ever had. Yet the results gave me joy only comparable to my son's birth.

Now, I know everything will be OK when I live in universal alignment. During tough times, I continually repeat, "Thy will be done," which centers me and eases stress.

The only things that matter in life are not living in fear and loving each other. To not live in fear, we must let go and allow things to unfold. "Letting go" does not mean waiting for something to happen or relinquishing your will and desires.

"Letting go" releases things that do not benefit your best self. It is asking for universal guidance and looking for meaningful signs and coincidences that offer direction. It is acknowledging the ebbs and flows of all life and seeing all the beauty and synchronicity.

All the religions and philosophies are based on love and taming the ego; the rest is just manufactured junk. This religious junk clutters our hearts and lives and causes anxiety, insecurities, and division. It should be disregarded as any path to righteousness. It is only about control.

It is not our faith that matters but our actions. My mom repeatedly said: "Your actions speak so loudly I cannot hear what you are saying." (Emerson, 1875)

How we treat others is how we will be remembered; not how religious we were.

Jesus said,

> *"Love one another. As I have loved you, so you must love one another.*
> *By this, everyone will know that you are my disciples if you love one*
> *another." John 13:34-35)*

When love is the foundation of our interactions, we walk with
God. When love is our religion, peace will be our intention.

Love calms, heals, and unites. We search for love from the time
we are born until the day we die. It gives life to our lives and meaning
to our existence. Science has documented that without love, children
can die. Even if the necessities of food, clothing, and shelter are met, a
child's survival is at risk if love is nonexistent.

A society without love is dysfunctional and chaotic; it is selfish
and rooted in greed, dominating the weak and elevating the unjust.
When control is more important than compassion, or wealth is
paramount to charity, it is a culture based on ego, not love.

"WWJD—What Would Jesus Do" was the best marketing
campaign the Church ever did. It was also the most hypocritical.
If they believed and lived their advertising, there would be no
starvation, malaria, or AIDS. The Church would give all its wealth
to developing countries and demand the best care for all God's
children. Instead, religious leaders look upon the marginalized with
disdain and ask what sins they have committed to incur such horrible
situations.

Any position of supremacy is anti-Christ.

At the Last Supper, Jesus washed the feet of his disciples.

> *"You call me 'Teacher' and 'Lord,' and rightly so, for that is what I*
> *am. Now that I, your Lord and Teacher, have washed your feet, you*
> *also should wash one another's feet. I have set you an example that you*
> *should do as I have done for you. Very truly, I tell you, no servant is*
> *greater than his master, nor is a messenger greater than the one who*
> *sent him." (John 13:13-16)*

Unconditional love means without condition. Pure, divine, all-
encompassing, unequivocal, genuine love is all that God offers.

It is up to us whether we access and implement it. But we must acknowledge it for what it truly is instead of molding this pure energy into a flawed Being.

There is nothing harder than constantly exemplifying love. Examples of where love is challenging are road rage, when someone receives a promotion over you, or ending a relationship. The easiest thing to do is to react and retaliate. Love requires the strength of control and consciousness.

Love is an expansive vibrational field of energy, and because of that, it is hard to initiate. At first, it requires a conscious effort. But because it is an open frequency, it can physically and emotionally rejuvenate us instead of exhausting us. When we focus on love, it rebounds.

But fear is the bedrock of hate. It has a reductive vibrational energy, so it is easy to maintain. Fear is not an active energy but a reactive one. Even though it requires little or no effort, thought, or control, fear is exhaustive.

Every moment, we choose which energy to access, but that choice can become habitual.

Reductive energies (fear/hate) are based on instinct instead of intent. They are our primal nature. These energies quickly multiply, signaling to everyone around us that there's danger. The energy makes us flee when we sense trouble without thought or examination. It is the same energy/instinct that focuses on retaliation when threatened. Or, in the most sublime cases, only realizing that you ate an entire bag of chips because the bag is empty. These energies invoke actions before thoughts.

Expansive energies (love/empathy) require thought before action. It is an override of instinct and into conscious awareness. This energy is reassuring; it dissipates confusion and elicits trust. We see it in a calm person during the storm, directing the fearful. Maintaining expansive energy in dire situations automatically elevates someone to a "hero"—the firefighter running into the burning building or the parent stepping between danger and their child.

And it is not just about you. Each vibrational action affects the field of energy in all who see it. Have doubts? Think of a heart-warming video and how you felt as the "hero" saved the day. Remember the smile, possibly a tear of joy, and how it warmed your heart? You probably knew no one in the video, but by witnessing their positive energy, you felt it, too.

Consider when you saw cruelty or injustice and how that made you feel. Were you full of anger, rage, and thoughts of retaliation? Probably. Because energies are contagious. Your happiness, and the happiness of those around you, depends on the energy you access. Each day, we must ask ourselves, "What am I spreading, and what am I catching?"

In every story, the Hero embodies the expansive energies, and the antagonist perpetuates the reductive. It takes true strength and courage to maintain restraint and remain intentional. The Hero stays calm while everyone else flees. Only a few will be strong enough to stand in love.

Situations and surroundings affect and influence fear and hate. But love embodies pure strength that stands committed, regardless of the experience. Integrity, honesty, compassion, and resilience are some qualities of love. Love is healing and can cause meaningful change. Unreasonable fear is destructive. and hurts everyone involved.

Our experiences of joy and pain influence our perspectives. Everything we encounter leaves imprints that alter our inclinations. These events are usually forgettable as far as memories go. Still, they change our day-to-day lives and how we view our environment. They are subtle and sometimes go unnoticed because they become who we are. They drive our subconscious, which affects our actions and reactions.

Our fears are based on perceptions and preconditioning and require reconditioning and realignment. I make conscious decisions throughout the day to not let fear overcome and paralyze me because I am walking in love and trusting the natural flow of life. Walking through and away from fear requires mindful determination and progress. Fear causes irrational actions and mindless decisions. I am, of course, not talking about logical fears like a hungry lion stalking you.

My dog Bailey was terrified of thunderstorms and fireworks. Frequently, he would awaken me in the middle of the night by jumping on my head, trying to escape the flashes of light and thunderous booms. His body shook as he tried to run away, like he could escape it.

Regardless of how much I comforted him, he looked at me like I was insane for staying calm. He assured me we must run for our lives. We lived in the world's lightning capital, so I often had to reassure him it was just a storm and the world was not ending. "Everything will be OK!" I was his emotional support human.

These experiences with Bailey gave me patience with myself. Thunderstorms and fireworks do not scare me, but uncertainty, injustice, inequality, and hate make me shake and want to run for cover. And while I cannot control lightning storms or life's ups and downs, I can control my fears.

As a control freak, uncertainty still challenges me, but I am learning to ride the ride without knowing what will happen next. Injustice, inequality, and hate are things I can do something about. By doing my part, the fear dissipates, and strength resonates.

An alignment occurs when your focus in life is less about control and more about letting go; less fear and more love. You are guided into your own Hero's journey. We are all looking for our reason for being, but we rarely stop to listen and just Be.

Since we were born, every interaction, emotion, duty, and desire left an imprint on our psyche. Our brains store the data, and our reactions are based on that information. Painful events leave deep impressions that (often) cause irrational fears, which affect not only our lives but also the lives of those around us. Joey is terrified of spiders because of my fears, which originated with my father being bitten and nearly dying.

Since the dawn of man, what kept us from getting killed by animals or rival tribes was fear. The "fight or flight" instincts enabled all life forms to thrive and survive. Within milliseconds, our brains analyze, conceptualize, and label everything—people, places, and things—placing them within the confines of our understanding.

We establish who a friend or a foe is during these fractions of time. And these instinctual reactions are based on memories and the lessons we encountered throughout our lives. Our history of pain, or what we were taught to fear, determines our impulses.

Vince's mother was the most fearful person I have ever met. Consequently, she also taught her children to be afraid. I was one of the many people she distrusted, so we were never close, but even from a distance, her fears affected me.

I had not spent more than a few hours with her in the 20 years before she passed. But to this day, if I complain at a restaurant, I immediately hear her voice. "Now they will spit in your food!" Whenever I see a bag on the side of the road, I hear her say, "There are probably babies or puppies dying in that bag!" She was afraid of everything and was always waiting to be attacked.

The first of only two times I ever saw her leave the house was to come to our wedding. Her fear locked her in her home and taught her children to be skeptical and afraid of everything and everyone. She created a foundation of mistrust, insecurity, and instability, and she probably had no idea. She would have viewed it as caring and concern for her loved ones, but fear is contagious, systemic, and life-altering.

Obviously, my mom's fears were even more impactful on me. Her fear of eternal damnation and the consequences of her denial created a life full of shame, hypocrisy, and isolation. She focused on the law instead of love, preventing her from having authentic or vulnerable connections. The Hell she feared became the life she lived because the one thing that was always missing was love. As her daughter, it forced me to walk through Hell with her, burning my own soul and teaching me nothing but fear and abandonment.

We are instructed to "fear not" because of the pain it inflicts on our lives and everyone around us. Fear's ability to influence us is why politics and religion abuse it.

Those in power use fear to push their agenda by manipulating the masses. Scared people are irrational, compulsive, prone to violence, and influenced by any form of leadership. Along with the crowd size, the insecurity multiplies.

Religion became the ultimate Ponzi scheme of fear.

Leadership does not mean domination. The world is always well-supplied with people who wish to rule and dominate others. The true leader is a different sort; he seeks effective activity which has a truly beneficent purpose. He inspires others to follow in his wake, and holding aloft the torch of wisdom leads the way for society to realize its genuinely great aspirations. (Selassie, n.d.)

In First World countries, we no longer fear being eaten by animals, so we turned our fears towards each other. Our concern has shifted to family, neighbors, strangers, or other countries. Fear made us irrational and defensive. We fear diversity, becoming suspicious and afraid of our neighbors. We fear intrusion, loss, and sometimes retaliation, all because an ancient instinct tells us to. Living with such anxiety resulted in a society that is sickly, drugged, easily offended, retaliatory, and often violent.

"The foundation of the Buddha's teachings lies in compassion, and the reason for practicing the teachings is to wipe out the persistence of ego, the number-one enemy of compassion."
~ Dalai Lama XIV

Compassion for others and ourselves.

Our egos focus on differences and assign various levels of fear. We may fear they are better than us (more affluent, more attractive) or deem them lesser and fear they could harm us. Our ego is satiated only when we can put others in a box—a box of confidence or concern. We need to understand what they are before deciding who they are.

So, many people fear the LGBTQ+ community because of the uncertainty of which box to place them. The ego becomes frustrated and afraid when we struggle with which category to assign someone. How we categorize people dictates who to fear and who is safe.

An unchecked ego has resulted in every injustice, inequality, and cruelty since the beginning of time. When in check, our ego is a motivator and the driver behind success. If the ego is unbridled, death and destruction occur. Love, through compassion, kindness, and empathy, are not the ego's priority.

These concerns also occur with different ethnicities, societal statuses, differently-abled people, and religions.

Having known dozens of differently-abled people, verses like Leviticus 21:17-23 reaffirmed the lack of absolute holiness, kindness, or validity of the Bible.

> *The Lord said to Moses, Say to Aaron: "For the generations to come, none of your descendants who has a defect may come near to offer the food of his God. No man who has any defect may come near: no man who is blind or lame, disfigured or deformed; no man with a crippled foot or hand, or who is a hunchback or a dwarf, or who has any eye defect, or who has festering or running sores or damaged testicles. No descendant of Aaron, the priest who has any defect, is to come near to present the food offerings to the Lord. He has a defect; he must not come near to offer the food of his God. He may eat the most holy food of his God, as well as the holy food; yet because of his defect, he must not go near the curtain or approach the altar, and so desecrate my sanctuary. I am the Lord, who makes them holy."*

I no longer care where it is written or who said it. If it is not offered through the lens of unconditional love, it is not of God—it is ego-based and, therefore, not worthy of consideration.

The ego does not care about the soul; it only focuses on the superficial. We appease the ego when we are secure within our tribe because it knows there is little chance of disruption. It does not like uncertainty; it needs constant reassurance that what it tells you is the truth, even if it is not. The ego is a liar, and our ignorance of that fact creates the division it wants. "There's only room at the top for one!" is a perfect example of an ego-driven mentality.

We do not grow without learning, and we do not learn from people who know and experience the same things we do. There are no "other people". We are simply people. There are only other ideas which are flexible and ever-changing. Once we realize that, the ego loses power, and we are open to growth, not rigid in our beliefs.

"The problem is that we have allowed our egos, the part of us which believes that we are separate from God and separate from each other, to dominate our lives." ~ Wayne Dyer

We grow when we discover things through the eyes of others— through their understanding and life lessons. We must get out of our heads and focus more on our hearts. Our focus needs to shift to how we can grow, learn, and what we can do to help others. Growth is detestable to the ego, so be prepared for the cognitive dissonance once you open your heart and mind to all the world offers. You might experience some fear and disillusionment. Keep moving forward. You can do it!

We should fear hurting others. Or not doing enough to be helpful and loving. We should worry about following anyone who places anything above love, compassion, and equality. We should fear not easing the suffering of others. Injustice should terrify us.

But we fear someone's skin color, the status of their souls, and how we believe they will spend eternity. Religion took the importance of the here and now and replaced it with fear of the afterlife and "God's" ever-changing preferences.

Living with love as the foundation of every interaction naturally aligns with our life's mission. When we practice acts of love, we work the muscles of our soul, uncovering our oneness. In that realization, we become united and one with God.

Living in the universal flow offers the clarity of hindsight, affording us recollection and recognition of how wonderfully it turned out. It is often beyond what we understood or assumed and more beautiful than we imagined.

When we are out of universal alignment, we neglect to notice that fighting the situation caused the bumps, or the bump was just part of the lesson. It is never because of an angry and vengeful God.

"If your understanding of the divine made you kinder, more empathetic, and impelled you to express sympathy in concrete acts of loving-kindness, this was good theology. But if your notion of God

made you unkind, belligerent, cruel, or self-righteous, or if it led you
to kill in God's name, it was bad theology."
~ Karen Armstrong.

Living a life full of unconditional love is virtually impossible. The ego is always present. And it is not a straightforward path. It can be perplexing, laborious, and sometimes painful. An Olympian must work for his medals.

If it were easily attainable, it would not be godly. We are inspired, humbled, and kind when we use love as our intention. Those were the founding principles of most religions. Still, they were obscured by the ego's reign instead of the influence of love.

Walking in constant love is hard enough, but sometimes, when trying to be compassionate and godly, it triggers others. When someone fearful witnesses the strength of love, they can become enraged, making the commitment to peace even more challenging. The proof is in the uprising against Pope Francis. He opened his heart and the doors of the Church to people who, for centuries, were considered unworthy. He took the stance of "Who am I to judge?" and was charged with heresy by dozens of Catholic scholars and clergy.

Such a charge against the Pope has not happened since 1333. Pope Francis is not allowing dogma to supersede love, the core of Jesus' mission, and for this, he was chastised. The Pope's declarations are infuriating many political and religious leaders who justified their judgment and hate under the guise of biblical law and ordination.

It is not just Christianity. All the belief systems (except Jainism) justify their immoral behavior as something divinely ordered. They are all guilty of focusing on power and control, and too many have lost sight of their core principles. Buddhism was founded on enlightenment and peace but is currently performing the ethnic cleansing of a Muslim sect in Myanmar.

Humans have always committed atrocities and justified them by claiming divine appointment.

It does not take religion to cause mass casualties; all it takes is unrestrained power.

Evil, under the pretense of righteousness, is still evil.

"The personal ego already has a strong element of dysfunction, but the collective ego is, frequently, even more dysfunctional, to the point of absolute insanity." ~ Eckhart Tolle

Greed and power are at the core of all unnatural tragedies. For centuries, the alignment of religion and politics fostered the ultimate control mechanisms.

Our holy commandments should include deep breaths and surrender. Not, "My way, or it's the wrong way!" When we act with love, we realize things are happening just as they should. We grow to where there's laughter instead of tears as another door slams in our faces. The goal is to understand that we are meant to adjust and keep moving forward through love.

If religion gives you a path to being more loving, it serves its purpose. Someone once told me that attending Church made them feel better and encouraged them to do better. That is the point. Without the foundation of love, religion is just an extension of high school cliques.

We are all connected, not just to each other, but with everything in the Universe. We can let love bring everything together or let fear tear us apart.

Living a life without love is Hell. There is no need for punishment in the hereafter. Through this process, I grew to believe that "God" is not a Being, and there is no Being who is Satan.

In the Torah, Lucifer was not the fallen angel who became the demon of death. Satan was an adversary, and proof of anything more simply does not exist. Christianity, via Zoroastrianism, created the beast, a Being whose goal is our destruction. There is no Being causing us to fall. Pride does that (Proverbs 16:18).

Demons cause no hostile forces, only our actions driven by narcissism, greed, and dominance. Living in fear invokes Hell on Earth for all who encounter it. Wayne Dyer said EGO is an acronym for Edging God Out, which aligns with the Jewish belief that Hell is being separated from God. Nothing does that better than the ego.

The Bible has excellent examples of people claiming to be better, more loved, special, or chosen. The tales always end in death and destruction.

Love does not say things like,

> *"Then in my anger I will be hostile toward you, and I myself will punish you for your sins seven times over. You will eat the flesh of your sons and the flesh of your daughters." (Leviticus 26:28-29)*

The God of unconditional love wants us to eat our children?

Christianity now scoffs at people experiencing poverty and denies the needs of immigrants fleeing war. Too much of the Christianity has become the antithesis of Christ. Jesus' message was distorted or negated and used for precisely what he abhorred.

The Church became the anti-Christ we feared for 2000 years. It was not an individual. It is the millions of followers who use Jesus' name to judge, condemn, divide, get rich, and hate their neighbors. The anti-Christ was not a single person destroying everything. It is those who use Jesus to push xenophobia, racism, misogyny, and wars. The anti-Christ is real and present in all the hateful, judgmental, divisive churches.

The sad irony is that if Jesus returned today, they would not welcome him. Jesus was a poor Middle Eastern immigrant who fought for equality and love—the opposite of what too many "Christians" value.

The corrupt and powerful killed Jesus for his radical views. Two thousand years later, church leaders are again challenging Jesus' teachings.

Much of the Church has become anti-Christ.

For some reason, the most vocal Christians among us never mention the Beatitudes (Matthew 5). But, often with tears in their eyes, they demand that the Ten Commandments be posted in public buildings. And, of course, those are Moses', not Jesus'. I have not heard one of them demand that the Sermon on the Mount, the Beatitudes, be posted anywhere. 'Blessed are the merciful' in a courtroom? 'Blessed are the peacemakers' in the Pentagon? Give me a break! ~ (Kurt

Vonnegut, 2004)

Due to human imperfection, religion has become corrupt, political, divisive, and a tool for power struggle. Spirituality is not theology or ideology. It is simply a way of life, pure and original as was given by the Most High. Spirituality is a network connection linking us to the God, the Universe, and each other." ~ (Nvenge, 1994)

If you want to reach a state of bliss, then go beyond your ego and the internal dialog. Make a decision to relinquish the need to control, the need to be approved, and the need to judge. Those are the three things the ego is doing all the time. It is very important to be aware of them every time they come up."~ (Chopra, n.d.)

I also learned that everyone will never agree on anything. No matter what it is, there will be people who disagree because they view things differently. This is especially true in religion. Whatever your beliefs, there is a scripture to support it. If there isn't a verse that fits your agenda, then one can be constructed. Because, in the Bible, there are dozens of contradictions. Every law has a loophole; there is a new order for every command.

But even without religion, as a planet full of humans, we will never completely agree on anything. Gravity, the shape of the Earth, the moon landing, and even the color of the sky and oceans are fitting examples of lacking universal agreement.

So, with a God figure, the supernatural, and all things unseen, hope or demand for any global agreement is naive at best. At worst, it is fatal.

"Everything we hear is an opinion, not a fact. Everything we see is a perspective, not the truth." ~ Marcus Aurelius.

Our Universe is up to individual belief systems and perspectives. Our beliefs are not reality; they are just our reality. Beliefs are not truth; they are only our truth. The truth is rigid, and beliefs are always fluid. Our beliefs are often reflections of our fears.

Our beliefs should never become our final conclusions because we ignore the facts when we are closed off because of feelings. And sometimes, ignoring those facts because of your feelings can get you and your loved ones killed, literally.

This book details my journey and encompasses most of what I learned, but there are a few things that I am now confident are my truths.

Love is my religion, peace is my intention, and unity is my goal.

I no longer place my faith in ancient humans, so I no longer believe in the god of religion. I believe in the divine energy of the Universe that we call love, which is my compass.

I believe in Newton's third law and the Golden Rule.

I understand people are on their own paths and struggle with the ego. We are here to help, not judge.

"Be tolerant of those who are lost on their path. Ignorance, conceit, anger, jealousy, and greed stem from a lost soul. Pray that they will find guidance. Search for yourself, by yourself. Do not allow others to make your path for you. It is your road and yours alone. Others may walk it with you, but no one can walk it for you." (Tribe, 2019)

Jesus never cared about "victory." His concern was with loss—loss of ego, greed, superiority, judgment, and resentment.

We may never agree entirely, but we can disagree respectfully and compassionately.

"Being positive and present" is not about living in denial or delusion of reality. It is finding good in each moment so that suffering does not overwhelm you. It is about being "positive" that things will work out as they should, even if we do not understand or see it.

I learned that sometimes, the most loving thing you can do is walk away with an open heart. To preserve peace and remain living in love, sometimes walking away is the right thing to do.

I discovered I will never know everything, but I want to try.

The ego bases our worth on opinions, titles, wealth, or possessions. But only those who loved us will keep our memory alive.

The Beatles' "Let It Be" gets me through the intense trials of life because of its accuracy and guidance.

I start my day with a simple prayer: "I release myself into the arms of Love. I am safe and supported. I am Love!" by Louise Hay.

I no longer fear God's wrath. I now live my days in Pronoia, believing that the entire Universe is conspiring to fulfill my dreams because I am living in Divine Will.

Anyone who says they have all the answers does not.

I am confident that God is love, nothing more and nothing less.

And it is a fact that we have ruined God. But now that we know better, we can be better.

With love,
The End

Acknowledgments

Everyone whom I have ever engaged with left a mark. Some left scars, some brought knowledge, and some gave me hope and love. I thank you all. My story would only be complete with all the pieces.

My grandson Ayden was the impetus for this book. The need to protect him from the trauma I incurred grew into the hope of protecting so many others. He forever changed my life, and I am eternally grateful for that. Thank you, Ayden, for bringing so much light and love into my life. I love you, honey.

The one person who has always been there for me is my aunt Fran. She has always been my biggest fan. She gave me my laugh, my tenacity, and my handyman skills. She also gave me laughs, love, consistency, and the true meaning of "family." I love you, Auntie, thank you.

Because of our dad, I missed much of my brother Tim's childhood. However, because of Dad's lack of influence, Tim became a great man and father. Tim, I am so proud of you. My nieces and sister-in-law are perfect (unbiased opinion!), and that is because of how wonderful you are. Thank you for your unending love, support, and friendship. I love you.

With that in mind, my sister-in-law Michelle deserves a shout-out for loving my brother and being such a fantastic mom. You helped stop the dysfunction associated with the Pallas name. Thank you; I love you.

My spiritual mentor, Michele Sevacko, got me through my darkest days. She was always just a phone call or text away, and her amazing heart and knowledge have been an inspiration. She guided me in getting my Ph.D. and has been a fantastic friend through it all. Michele. I love you and am so thankful you came into my life.

This book would not have been published without Kathy Ver Eeck's professional guidance and friendship. She showed me all the pieces needed for its success. Her online group, Pitch to Published, offered support, guidance, professional and peer reviews, and friendships I will forever cherish. Kathy changed my life, and I am forever grateful.

My childhood best friend, Anne Marie, taught me accountability, kindness, and love without religion. She showed me that love and goodness had nothing to do with the church. And when the church said she was going to Hell for being an atheist, I wanted nothing to do with them and their "God." Her kindness and warm heart always set an example for me. She was the "good angel" on my shoulder and the antithesis of the hatred in the church. Thank you. I love you.

My high school best friend, Joy, has been more like a sister than a friend. She loved me through it all and has been a cheerleader for me and this book. I appreciate your friendship, all the memories, support, and love. I love you.

Heidi and I have been friends since our twenties. We stayed connected through all of life's phases. She has been a dear friend and a dedicated supporter of my work: so many memories and life's ups and downs. I am grateful to have called you "friend" for almost thirty years. Thank you for sticking by me and supporting me through it all. I love you.

For almost 30 years, Melisa showed up whenever I needed her. She somehow knew and was there to give me love and wisdom. After my mom passed, Melisa gave me the book *Embraced By the Light*, and she has been an integral part of my growth. I love you, Melisa, thank you.

Lisa Marie Messex and her life coaching focused on trauma and loss helped me through my darkest days. She helped me embrace my "too muchness" and love that part of me. She showed me my beauty and uniqueness and taught me to value what others claimed were flaws. Lisa was a big part of finally accepting and loving myself. Thank you.

I met Amey in Pitch to Published, and she taught me that my value was not dependent on what I could offer or what others said. She taught me that my life had value simply because I was alive. I was nearly 50 years old and had never heard that before. Thank you so much for helping me see my value. You gave me a priceless gift.

I am so grateful for my editing team. Joppa Editing, Amey Aubry, Kevin Maxwell, Paula Skillicorn, and Timothy Warren worked to make the book shine. Thank you for seeing everything I did not and helping to deliver this "baby" of mine. You rock!

My Facebook Launch Team deserves a huge thank you! In alphabetical order, Amey, Andrew, Anne, Beth Anne, Brendan, Cal, Charlie, Claiborn, Dan, David Keith, David, Friar Nicolas, Greg, Harold, Jeff, Jess, Kevin, Lynn, Michael, Michelle, Mike, Nancy, Paula, Pete, Ray, Scott, Shikera, Terry, Tim K., Tim H., Tim W., Timothy, and Todd, your willingness to help and offer input, support, and friendships made my heart explode. I could not have asked for a better team to start the launch with. Thank you all so very much!

Thank you to all my guests on *Fireside Creators*, and social media friends and followers. Your support, input, advice, and love mean the world to me. *You are the best friends I have never met!*

Thank you, and I love you all!

References

Adamantius, O. (275). Princ 4.2.4. Butterworth.

Archdiocese, C. (n.d.). Catechism of the Catholic Church - PART 3 SECTION 2 CHAPTER 2 ARTICLE 7. 2408. http://www.scborromeo.org/ccc/p3s2c2a7. htm#2408.

Arky Arky Song - 3LittleWords - Volume 2. (2022, Nov 14). Retrieved from YouTube (3LittleWords): https://www.youtube.com/watch?v=Zuu_InUIbls

Augustine, H. (1853). The Writings of Thomas Jefferson (Vol. 3). Washington DC: Taylor & Maury.

Berridge, K. C. (2011). Building a neuroscience of pleasure and well-being. Psychology of Well-Being. doi:https://doi.org/10.1186/2211-1522-1-3

BG, B. G. (n.d.). Chapter 2: Sānkhya Yog verse 22. Retrieved from https://www.holy-bhagavad-gita.org/chapter/2/verse/22

Buddhānusmⱥti - A Glossary of Buddhist Terms. (n.d.). Retrieved from https://www2.buddhistdoor.net/dictionary/details/dharma

Caldwell, L. (1996, Feb 18). The Secret History of Mark. Retrieved from Fordham Edu: https://sourcebooks.fordham.edu/pwh/secretmark.asp

Campbell, J. (2008). The Hero with a Thousand Faces. San Francisco: New World Library.

Carr, B. (2004, 10 August). Papal Infallibility. Retrieved from Catholic Answers: https://www.catholic.com/tract/papal-infallibility

Census of Marine Life. (2011, Aug 24). How many species on Earth? About 8.7 million, new estimate says. Retrieved from Science Daily: https://www.sciencedaily.com/releases/2011/08/110823180459.htm

Chodron, P. (2017, March). The Essential Pema. (L. Calder, Ed.) Retrieved from The Pema Chödrön Foundation: https://pemachodronfoundation.org/wp-content/uploads/2017/03/The-Essential-Pema-Study-Guide.pdf

Chopra, D. (n.d.). Deepak Chopra Quotes. Retrieved from AZQuotes.com: https://www.azquotes.com/quote/519463

Cirlea, J. A. (2021, April 15). The Four Noble Truths from the Jodo Shinshu perspective. Retrieved from Amidaji International Temple: https://amida-ji-retreat-temple-romania.blogspot.com/2021/02/the-four-noble-truths-from-jodo-shinshu.html

Coles, A. (2008, July). God, Theologian and Humble Neurologist. Brain, 131(7), 1953–1959. doi:https://doi.org/10.1093/brain/awn128

Collins Dictionary. (2023).

CSB Bibles by Holman. (2019). CSB Ancient Faith Study Bible. B&H Publishing Group.

Dass, R. (2013, March 10). Dying is Absolutely Safe – Awareness Beyond Death. Retrieved from Ram Dass Foundation: https://www.ramdass.org/dying-is-absolutely-safe/

Department of Economic and Social Affairs Population Division. (2023, Nov 25). World Population Prospects 2022. Retrieved from United Nations: https://statisticstimes.com/demographics/world-sex-ratio.php

DeSouza, T. R. (1975). Goa-based Portuguese Seaborne Trade in the Early Seventeenth Century. The Indian Economic & Social History Review, 12(4), 433–442. Retrieved from ACTA Indica: https://journals.sagepub.com/doi/abs/10.1177/001946467501200405

Dobzhansky, T. (1973). Nothing in Biology Makes Sense Except in the Light of Evolution. American Biology Teacher, 35, pp. 125-129.

Dyer, D. W. (2009). Change Your Thoughts - Change Your Life: Living the Wisdom of the Tao. ● Hay House Inc.

Emerson, R. W. (1875). Social Aims.

Encyclopedia Britannica. (2015). The Council of Lyons. Encyclopedia Britannica, Inc.

Faggin, F. (2011). About Us. Retrieved from Faggin Foundation: http://www.fagginfoundation.org/about-us/

Faggin, F. (2013, August 7). Federico Faggin Explores the Fabric of Consciousness. (M. Battocchi, Interviewer) Retrieved from https://sanfranciscoitaly.com/post/57614873633/federico-faggin-explores-the-fabric-of-consciousness

Faggin, F. (2014, August 25). Explaining Consciousness. Retrieved from the

Faggin Foundation: https://web.archive.org/web/20181031005507/www. fagginfoundation.org/articles-2/explaining-consciousness/

Farrand, M. (1929). the Laws and Liberties of Massachusetts (1646). Harvard University Press; First Thus edition.

Feather, R. (2005). The Secret Initiation of Jesus at Qumran: The Essene Mysteries of John the Baptist. Bear & Company.

Fideler, D. R. (1995). Alexandria: The Journal for the Western Cosmological Traditions (Vol. 3). Phanes Press.

Francis, P. (2014). Evolving Concepts of Nature. Address on the Occasion of the Inauguration of the Bust in Honour of Pope Benedict XVI. Vatican. Retrieved from https://www.pas.va/en/magisterium/francis/2014-27-october. html

Ghosn, S. (2018, Sept 21). "Good Thoughts, Good Words, Good Deeds" Has Been the Constant Motto of Bakhtavar & Fred Desai Throughout Their Life and One of the Essential Teachings of Their Zoroastrian Faith. Retrieved from SOS Art Cincinnati: https://sosartcincinnati.com/2018/09/21/good-thoughts-good-words-good-deeds-has-been-the-constant-motto-of-bakhtavar-fred-desai-throughout-their-life-and-one-of-the-essential-teachings-of-their-zoroastrian-faith/

Global Research Society and the Institute for Social Research (Ipsos). (2011). Ipsos Global @dvisory: Supreme Being(s), the Afterlife and Evolution. Reuters.

Graney, C. (2018, April 21). The Inquisition on Copernicus, February 24, 1616. Retrieved from Vatican Observatory: https://www.vaticanobservatory.org/ sacred-space-astronomy/inquisition-copernicus-february-24-1616-little-story-punctuation-re-run/

Griffiths RR, J. M. (2016). Psilocybin produces substantial and sustained decreases in depression and anxiety in patients with life-threatening cancer: A randomized double-blind trial. J Psychopharmacol, (12):1181-1197. doi:10.1177/0269881116675513

Jarnick, S. (2013, Dec 27). The Power to Forgive. Retrieved from Red Letter Christians: https://www.redletterchristians.org/power-forgive/

Jefferson, T. (1813, August 22). To John Adams from Thomas Jefferson. Retrieved from Founders Online, National Archives: https://founders. archives.gov/documents/Adams/99-02-02-6135.

Jefferson, T. (1825, January 17). From Thomas Jefferson to Alexander Smyth 17 January 1825. Retrieved from Founders Online, National Archives: https://founders.archives.gov/documents/Jefferson/98-01-02-4882

Johnson., D. (2023, Oct 2). Darren Johnson. Retrieved from AZQuotes.com: https://www.azquotes.com/quote/765790

Justinian, E. F. (543). Second Council of Constantinople., (p. 11). Retrieved from https://www.newadvent.org/fathers/3812.htm

Karma-gli◉-pa, a. 1. (1992). The Tibetan Book of the Dead: The Great Liberation Through Hearing in the Bardo. Boston: Shambhala. Retrieved from Buddhism Red Zambala: https://buddhism.redzambala.com/tibetan-book-of-the-dead/tibetan-book-of-the-dead-part-4.html

Katherine L Narr, R. P. (2007, Sept 1). Relationships between IQ and regional cortical gray matter thickness in healthy adults. Cerebral cortex, 17(9), 2163-2171.

Kids, C. (2023). Rise And Shine (Arky Arky). Retrieved from Musixmatch: https://www.musixmatch.com/lyrics/Cedarmont-Kids/Rise-and-Shine-Arky-Arky

Koenig, H. G. (2012, Dec 16). Religion, Spirituality, and Health: The Research and Clinical Implications. doi:https://doi.org/10.5402/2012/278730

Koenig, H. G. (2012). Religion, Spirituality, and Health: The Research and Clinical Implications. International Scholarly Research Notices. doi:https://doi.org/10.5402/2012/278730

Koran. (n.d.). (S. International, Trans.) doi:https://quran.com/4:34?font=v1&translations

Kurt Vonnegut, J. (2004). Cold Turkey. In These Times, 10.

Lidz, F. (2005, January). The Little-Known Legend of Jesus in Japan. Retrieved from Smithsonian Magazine: https://www.smithsonianmag.com/history/the-little-known-legend-of-jesus-in-japan-165354242/

Lovgren, S. (2005, Aug 31). Chimps, Humans 96 Percent the Same, Gene Study Finds. National Geographic. Retrieved from https://www.nationalgeographic.com/science/article/chimps-humans-96-percent-the-same-gene-study-finds

Luther, M. (1522). Luther's Works. In Volume 35 (pp. 398-399).

Luther, M. (1530). Luther's Works. In Volume 35 (p. 411).

Luther, M. (2005). The Smalcald Articles. In The Lutheran Confessions. (p. 289). St Louis: Concordia Publishing House,.

Mahabharata. (n.d.). (K. M. Ganguly, Trans.) 2013.

Marr JS, M. C. (1996). An Epidemiologic Analysis of the Ten Plagues of Egypt. Caduceus.

Masud, E. (1995). The Truth About Islam. Retrieved from https://archive.org/details/the-truth-about-islam-by-enver-masud

McClendon, C. H. (2017, April 5). Christians remain world's largest religious group, but they are declining in Europe. Retrieved from Pew Research Center: https://www.pewresearch.org/short-reads/2017/04/05/christians-remain-worlds-largest-religious-group-but-they-are-declining-in-europe/

Merriam-Webster Dictionary. (2023, Sept 9). sin. Retrieved from merriam-webster: https://www.merriam-webster.com/dictionary/sin

Miller L, B. R. (2014). Neuroanatomical Correlates of Religiosity and Spirituality: A Study in Adults at High and Low Familial Risk for Depression. JAMA Psychiatry, 71(2):128–135.

Notovitch. (2018). The Life of Saint Issa: The Lost Years of Jesus Christ in India and the East. lulu.com.

Notovitch, N. (1990). The Unknown Life of Jesus Christ. Progressive Pr.

Nvenge, A. P. (1994). African Unity: The Only Solution. African Unity Press.

Oxford English Dictionary. (2023, July). pagan, n. & adj. doi:https://doi.org/10.1093/OED/4846189747

Oxford University Press. (2023). Monism. In O. Languages, Oxford Dictionary. Oxford University Press.

Parnia S, S. K.-N. (2014). AWARE-AWAreness during REsuscitation-a prospective study. Resuscitation. doi:10.1016/j.resuscitation.2014.09.004

Pavlovitz, J. (2015, Aug 13). 3 Reasons "Love The Sinner, Hate The Sin" Is An Abomination. Retrieved from John Pavlovitz: Stuff That Needs to be Said: https://johnpavlovitz.com/2015/08/13/3-reasons-love-the-sinner-hate-the-sin-is-an-abomination/

Penrose, R. (2006). BEFORE THE BIG BANG: AN OUTRAGEOUS NEW PERSPECTIVE AND ITS IMPLICATIONS FOR. EPAC, (pp. 24-29). Oxford. Retrieved from https://epaper.kek.jp/e06/PAPERS/THESPA01.PDF

Pew Research. (2020). On the Intersection of Science and Religion. Pew Research. Retrieved from https://www.pewresearch.org/religion/2020/08/26/on-the-intersection-of-science-and-religion/

Pew Research Center. (2012, December). The Global Religious Landscape. Retrieved from Pew Research: https://assets.pewresearch.org/wp-content/uploads/sites/11/2014/01/global-religion-full.pdf

Pew Research Center. (2013). Religious Groups' Views on End-of-Life Issues. Retrieved from https://www.pewresearch.org/religion/2013/11/21/religious-groups-views-on-end-of-life-issues/

Price, D. (2010). The Missing Years Of Jesus: The Extraordinary Evidence that Jesus Visited the British Isles. Hay House Publishers.

Rettner, R. (2015, Sept 23). God Help Us? How Religion is Good (And Bad) For Mental Health. Retrieved from Science Daily: God Help Us? How Religion is Good (And Bad) For Mental Health

Robinson, J. (2010, April). The God of the Patriarchs and the Ugaritic Texts: A Shared. Retrieved from BYU Scholars Archive: https://scholarsarchive.byu.edu/cgi/viewcontent.cgi?article=1116&context=studiaantiqua

Sastri, S. S. (1928). Katha Upanishad with Shankara's Commentary. Upanishad Book.

Schroeder, G. L. (2001). The Hidden Face of God: How Science Reveals the Ultimate Truth. United Kingdom: Free Press.

Segan, C. (1987). Keynote Address. CSICOP.

Selassie, H. (n.d.). Haile Selassie Quotes. Retrieved from Good Reads: https://www.goodreads.com/quotes/10249183-1-leadership-does-not-mean-domination-the-world-is-always-well

Slocum, S. (2018, March 18). Section Review. (R. D. Pallas, Interviewer)

Souvay, C. (1910). St. Joseph. Retrieved from The Catholic Encyclopedia: https://www.newadvent.org/cathen/08504a.htm

Spar, I. (2009, April). The Gods and Goddesses of Canaan. Retrieved from

Department of Ancient Near Eastern Art, The Metropolitan Museum of Art:

https://www.metmuseum.org/toah/hd/cana/hd_cana.htm

Spong, J. S. (2006, August). Priest says Hell is an invention of the church to control people with fear. Television. (K. Morrison, Interviewer) NBC. Retrieved from https://www.youtube.com/watch?v=QGzc0CJWC4E

Tatchell, P. (1996, March 18). Was Jesus Gay? Retrieved from Peter Tatchell: https://www.petertatchell.net/religion/jesus/

The Gnostic Society Library. (n.d.). The Gospel of Mary. Retrieved from http://www.gnosis.org/library/marygosp.htm

The Natural World: Science and Technology. (2016). In T. U. Church, 2016 Book of Discipline (p. 160. F). The United Methodist Publishing House. Retrieved from Church and Society: United Methodist Church: https://www.umcjustice.org/who-we-are/social-principles-and-resolutions/the-natural-world-160/the-natural-world-science-and-technology-160-f

The University of Calgary. (2022, Dec 31). Law of Conservation of Energy. Retrieved from Energy Education: https://energyeducation.ca/encyclopedia/Law_of_conservation_of_energy

Tribe, L. (2019, Sept 5). LAKOTA Code of Ethics. Retrieved from The Sanctuary: https://www.thesanctuaryheal.com/post/lakota-code-of-ethics

Valencia College West Campus. (n.d.). THE FOUR FUNCTIONS OF MYTH Mythologist Joseph Campbell. Retrieved from Valencia College: https://online.valenciacollege.edu/files/22775646/download?download_frd=1

Vedas. (2018). Nasadiya Sukta: The Hymn of Creation. In Rigveda (A. L. Basham, Trans., p. 10:129).

Veen, R. A. (2006). Justification and the Law. lulu.com.

West, D. (2014, March 22). The Brain Does NOT Create Consciousness. Retrieved from Waking Times: https://www.wakingtimes.com/brain-create-consciousness/

Wilhelm, J. (1911). Protestantism. New York: Robert Appleton Company. Retrieved from The Catholic Encyclopedia: http://www.newadvent.org/cathen/12495a.htm

William, M. M. (2013). Sanskrit-English Dictionary Motilal Banarsidass.

What Now?

Use the QR code below, or go to
SheriPallas.com/book-club

There, you will find resources, a social media
community, and a follow-up course:
BEYOND "We Have Ruined God"!

It features guest speakers who helped me though my
journey, and are experts in their fields!
The course goes deeper into the subjects and teaches
how to live a more love-centered life.

I will see You there!

www.ingramcontent.com/pod-product-compliance
Lightning Source LLC
Chambersburg PA
CBHW011227120626
46549CB00008B/3179